FLY-FI
WESTERI
STREAMS

D0760621

Other books by Jim McLennan

Trout Streams of Alberta

Blue Ribbon Bow

FLY-FISHING WESTERN TROUT STREAMS

Jim McLennan

STACKPOLE
BOOKS

Published by
STACKPOLE BOOKS
5067 Ritter Road
Mechanicsburg, PA 17055
www.stackpolebooks.com

Printed in the United States

First Edition

10 9 8 7 6 5 4 3 2 1

Cover photograph by the author
Cover design by Tracy Patterson
Color fly plates by Michael Radencich
Illustrations by Dave Hall
Photographs by the author

Library of Congress Cataloging-in-Publication Data
McLennan, Jim, 1953–
    Fly fishing western trout streams / Jim McLennan.—1st ed.
        p. cm.
    ISBN 0-8117-2636-3 (pbk.)
    1. Trout fishing—West (U.S.) 2. Fly fishing—West (U.S.) I. Title.
SH688.U6 .M388 2003
799.1'757'0978—dc21
                                                                    2002009150

*To the memory of the western fly-fishing greats
who now fish the other side of the divide:
Joe Brooks, Dan Bailey, Roderick Haig-Brown,
Charles E. Brooks, and Gary LaFontaine.*

CONTENTS

FOREWORD

I first met Jim McLennan forty-two years ago. I was selling welding equipment and his dad, Doug McLennan, was a good customer and good friend who ran Mechanics Supply in Edmonton, Alberta. Doug arranged to have his welding seminars for the staff on Sunday because there was no hunting in Alberta on Sunday, and that way he and I could hunt Friday and Saturday. He took me on some wonderful duck and sharptail grouse hunts. I had the added pleasure of staying in Doug and Eleanor McLennan's home during my visits, and young Jim, age seven, talked to me about fly fishing. He didn't catch the fly-fishing bug from his dad, as Doug's interest was shooting and hunting. But young Jim sure had the bug at the ripe age of seven.

Shortly after I acquired the Orvis Company in 1965 Jim started writing me about fly-fishing on the Bow River near Calgary and invited me to come out and fish with him. I wasn't able to do it until the seventies and *wow*, what a trip it was. We caught a number of browns and rainbows, some of which exceeded twenty inches, during a magnificent Trico spinner-fall.

Since that time I've had a number of occasions to fish with Jim, and I can assure you I've learned a great deal more from him than he has from me. He's a keen and astute observer and has developed a number of unique techniques for taking trout. And above all, he understands that fly fishing for trout is supposed to be fun. He spends most of his time fishing with his wife, Lynda, and daughter, Deanna, both superb anglers who squeal with joy when a trout rises to their fly.

I've just reviewed Jim's chapter on spring creek fishing. This is my favorite kind of fishing, and as I write, I'm looking out on a beautiful spring creek in Wyoming. Jim is a wonderful writer and his description of spring creeks, which includes the delights, the frustrations, and the techniques that sometimes work, is the best I've ever read. You will enjoy this book.

—Leigh H. Perkins
CEO, the Orvis Company,
and author of *A Sportsman's Life*

ACKNOWLEDGMENTS

Like most, this book began as an idea that wouldn't go away. And like all, this book had help with its birth. Near the beginning of the process Dave Hughes, probably the most prolific writer in the history of fly fishing, provided information, inspiration, and advice. From an idea, it became a query, sent to Judith Schnell at Stackpole, who seemed to think it might be possible to turn this pesky idea into a book. Through the rest of the process Judith and Amy Dimeler and the staff at Stackpole were polite, patient, and astute, answering e-mails and directing the book's course wisely.

Long-time friend Ross Purnell, of *Fly Fisherman* magazine, read and commented on parts of the manuscript dealing with tailwater trout streams. George Anderson, of Livingston, Montana, helped with some of the spring creek methods. I leaned heavily on Dave Hughes's book *Wet Flies* for the information on that method of fishing.

I also called on a number of fishing friends for information in the hatch charts—Ken Beatty, Chuck Echer, Gary Gould, Tyler Thomas, and Tim Wade.

For help in other ways, thanks to Ken Kohut, Bob Scammell, Jim Gilson, Tim Tollet, and Leigh Perkins. Thanks to Glenn Smith, of Calgary, Alberta, the vise magician whose flies appear in the photographs. Big thanks to my wife, Lynda, for bringing coffee and breakfast on those long mornings in the basement and for sharing western trout streams with me for twenty-five years.

INTRODUCTION

The first western fly fishers were probably homesteaders who put a fly rod in the trunk when they moved west to settle a new land. They wouldn't have known what to expect, but what they found, along with dry air, plains grizzlies, and elk, was an astonishingly beautiful and harsh landscape. They quickly learned that the West is a place where Mother Nature's grip is firm and compassionless. The extremes of winter weather and spring flooding were often more than just an inconvenience and occasionally extracted a toll in livestock, homes, and human lives.

The former easterners would have met and been impressed by the strength and power of two forces birthed in the loins of the Rocky Mountains: the rivers and the wind. Those few fly fishers among the early homesteaders found new fish—cutthroats, rainbows, and giant bull trout—that may have helped them overcome melancholic memories of their favorites from back home.

Just where, when, and for whom this first happened is open to speculation only, for fly fishing was surely a novelty during the early settling of the West. The earliest migrants had other things on their minds and precious little time for recreation.

But later, in the early to mid-twentieth century, more people came west, seeking economic opportunity, and some of them liked to fly-fish. Western fly fishing began to grow and take on an identity. It developed more or less simultaneously on several fronts, and each area had its godfather figure. In Wyoming's Jackson Hole country, curmudgeonly Bob Carmichael was the guru of the Snake River with its fine-spotted cutthroats, while Dan Bailey held forth from behind the counter of his soon-to-be-famous fly shop in Livingston, Montana.

Casting clubs in San Francisco and Pasadena fueled interest in fly fishing on the West Coast, and farther north, on Canada's Vancouver Island, Roderick Haig-Brown began his quest to articulate the ethics and esthetics of the sport.

But perhaps the best perspective on western fly fishing at that time was provided, surprisingly, by an outdoor writer from New York named Ray Bergman. He wrote compelling stories of his experiences on western trout waters, particularly those in Yellowstone Park, in the best-selling fishing book, *Trout,* first published in 1938.

The first fly-fishing methods used in the West were the methods that worked in eastern North America. They worked in a general way in the West, and they still do, but the differences between eastern and western watersheds and between eastern and western trout are substantial, and the development of distinctively western approaches to fly fishing was inevitable. Those differences and those approaches are the subject of this book.

As fishing pressure increases, western trout are becoming every bit as skeptical and selective as their eastern counterparts. Versatility is now the major prerequisite for consistent success on western streams. The skilled western fly fisher possesses the finely tuned finesse and hatch-matching abilities demanded by eastern streams, plus the casting, wading, and water-reading skills that western rivers require. Throw in an experimental, yet pragmatic, attitude and you have the type of angler that every western guide looks forward to taking out. The best of these fishermen are not only comfortable with everything from double streamer rigs and sinking-tip lines to midges and 7X tippets, but they know when to use each.

Western trout streams are best characterized by the words *abundant* and *diverse*. I recently made a business trip through Montana and Wyoming. I kept track of the named trout streams that I crossed along the way. Beginning with the Sheep River a few blocks from my home in southern Alberta and concluding with the North Platte in Wyoming a few days later, I counted over 70 streams, ranging from rivers large and famous to creeks small and unknown. This number does not count those that I came near but didn't cross, nor the ones I crossed but didn't notice because I was dozing behind the wheel. I saw big freestone rivers, tailwaters, spring creeks, mountain brooks. I saw streams with dozens of anglers and streams that seemed abandoned by humans. The intent of this book is to identify and explain the methods required to fish the abundant and diverse trout streams of the West; to help experienced fly fishers who plan to, but have not yet fished there; and to help new fly fishers who live in the West.

—Rock Creek, Montana,
August 8, 2002

CHAPTER 1

Western Trout
(and Some Relatives)

RAINBOW TROUT

If you were to design the perfect fish for fly fishing, you might end up with a duplication of the rainbow trout. Rainbows possess all the practical and esthetic qualities we want in a sport fish. They live comfortably in streams and lakes and will go to the ocean if there's one handy. They feed heavily on aquatic insects and are happy to do it at the surface of the water. They are beautiful, sleek creatures that, like European sportscars, look fast even when they're parked. Add the fact that they can be reared quickly and easily in hatcheries, and it's not hard to understand why rainbow trout are now favorites of anglers around the world.

What anglers like best about them is their exceptional fighting ability. When hooked, rainbow trout are the uncontested champions of performance. No freshwater fish runs as far, jumps as high or as often. This was made clear to me for the umpteenth time when I fished a small western spring creek a number of years ago. Pale morning dun mayflies were on the water one cloudy, showery afternoon, and the fish were rising to them nicely. They were mostly cutthroats, and I had been having a pretty good day, catching some good-size fish when I did everything just right. At a spot where a gentle run ducked beneath a round, plump willow bush, several good fish were rising, quietly sipping the duns that drifted on the placid surface of the spring creek. I slipped gently into the water downstream of the willow and made a few casts to the nearest fish. After a while, it took my fly. It was an eighteen-inch cutthroat and it thrashed about a bit, but I was able to keep it from disturbing the other fish while I brought it to my net.

The next fish was rising a bit farther back under the willow, and it took several tries to get the cast right. Finally the fly settled like a piece of lint on a billiard table and bobbed along until the head of a trout politely creased the surface to take it. I tightened up gently, congratulating myself for show-ing restraint and remembering to set the hook with my "6X strike." When the fish felt the prick of the hook, it bolted upstream, ripping the fly line out of my hand. The reel stuttered, the handle stung my knuckles, and the tip-pet broke about the time the fish reached the shallow water beyond the willow. After breaking off, it jumped, going hard around the next corner, and as it left the water, I saw the pink stripe on its side that explained every-thing. This was not a bigger fish; it was a different fish—a rainbow, just doing its thing.

Few fishermen get confused when rainbow trout are mentioned in a conversation. Other species of fish, especially Pacific salmon, have many localized names that can make it difficult to know just what is being dis-cussed. A taxonomist might disagree, but to most anglers a rainbow is a rainbow is a rainbow, whether it lives in Alaska, Montana, New Zealand, or South America.

Rainbow trout are native to North American waters draining the Pacific Ocean, from Alaska to northern Mexico. With a few exceptions, one being the Athabasca strain in Alberta, they are not native to waters draining the eastern slopes of the Rockies. In general, rainbow trout are spring spawners, though their longtime affiliation with fish hatcheries has allowed human tampering to the point where fall-spawning strains now exist.

The rainbow has been the subject of a classic "lumper versus splitter" debate among taxonomists for decades. For many years it was believed there were two species—the oceangoing rainbow, called steelhead, and the non-migratory stay-at-home version, simply called rainbow. Then the lumpers took the lead, and for a time both migratory and nonmigratory rainbows were called *Salmo gairdneri*. It's been a seesaw battle, though, and in the 1990s the splitters had their way and steelhead were removed from the rainbow trout list and assigned a new classification, called *Oncorhynchus mykiss*.

The ease with which rainbow trout eggs and fry can be reared in hatch-eries and transported great distances is the reason they are the most common trout in the West today. In the early days, before the practice of non-native introductions was governed by sound biology and political correctness, fish planting was a "make it up as you go" proposition. Consequently, migra-tory and nonmigratory strains of rainbows were mixed, resulting in incon-sistent success in establishing rainbows in new waters.

Rainbows were also introduced to many waters already occupied by native cutthroats and bull trout. In some cases, this reduced the stocks or compromised the purity of the native fish. In other cases, rainbows may have accidentally saved the day by giving a stream a species hardier than the natives. In Alberta's Bow River, the introduction of rainbows has been a huge blessing, simply because they are more capable than the native cutthroats and bulls of withstanding the pressures caused by the proximity of a major city.

Throughout North America, the heritage of most non-native rainbows can be traced to California and Oregon. Both resident and migratory fish from rivers such as the Rogue and McCloud were used for transplantation as early as 1870. In 1874 fertile California rainbow trout eggs destined for New York State were packed in ice-chilled trays and placed in the bowels of a steamship. Their route was around South America, but the eggs survived, with the result that California rainbow trout reached the eastern United States nine years ahead of European brown trout. The expansion of their range continued, and today there are great rainbow trout fisheries around the world.

In western North America, there are great, heavily spotted Alaskan rainbows in the Bristol Bay drainage. There are the silver bullets from British Columbia's Babine and Alberta's Bow. There are the Ph.D. rainbows of Idaho's Silver Creek and Henry's Fork. The Deschutes River in Oregon, Hat Creek and Fall River in California, the Roaring Fork in Colorado, the San Juan in New Mexico, and Arizona's wide Colorado all are home to the glorious fish Ernest Schwiebert called "The Trout on the Flying Trapeze."

It's hard to generalize about the type of water rainbow trout prefer. Most books tell us they like fast water, and there are plenty of fast-water rainbow streams, such as the Deschutes in Oregon and the middle Madison in Montana. But there are also first-rate rainbow waters that are very docile. Much of Fall River in California and the Harriman State Park (Railroad Ranch) section of the Henry's Fork of the Snake are smooth and flat. Rainbows also thrive in many gentle spring creeks, so I guess the word we're left with is *adaptable*. Rainbows make out well in a variety of habitats, as long as their needs for food, shelter from current, and safety from predators are met.

As for the influence of weather on their behavior, rainbows sit somewhere between the sun-worshipping cutthroats and the nocturnal brown trout. Rainbows are often most active in low-light periods, but it's not impossible to find them chowing down in the bright sun either. Here's that word again—*adaptable*.

A black cloud drifted over the trout-fishing horizon in 1994 with the discovery of whirling disease in Montana's Madison River. A parasitic infection originally thought to exist only in hatcheries, whirling disease affects immature rainbow trout and can cause severe declines in rainbow populations in streams where conditions are conducive to the spread of the disease. Though its presence has not had the devastating affect that was originally feared, in the early twenty-first century a great deal of research is being done to seek a biological and/or management antidote to whirling disease.

In writing this, I almost called rainbow trout "the Chevrolets of the fish world," and if I had, my point would have been that these fish are common, reliable, and almost universally appreciated. But even though that's all true, I'd still feel I was shortchanging them. Could the sport of fly fishing exist without rainbow trout daintily taking dry flies and then running hard for the ocean? It probably could, but it sure wouldn't be the same.

CUTTHROAT TROUT

Though they've been here all along, fishing for cutthroats has become more popular and even somewhat fashionable in recent years. There are two reasons for this. First, cutthroats are a native species in the West, and anglers have recently begun to take greater interest in, and place more value on, native fish. Second, cutthroats respond especially well to catch-and-release regulations, because they are capable of surviving a number of catchings without apparent difficulty. So in many places, the fishing for cutthroats is improving as more streams are placed under no-kill or limited-kill angling regulations.

It's also become fashionable, I'm afraid, to consider cutthroats to be a little—well, a little *thick*, as in not the sharpest knives in the drawer and a little slow on the uptake (or maybe that should be a little *quick* on the uptake), because they're usually pretty easy to catch. And while there's no denying the fact that cutts are generally easier to catch than rainbows or browns, there are exceptions.

Take, for example, the day I was fishing in southeastern British Columbia with a friend from Vermont. Tom works for a large fly-fishing company and previously earned his living by guiding anglers in his native Colorado. He knows about dumb cutthroats.

We parked at the top of a hill on a bluebird August day and scrambled down a gravelly slope to a perfect cutthroat creek that gurgles through the spruce forest below. Right at the bottom of the hill is a beautiful clear pool, which on this particular afternoon was alive with big cutthroats chugging at the surface, scoffing juicy green drake mayflies that hopped and fluttered down the rocky run.

We were so sure this was going to be a slam-dunk affair that we decided the gentlemanly thing would be to take turns on these gullible fish. Being a gracious host, I told Tom to go first. I think he said something like, "OK, but don't worry, this won't take long."

About the time the battery in my watch died, Tom decided it was my turn, even though he hadn't caught a fish yet. I was still pretty cocky about things and figured I had a big advantage over some guy from Vermont, because I had fished this creek before and knew what these trout liked.

We took turns, all right—trying every Green Drakish thing we could find in our vests, all with equally dismal results. Through it all, the fish fed merrily on, occasionally drowning one of our sorry artificials with the backwash of a rise, but never making the mistake we were waiting for. When we ran out of clever ideas, we looked at each other, shrugged our shoulders, and headed upstream. Dumb cutthroats indeed.

If there's a point to all this, it might be that not all cutts are pushovers, and even those that start out easy get tougher as they encounter more anglers. In the old days, when somebody said the cutthroats were getting fussy, he meant you had to go all the way down to a #14 Royal Wulff to fool them. In lightly fished backcountry streams, you can still do well with standard attractor patterns, but by late summer on the most popular rivers, the fish are generally underwhelmed by #8 Stimulators and clumsy, rubber-legged foam flies (or fancy Green Drake Emergers). One of the side effects of no-kill regulations is that the fish get tougher to catch, and hard-fished cutthroats get as tough as any. I know I'm convinced, and I now wince whenever somebody refers to cutthroats as dumb, gullible, or easy.

Cutthroats are native to watersheds draining both slopes of the Rocky Mountains in headwater streams of the Saskatchewan, Columbia, Missouri, Colorado, Arkansas, Platte Rivers, and the Rio Grande. The three best wild cutthroat river systems today are the Snake in Wyoming, the Yellowstone in Yellowstone Park, and the Elk in southeastern British Columbia. Each system has a different strain of native cutthroats. In the Snake and Yellowstone, the fish are named after the rivers—Snake River cutthroats and Yellowstone cutthroats—and in the Elk system, the fish are the westslope strain. Though the subspecies are different, cutthroats are cutthroats, and they all are found in the same exquisite high-country settings, in postcard streams that run clean, cold, and clear. And, they all exhibit the quality that most endears them to fly rodders: a willingness to feed on the surface.

Rainbows and browns become candidates for dry flies when they are drawn to feed at the surface by a heavy hatch of natural insects. Cutthroats are different. They live in cold streams where the hatches are sparse, and as a result, they have learned to be opportunistic. Through the summer, they will often come to a dry fly, hatch or no hatch.

Because of this wonderful trait, cutthroats are perfect fish for newcomers to fly fishing—especially children. Many western anglers have cut their teeth on little creeks full of small but eager cutthroats. These great fish provide what psychologists call positive reinforcement and what dry-fly anglers call red-letter days.

The best time of year to fish for cutthroats is the second half of the summer, when the weather and water are warmest. Unlike brown trout, and to a certain degree rainbows, cutthroats are most active on the afternoons of bright, sunny days. I've never heard an explanation for this, except that all life in a cold creek takes a while to warm up and get going. On cutthroat streams, it's often a good plan to fish with nymphs or streamers until early afternoon, and then switch to drys after the water has warmed up a bit.

One similarity between cutthroats and brown trout is their preference to lie near debris in the stream. Undercut banks, logjams, and deadfalls are prime places to find both fish. On big, rocky rivers, cutthroats also lie along current seams on the insides of big corners. They seem to have a preference for currents of medium speed. I seldom catch them in either the quickest or the slowest water in the stream.

Because they are both true trout that spawn in the spring, cutthroats and rainbows hybridize easily, producing offspring that are fertile. Over time, rainbows come to dominate this game, eventually taking over the stream. Mother Nature's plan was to keep these two fish separate, but as is often the case, man thought he had a better idea and made many introductions of rainbows into native cutthroat waters, with the result that many former cutthroat fisheries are now rainbow fisheries. The best cutthroat streams today are those where rainbows have never been introduced, or where the cutthroats are isolated from rainbows by natural barriers like waterfalls. In Yellowstone National Park, cutthroats are the only trout species living above two large sets of falls on the Yellowstone River.

While the Yellowstone, Snake River, and westslope strains are the most common cutthroats, there are a number of additional subspecies, including the Gila and Apache strains, whose native range extends as far south as New Mexico and Arizona. A relative from the north and west is the sea-run cutthroat of British Columbia, Washington, and Oregon. This is one of the fish immortalized by Roderick Haig-Brown in *A River Never Sleeps*. It is pursued by anglers where the coastal rivers meet the ocean. Sea-run cutthroats are favorites of anglers who fish minnow patterns near beaches and rocky points within sight of Vancouver's and Seattle's office buildings and elsewhere along the northern Pacific coast.

One of the reasons I hunt and fish is because doing so allows me to occasionally experience brief, fleeting contacts with perfection. These come in varied and surprising ways, but none better than the sight of a peach-and-rose-hued cutthroat turning up from the bottom and sliding gracefully toward a dry fly.

BROWN TROUT

One of my best fishing trips was a visit to Yellowstone Park with my wife and daughter a number of years ago. I wanted my daughter to see and experience some of the things that gave me fond memories from my teenage years. So we visited the geological wonders like Old Faithful and the Grand Canyon of the Yellowstone, and the piscatorial wonders, too, like the Madison, Firehole, and Gibbon Rivers. Along the way, we spent a few days with our friend Leigh Perkins at his home in Wyoming. Leigh's house is about thirty feet from one of the juiciest spring creeks I've ever seen.

During trout talk over dinner one night, Leigh mentioned that the biologists who study the creek find a surprising number of brown trout in it, even though the majority of the fish anglers catch are Snake River cutthroats. "They told me there're some big browns in the pool right in front of the house," Leigh said.

It was a temptation I couldn't resist. After dinner, when it was good and dark, I cut back my dry-fly leader and tied on the biggest Clouser Minnow I could find in my box. I walked out the door and started casting, taking care not to break the dining room window with a backcast. The fly sailed out into the gloom, landed with a splat, and settled. I waited a few seconds, and then began a stripping retrieve. About three casts into the proceedings, something mugged the Clouser out in the deepest, darkest part of the pool. A few minutes later Leigh was there, after-dinner drink in hand, while Lynda and Deanna leaned into the flashlight beam that illuminated a four- or five-pound brown trout. "I'll be damned," Leigh said. "I thought I'd caught every fish in this pool twice. But I've never seen this guy before."

The fact that this fish was unknown to the man who fishes the stream every day would be portrayed by scientists as an example of the nocturnal tendencies of brown trout. But such pragmatism makes for dull fishing stories, and the outdoor press gives us a different spin. The fishing magazines tell us that brown trout are smart, elusive, and difficult to catch. Sometimes they use the word *wily*. They tell us that this is because browns have been fished over for hundreds of years in their native Europe, where they gained a several-century head start on our native fish in the business of outwitting anglers.

It is true that brown trout are a hardy, adaptable species, capable of withstanding heavier angling pressure and lower-quality water than other trout. These qualities allow brown trout to thrive in circumstances in which native trout cannot. Like the white-tailed deer, the brown trout lives unnoticed at the very threshold of civilization. And also like whitetails, brown trout have attained near-mystical status among those who pursue them. In truth, this sacred regard for brown trout is a little hard to explain. Browns don't fight as well as rainbows, and they aren't as pretty as some other trout. Still, there's something special about a brown trout. Maybe it's those outdoor magazines again. They have convinced us that when we catch a brown— especially a big one—we can be sure we've done something miraculous. And everybody likes to think they've beaten the odds and achieved the near impossible.

So maybe we like to catch brown trout simply because we don't catch them as often as other trout. That might just be human nature. And it doesn't hurt that brown trout have the ability to get big just about anyplace they live, with huge specimens periodically materializing from surprisingly small streams.

Brown trout are one of the mainstays of North American fly fishing today, but their star ascended slowly. When they were first brought to the Catskill streams of New York from the Black Forest of Germany in 1883, browns were perceived as a threat to the stocks of native brook trout that were dearly loved by the fly fishers of the day.

The brown trout used in early North American plantings are thought to have been of two strains, the Von Behr strain from Germany and the Loch Leven from Scotland. Today, after a century of mixing and matching, the two are generally indistinguishable, though you still occasionally hear an old-timer refer to a beautiful, red-spotted specimen as a "German brown."

It sounds strange when you say it out loud, but people sometimes develop relationships with brown trout. These are usually people who spend a lot of time on the same small streams. They might have a cabin or house near the creek, and they fish the same water so often that they come to know the habits and lies of individual fish. The first time I encountered this was with my friend Bob Scammell, who has a cabin on a good brown trout stream. We were supposed to be fishing together, but in reality Bob was guiding me, which seems to give him as much pleasure as fishing himself. He took me to a slow, deep bend and pointed at the far bank. "The fish is under the dead spruce branch," he said. "Not the green branch, and not the stump." When I finally made the right cast, a fish appeared at my fly. And when I landed the fish, Bob looked knowingly at it and said, "This one is called 'The Shark.' He's wintered well." In the years since, I've been intro-duced to trout—all browns—named Cedric, Walter, the Tree Hole Trout, and Hooper. All this is possible because browns in small streams are home-bodies. They live where they live until somebody or something eats them or chases them out. It's a wonderful trait in a fish.

Some of the best western brown trout rivers are the Beaverhead, Big-horn, and Madison in Montana; the Bow in Alberta; the Provo in Utah; the

Owens in California; and the Cowichan on British Columbia's Vancouver Island. Brown trout often share these waters with rainbows or cutthroats (or with steelhead and salmon in the Cowichan), and it's possible to have good fishing for the other species when the browns are pouting and don't want to play. Many of the West's biggest browns are caught in autumn when they move from lakes and reservoirs into the rivers in preparation for spawning. Streamer fishing for big browns is an October tradition on rivers like the Madison above Hebgen Lake in Yellowstone Park.

The fundamental strategies for finding brown trout are to fish late in the evening and on overcast days, when the fish are most likely to be feeding. When the weather is too nice, concentrate on parts of the stream where direct sunlight doesn't hit the water. Brown trout favor cover and like to lie along undercut banks or beneath overhanging trees and bushes. Most books will tell you that brown trout prefer slightly slower water than other trout, and though I've caught them there, I've also caught enough of them in rough-and-tumble pocket water that I tend to disregard that generality. They are where they are.

In the late nineties, I traveled to British Columbia's Cowichan River to film a winter steelhead-fishing episode of the TV series *Iron Blue Fly Fishing.* Understand that trying to catch a steelhead is a lonely and daunting task under the best of conditions, but when the camera is rolling, the director is drumming his fingers nervously, and time and money are evaporating with each steelheadless moment, you begin to feel some pressure. It's a little like sitting under the bright light in the small room with the snarly police seargent—with your waders on. At lunch the second day, I sought relief from the stress and wandered down the river to a good run pointed out to me by the guide and guest on this episode, Joe Saysell. I fished carefully, trying to get a big egg fly to dead drift through the heart of the run. After a few casts, the line stopped drifting. I struck hard and hung on as a fish made a determined track for the middle of the river. I yelled, and the cameraman came stumbling down the bank, trying to run and fire up the machinery at the same time. We filmed the rest of the fight, which was solid, if a little unspectacular, but after a few minutes I began to get a funny feeling about things. It turned out that the fish was a brown trout—a very good brown trout, but still, a brown trout, which meant it wasn't a steelhead. And we were on a steelhead river, supposedly making a TV show about steelhead fishing. It was the first and last time I've been disappointed by a twenty-inch brown, but it confirmed once again the fact that brown trout are where you find them.

You can often do well with browns when the water is slightly off-color. I don't mean water that is muddy, but water that is stained a little from spring runoff or a recent rain. The fish are often more active when the water has two to three feet of visibility than when it is completely clear. I think the dark water accomplishes the same thing as a dark sky—it keeps the sun off the fish and makes them a little less shy and a bit more willing to move about and feed.

Several years ago a friend from Pennsylvania fished the Bow River with me during a hot spell in August. The bright and sunny weather continued through the first few days, and while Jim caught plenty of big rainbows, the knowledge that there were brown trout around began to eat at him. He wanted a big brown. He asked me what he could do to get one, and I told him to work on changing the weather. He took my suggestion (or somebody did), and his last day was cold, drizzly, and windy. Fishing the same water with the same flies and methods as we had all week, he caught four big browns the final afternoon. And they all appeared from out of nowhere, just the way the magazines said they could.

I may have inadvertently made the case here that brown trout are ordinary fish with some distinct behavior tendencies. The scientific side of my brain may even agree with this. But the side of my brain that stores memories and yearns for the unreachable—the side I fish with—does not. There is indeed something special about brown trout. They induce a deep craving in me to understand what's going on under the water. And on those rare occasions when I catch a hook-jawed dragon with golden sides and ruby spots, I feel as if I've performed an honorable bit of magic by reaching into the heart of the stream and pulling out something I wasn't even sure existed.

BULL TROUT

In the old days, the recipe for catching a bull trout went something like this: Step 1. Find a live mouse. Step 2. Tie a fishhook to the mouse. Step 3. Put the mouse on a small piece of wood. Step 4. Set the piece of wood adrift in a deep, eerie pool of a western trout stream. Step 5. Pull Mickey off his raft when it reaches the deepest part of the pool. Step 6. Well, I think you get the picture. This method doesn't pass the political correctness sniff test today, and I've never seen it featured on a fishing TV show, but it does provide insight into the character of the bull trout.

It's easy to ascribe noble and mystical qualities to bull trout—how they're a true symbol of wilderness, the canary in the mine of trout streams, a throwback to another era. And while bulls no doubt deserve most of these lofty attributes, I see them in a somewhat simpler light. My admiration stems from an appreciation for the bull trout's simple, honest creed, its all-encompassing mission in life, which is to kill and eat things. They are the top link in the predatory chain of trout streams draining the Rocky

Mountains, and as such, they aren't choosy about what they kill and eat. They take what comes along.

Perhaps the bull trout's most attractive characteristic to a sport fisher is its ability to grow big, even in small water. A two-footer is a big trout in a stream, but not a particularly big bull trout. In some of the more remote areas of British Columbia and Alaska, a bull must be bigger than fifteen pounds to be noteworthy. These are the only resident stream trout we have that warrant quantification in feet and pounds.

The bull trout's natural range includes most western drainages from southern Alaska to California along both sides of the Rocky Mountains. They are members of the char family, along with eastern brook trout, lake trout, and Dolly Varden trout. At one time Dolly Vardens and bull trout were considered the same species, but in the 1980s it was determined that bulls are distinct from Dollies, which only occur naturally west of the Continental Divide and usually spend part of their lives in the Pacific Ocean.

Though they can and do take up full-time residence in smaller streams, in many cases bull trout spend spring and summer in the larger main stem rivers and move into smaller tributaries in August before spawning in September. The best fishing is in the big rivers in midsummer or in the tributary streams shortly after the fish move into them. As spawning approaches, they become more difficult to catch.

Bull trout are pale olive in color, with a few pastel salmon pink spots as highlights. Like brook trout, bulls have white leading edges on their pectoral, pelvic, and anal fins, and anglers sometimes confuse small bulls with brookies. The bulls' identification badge is the absence of black markings on their dorsal fins. Like gawky teenage boys, immature bull trout often have large heads and skinny bodies. But when they mature, they begin to put on weight. Most bulls over two feet long are heavy-bodied and perfectly proportioned, both fierce and handsome, in the manner of a raptor.

As the grand poobahs of our streams, adult bull trout have few natural enemies and view themselves as more *predator* than *predatee*. However, their aggressive nature and lifestyle of killing and eating make them vulnerable to the same kind of treatment at the hands of human predators. They are especially susceptible to big spoons and live bait of the smelly variety. This trait didn't deplete the bull trout's numbers excessively in the first half of the twentieth century, because many of the places they lived were simply too difficult for people to get into. But these days it's easy to penetrate the wild places where bull trout live, thanks to mountain bikes, quads, ATVs, and the opening up of the backcountry by the tourism, mining, logging, and oil industries. When you combine the bull trout's susceptibility to angling with the increase in wilderness accessibility, and throw in the fact that bulls don't spawn until they are five or six years old, you have a recipe for eradication—which is just what happened through much of their range in the last sixty or seventy years. Currently there are some western states where not only are bull trout protected from harvest, but angling for them is not allowed. In other areas, such as Alberta, angling for bull trout is allowed, but all bulls caught must be released.

In the early days, bull trout were considered second- or third-rate game fish, especially by snobby fly fishers. The bull trout's receptiveness to big lures and liver-baited treble hooks was thought to make it less sporting than other species. In truth, this was an angling version of the sour grapes story. Fly fishers couldn't figure out how to catch bull trout, so they decided they weren't worth fishing for. But things are changing. We have learned that bull trout will take streamer flies that imitate the small fish they eat, and in places where their numbers are recovering and where angling is allowed, they have undergone a serious upgrade in status. They have become the darlings of the outdoor press, and for some anglers, catching a bull trout is like getting an autograph from a movie star.

Most anglers still focus on the rainbows, cutthroats, and grayling that usually share the streams with the bulls, but in some places, like the Elk system in southern British Columbia, there is a growing number of hardcore bull trout hunters wandering the streambeds these days. You'll recognize them because they carry 8- and 9-weight fly rods rigged with sinking-tip lines. If you can get one of these guys to let you look in his fly box, you'll see rows of pink, yellow, and orange lead-eyed streamers up to 6 inches long. This might seem like overkill, but a #2/0 streamer is not too large for a fish that's willing to take a bite out of a ten-inch cutthroat.

Bull trout are often large enough that they can be spotted in the deep pools, and some fishermen routinely climb high banks above such places to scout for bulls before fishing. There's also the unintentional method of locating a bull trout, which my daughter and I witnessed a couple of years ago. We were fishing a small "kids' creek" for cutthroats, and I was doing my angling-mentor routine, spouting off about reading water, matching hatches, fancy casting, and anything else I thought would impress a twelve-year-old. As a demonstration of the relevance of all this, I cast my dry fly up beside a fallen log. "There should be a fish right about . . . there," I said smugly as a little blip appeared at the fly. The twelve-inch cutthroat raced around the pool for a moment, and then made an unexpected beeline straight toward us. When he got about a yard from our feet, it became apparent that we were the least of Mr. Cutthroat's worries. A two-and-a-half-foot long bull trout was after him, charging and snapping, and disinclined to give up on a good chance at an easy lunch. When the bull bumped into our feet during one of his charges, Deanna and I both involuntarily stepped back out of the water. The experience rattled both of us a little. The bull didn't get the cutthroat, but it was a graphic example of the predator-prey relationship. After it was all over and the bull trout had disappeared back under his log, Deanna looked up at me with eyes like hubcaps and said, "What the heck was that?" On the whole, I think she was more impressed with the bull trout's ferocity than with her father's clever demonstration that started the whole episode.

Bull trout need one of two things to survive these days: isolation from people or regulations restricting their harvest. As the former declines, the latter become more critical. In many parts of the West where there is neither, bull trout are either extremely rare or, simply and sadly, gone.

Today's recipe for catching a bull trout is a little different: Step 1. First hook a small trout, grayling or whitefish. Step 2. Watch closely behind that fish as you bring it in. Step 3. When a big green ghost materializes from the deep and tries to steal your fish, release the little guy, tie on a big streamer, and swim it around the pool like a little fish with a problem. Step 4. Hang on tight.

EASTERN BROOK TROUT

Eastern brook trout are native to the northeastern quarter of North America, east of the Mississippi from Hudson Bay to South Carolina. They were the fish that charmed early sportfishers in dainty hemlock-lined streams of New York's Adirondack Mountains and Pennsylvania's Poconos prior to the American Revolution. They satisfied the immigrant fly fishers who had left their beloved brown trout behind in the chalkstreams of the British Isles. Ironically, a century later, when browns and rainbows were introduced to the streams of the northeastern United States, they were viewed as interlopers that threatened to displace the native brook trout. The early American fly fishers had become fiercely loyal to both their new land and the trout that lived there.

Since then, brook trout have been transplanted widely throughout North America, and some western waters, particularly lakes like British Columbia's Fortress Lake and Idaho's Henry's Lake, provide exceptional fishing for big brook trout.

In large measure, however, the introduction of brook trout to western waters is now viewed as a mistake. Most of the streams to which brook trout were introduced originally held native cutthroats, rainbows, or bull trout. Brook trout spawn at an earlier age and do so more successfully than the native western fish, and this allows them to outcompete the natives and eventually dominate the streams. The result is frequently an overabundance of stunted brook trout and serious decline or even elimination of the native fish. Brook trout have been identified as an obstacle to the recovery of native bull trout and cutthroat populations in parts of the West.

Perhaps the best example of this is in my home province of Alberta. There are brook trout in many of our small mountain streams and beaver ponds, invariably waters that once held good numbers of native cutthroats and bull trout. In many of these places, brook trout are now exempt from the catch-and-release regulations that apply to other species, and anglers are encouraged to harvest them to make room for the natives. On one stream, from 1999 through 2001, anglers were allowed to fish but only if they killed every brook trout they caught. This was done as an experiment to determine if brook trout numbers could be adequately reduced by angling.

Early indications are that the experiment is working; that is, that the population of brook trout has decreased and the population of natives has increased. The question, though, is whether these results can be sustained while there are still brook trout in the stream.

There are some colliding ideals here. It's a little hard to explain this project to people who are under the impression that modern fly fishing is a low-impact, nonconsumptive, ecologically sound, compassionate, and politically correct sport. And even though there is scientific justification for the project, some people see the "ethnic cleansing" of the dainty and beautiful brook trout as a little like putting out a contract on the Easter Bunny.

Brook trout are members of the char family, which also includes bull trout and lake trout, and like all char, brookies spawn in the fall. Their sporting qualities would be comparable to brown trout, except that they rarely if ever jump when hooked. Their fighting style is more George Foreman than Muhammad Ali—strong, persistent, effective, but not flashy. Small brook trout are generally easy to catch, but the late western fly-fishing guru Charles E. Brooks considered large brook trout as difficult to fool as big browns.

Even in view of their recently tarnished reputation, I can't deny the fact that I like brook trout. They somehow still seem correct in the small, pristine mountain creeks and beaver ponds where I most often find them. In these places the brookies rarely get big, and consequently they don't get the attention that other species might. Many people, though, consider them the prettiest of all trout, and I hope there will always be a place in our sport, even in the West, for small creeks full of small brook trout, where small kids can catch them.

MOUNTAIN WHITEFISH

Whitefish are the blue-collar, hard-hat residents of our western watersheds. There may be more whitefish than trout living in our streams, and there may be more whitefish caught than trout, but whitefish still don't get much press coverage. You don't see their images on computer screen savers, and eloquent outdoor writers never wax poetic on their virtues. Not that I'm some kind of champion of whitefish either, mind you. I'd rather catch a trout than a whitefish, but I'd sure rather catch a whitefish than nothing. And there have been plenty of times when I've caught whitefish only and was glad to have them. Perhaps their status, or lack of it, is best summarized by the angling regulations for Montana, wherein you'll find that the limit on whitefish is one hundred per day.

Mountain whitefish are relatives of trout but are not trout. They are native to western watersheds on both sides of the Rockies. They feed on the same things as trout and are prime candidates for well-presented nymphs. Whitefish feed on the surface at times, though not as readily as trout. And that might be a good thing, for when they are rising, whitefish can be maddeningly hard to fool, thereupon morphing into yet another piscatorial sour grape.

Their fighting qualities are likewise underrated; they don't run very far and they don't jump at all, but their strength is impressive, and they make good use of current by turning their bodies perpendicular to it and daring the angler to bring them in. Often they seem to do their most vigorous fighting after they're in your net or your hands.

Whitefish are perhaps most numerous in the larger western rivers and are not generally hard to locate. Stand on a high bank above a freestone stream and watch for movement on the bottom or fish a nymph in the riffly water, and you'll probably find them. They move from the big rivers into tributaries to spawn in September. When the spawning migration peaks, there can be so many whitefish crammed into a pool that the entire bottom of the stream appears to be gently writhing.

It's hard to say which western streams are the best whitefish rivers. The Madison? The Missouri? The Deschutes? Getting this information is a little like asking which store in Las Vegas has the best selection of Bibles. It's not that the question doesn't have an answer; it's just that nobody's trying very hard to find it.

ARCTIC GRAYLING

Most western fly fishers have not caught a grayling, and because of that, they're missing something. Of all western coldwater fish, grayling best symbolize two things once thought to be fundamental to the heart of fly fishing—wilderness and wildness. Arctic grayling are not sophisticated, not particularly strong, and not the least bit selective. They are beautiful and fragile-looking, and are probably the easiest fish to catch on a fly. An outdoor writer friend once called arctic grayling "the eager ones," and it's a phrase I wish I had thought of.

Catching a grayling is not difficult, and doing so is not evidence of particular angling prowess. Catching one is instead evidence of the faithful existence of true wilderness, something sadly missing from much of the modern fly-fishing experience. Grayling live in places where the summer passes in the blink of an eye and darkness rules much of the year. They are soulmates of the caribou, scratching out an existence in the harshest of circumstances, thriving in streams where the tracks in the sandbars were more likely made by wolves or grizzlies than by fishermen.

Grayling are distinguished by their large, sail-like dorsal fins, which are most impressive in males, and by their overall iridescent purplish cast. They have large scales and small mouths. Grayling are gregarious fish, and when you find a feeding school, stand back. No fish, not even cutthroats, come close to the eagerness with which feeding grayling take dry flies. It seems possible at times, and maybe it is, to catch and release every grayling in the pool. This is where the mythical hundred-fish day becomes a possibility. Grayling are good jumpers, but they don't run much and they seem to run out of gas quickly. Even in the far north, a two-pounder is a big one.

In my experience, grayling appear never to have been taught the basic drag-free drift concept of dry-fly fishing. This was pointed out to me by a guide on the Fond du Lac River in northern Saskatchewan. It was mainly a pike trip, but we were trying to catch a couple of grayling for a shore lunch. I did my spring creek bit, trying to get a perfect natural drift with my dry fly. When I had made three casts without success, the guide, J. B. Bigeye, said, "No, no, no, not like that. Like this," whereupon he took my rod, made a cast across stream, and held the rod still while the current straightened out the line. The fly started water-skiing, and a grayling popped up from below and inhaled it. J. B. made a second cast, caught a second grayling, and we had our lunch.

Native to Montana and Michigan as well as the north, grayling are today found in good numbers only in waters draining into the Arctic Ocean. In the backcountry of Alaska and the Yukon, as well as in northern British Columbia, Alberta, and Saskatchewan, schools of grayling still glide over the gravel bars in great numbers. Northern fly-in fishing lodges list grayling in their brochures as one of the fish available to guests, but they are usually described in small print, below the bigger attractions of lake trout, northern pike, and walleye. Grayling deserve better.

CHAPTER 2

Western Trout Streams

A t nine thousand feet, on a steep, south-facing slope, dark shale absorbs and holds the warmth of a late-April afternoon. Up a little higher, a snowbank begins to soften under the heat of the spring sun and the prevailing winds from the warm Pacific coast. Snow starts to melt and drain away from the bottom of the snowbank. Small trickles marry and create a stream the size of those that float children's boats in street gutters. This miniature stream meets others like it to form a brook that flows for just a few weeks each spring while the snow is melting. The little stream accelerates across the rocks and tumbles off the mountain in a wispy waterfall. Where the water lands, it is below the treeline. The snow is deeper here in the scrub timber than on the exposed slopes above, and the vegetation holds it longer. As it melts, the snow gradually and steadily enlarges the stream. A bit farther along, in a hanging valley at sixty-five hundred feet, the clear water stalls briefly in a small pond surrounded by willows and crisscrossed with sunken deadfall. When it leaves the pond, the stream takes on a new identity. From here on it appears on some topographical maps—complete with a name—and from here on it flows year-round.

In the pond and in the slightly larger stream below, the first fish appear. They are native cutthroats with dark backs, large heads, and orange marks under their jaws. Some of the fish are old, and all of them are small. They live in the tiniest of pockets in the stream, balancing the needs for shelter and safety with the pull of hunger, which brings them darting across the miniature pools to nab an ant or beetle that has fallen in from the willows.

A mile farther, the stream is joined by another that does not look as bright and healthy. It carries a dirty gray tinge of silt, the result of clear-cut logging along its banks not far upstream. In another few miles, this new mix of clear and cloudy water joins a larger river flowing from the north through a wide gravel floodplain. Deposited along the banks and in the

17

brush well back from the water are debris, deadfall, and silt bars—remnants of a thousand spring runoffs, another of which will begin in a few weeks. If rains come with the melting snow, the river will again rise enough to take a new course through the bottom of the valley and will deposit new debris in new places.

As if life weren't arduous enough, the cutthroats now have something else to worry about. In the deeper pools live some large bull trout. They aren't as numerous as they once were, but those that remain still rule the river. The ancestors of the bull trout have preyed upon the ancestors of the cutthroats for generations. And when one of the big bulls slides out of the depths to take a look around, the cutthroats stop feeding. They don't flee, for that would surely provoke an attack. Instead they make a seemingly conscious effort at nonchalance, in that same peculiar way African antelope sometimes do when they find themselves in the presence of a hunting lion.

A few miles downstream, the river drops over an impressive set of falls, which adds oxygen to the water and keeps the cutthroats in the upper river separated from the philandering ways of the rainbow trout that were introduced below the falls in the 1940s. At the base of the falls this spring day, a hiker rests and watches the fish that seem to be attacking the white waterfall. Over and over they vault from the depths of the plunge pool, trying vainly to jump the falls and continue their upstream migration to spawn.

In the tailout below the pool at the falls, the fish that have given up high-jumping begin the spawning ritual. There are large, dark pairs where the shallow water flows quickly over fine, clean gravel, and as the females dig redds into which they'll deposit their eggs, the attending males, gnarly and bruised, slash at cocky fourteen-inch teenagers that are trying to steal their women.

For a time, the river flows through a tight, bouldery canyon that gets little sunlight even in high summer, but eventually it squirts eastward through an opening in the mountains and moves into less jumbled country. Here white-faced cattle graze on windswept hills that once fed bison and mammoths. Calves are born each spring on land that has been in the hands of the same ranching families for a hundred years. The presence of man is apparent in these foothills, but the ranch buildings, oil wells, power lines, and gravel roads are small parts of a landscape still dominated by wind, sky, and grass.

A few limber pines dot the hills, and tall cottonwoods are just starting to show green in the river bottom. In a few weeks, their white fluff will drop and blow in the persistent west wind that comes off the Rockies. Some of the fluff will land on the water and drift with the June hatch of pale morning dun mayflies. Some of it will fall on the gravel of the streambed, and in biblical fashion, some will fall on good soil—the rich silt that spring floods deposit on the downstream ends of islands. Here the seeds will germinate and saplings will begin to grow. Like fire on the prairie, flooding on a trout stream is not only tolerable, but necessary, and even crucial to the health and perpetuation of the ecosystem. Cottonwood trees can't reproduce without spring floods, and without cottonwoods, trout streams are less healthy. The big trees' roots hold soil and prevent erosion, and their canopy shades the stream and keeps the water cool. In the fall, the yellow leaves drop to the water and decay, providing phosphorus and nitrogen to the water, which allows the stream to feed aquatic plants, then insects, then trout.

After the stream has been joined by a few more freestone brothers, it is a big river by fishing standards. This warm spring morning, four or five McKenzie driftboats are on the water, their passengers casting sinking-tip fly lines and streamers but hoping to find the first rising fish of the year this afternoon when the *Baetis* mayflies begin to hatch.

Far down the valley, the river takes a sharp right turn. On the left bank, the water drives hard against rock riprap that was placed there after the last big flood to protect the small ranch town from further damage. Across the river, another small tributary adds its flow, but this one is different from the others. A few rainbows are spawning in the first pool above the confluence, and a few yards above that, a bed of aquatic plants waves seductively in the oily current. The water in this stream is clear, noticeably clearer than that in the main river. This stream is also quiet, without the rattling clatter that has been part of the main river's personality for forty-five miles.

This small creek begins a mile upstream, beneath a crack in the bedrock, in an underground place where water from rain and snowfall collects. Some water seeps out the crack and percolates through the gravel into a small pool. Constant flow from the spring overfills the pool, and the water falls a few feet down a low bench into the streambed, where it is joined by another, smaller spring creek that begins similarly a quarter mile to the east.

The spring creek moves gently and quietly, slowing in pools and flats and tiptoeing delicately through shallow riffles. Along one of the flats, a barbed-wire fence parallels the water, with one small indentation into the stream. There is gravel in the indentation, placed there by the third-generation cattle rancher who owns the land the creek flows through. The fence allows cattle to drink from this spot only, and the gravel prevents them from muddying the water. The rancher's father and grandfather had allowed the cattle to wander unchecked in and around the stream. Over forty years, bovine hooves had turned a deep, narrow run into a shallow, silty flat. The trout stopped using this part of the stream, and for years there were few fish upstream of this point.

It has been fifteen years since the fence was installed, and the creek has recovered well. There are gravel patches on the bottom where more spring water enters, and willows along the banks again. Midges hatch every day of the year, and trout cruise slowly and constantly, tipping upward to take an adult midge or flashing beneath the surface to take a pupa.

The rancher has done other things to restore the spring creek to its original productive state. In return for granting permission to fish, he asked anglers to abide by a catch-and-release rule. Over just a few years the fishing improved, and the rancher was approached more often by people who wanted to fish. He began to charge a fee and to limit the number of anglers allowed to fish each day. He was surprised how many people were willing to pay to fish, and a few years ago he began using the money to pay a stream-keeper to manage and improve the spring creek. The keeper brought in gravel to provide more good spawning habitat, planted some willows along the streambed, did more fencing, and removed some of the agricultural junk that littered the yard and the stream itself. The small spring creek is now treasured in the fly-fishing world and has an important place in the culture of the sport.

Downstream ten more miles, the main river is joined by one last major tributary, this one already dirty from rains in its headwaters to the south. For several miles the clear water refuses to completely mix with the dirty, and a curious line divides the river into two distinct halves.

After the waters have finally mixed, the current begins to slow, and after a mile or so the river is a river no more, but a long, narrow lake. Motorboats, water-skiers, and cottages appear, and the river has become a "recreational resource" of a different type. The lake is more than twenty miles long, and just above the face of the dam that creates it, one edge of the reservoir is peeled off and diverted into a sterile-looking irrigation canal. Some fish—whitefish, suckers, trout—follow the path into the canal, which takes them into farm country and an abrupt end to their lives when the canal's faucet is turned off in the fall.

The rest of the water is directed through large tunnels and is spit out from the bottom of the dam into the river channel below, clearer and colder than before, and with an injection of nutrients from the depths of the reservoir above.

Immediately below the dam, the river takes on a bright new personality. The most abundant new feature is the driftboat. A gravel boat ramp and parking lot sit a few hundred yards below the dam. This spring morning, there is a lineup of driftboats behind SUVs, waiting to launch. Benches and kiosks near the ramp provide places for fly fishers to sit and gear up, and dispense information on the special angling regulations that apply to this tailwater portion of the river. The kibitzing laughter of optimistic anglers drifts through the valley, along with music that pours out of quad speakers and spills through the open door of one of the trucks.

The river here is rich in aquatic life. The surface is cluttered with bugs—*Baetis* mayflies, midges, Skwala stoneflies, and scum lines of nymphal shucks collect along the banks and against the sides of anchored boats. Rainbow and brown trout pod up to tilt and tip at the surface. Along the slow inside corners, beds of *Potamogeton* and other plants reach the surface, even this early in the year.

Though the river itself is busier in nearly all ways, the river valley is getting less busy. Below the dam, the cottonwood trees are dwindling. Beavers are taking some down, but new ones aren't growing because the river here hasn't seen a spring flood in the sixty years the dam has been in place. Many of the remaining cottonwoods have been wrapped with chicken wire to reduce the beavers' success.

Fifteen miles farther downstream, the river passes another boat ramp and parking lot, and within the next few miles, it becomes apparent that the carnival is over. The river becomes a lonely river once more. The gravel roads that have accompanied it for nearly a hundred miles are gone. So are power lines. So are fences. So are driftboats and anglers. The trout are still here, but they are bothered little by humans, except for the kids who live on the Indian reserve where the river flows through it.

The next bridge across the river is thirty miles farther down, where the river leaves the reserve, and there it looks different. The water is cloudy, stained by used irrigation water that has been returned to the river after doing its work in the grain and potato fields. The trout are fewer in number because the riffles and runs have been replaced by uniformly slow and (to a trout fisher) uninteresting habitat. Pike, perch, and carp are now part of the new bio-mosaic of a western river.

The connections that lie within the ecosystem of a trout stream are not simply the obvious liquid links between upper and lower river, between tributaries and main stem, but also the more visceral links that reach in every other direction. There are upward connections with sky, cloud, sun, and wind that both remove and provide water. There are downward connections with the earth, to springs and bedrock. There are horizontal connections with plants and animals that live in and along the waterway and contribute nutrients, shade, and stability to the river. And there are the inevitable outward connections with man and his increasing ability to both wound and heal.

Western North America is ruled by mountains. The end result of their influence is *diversity*—diversity in landscape, climate, geology, geography, hydrology, flora, and fauna. Western North America has rain forests and deserts, and the mountains are a reason for both. But their influence extends beyond natural history to anthropology and culture. Everything about western life, from what people eat to what they believe and what they do for a living, is in some way influenced by the presence of mountains.

Likewise western trout streams, where the watchword is still *diversity*. Almost any water that is pulled downhill by gravity has at least the potential to be a trout stream. This includes tiny rivulets slipping off the Rockies, high-altitude meadow streams, small freestone rivers, large freestone rivers, giant freestone rivers, rivers flowing between lakes, lowland spring creeks, tailwater streams of all sizes, even irrigation ditches. Such variety in types of streams causes a corresponding variety in trout habitat, each of which demands a distinct approach from the fly fisher.

Though many streams have a mixed heritage, making them difficult to categorize, it is still worthwhile to consider most western trout streams as being one of three types: freestone streams, spring creeks, or tailwaters.

FREESTONE STREAMS

A freestone stream is one whose primary sources are the glaciers and snowfields of the mountains. Freestone streams can be any size. Typical examples are the Gallatin River in Montana and the Roaring Fork in Colorado. Follow such a river upstream and you'll find it getting smaller and smaller, breaking into numerous tributaries, with each of those getting smaller and smaller. Eventually, after much gain in elevation, you'll find the beginnings of a river.

The combining of many tiny trickles of meltwater creates a stream, but not all water draining off the mountains qualifies as a trout stream. If the creek stops flowing in summer when the snow is gone, or in winter when the snow isn't melting, the stream is seasonal only—that is, it flows only in spring or in times of high precipitation. This cannot be a trout stream. Trout streams need year-round supplies of water, and for many freestone streams these are provided by collecting basins in the headwaters of the system. These are lakes or ponds—often beaver ponds—into which the small tributaries flow. Such ponds collect enough water from the abundant flows of springtime to supply the outflowing streams with water the rest of the

A typical western freestone trout stream.

year. So although the source of most freestone streams is considered to be melting snow, these headwater basins provide trout streams with water when there is neither snow nor melting.

In the Rockies, the water near the headwaters is pure and cold, and much better suited for the production of beer and brokerage-house TV commercials than for the growth of trout. The clichéd photograph of a fly fisher fighting a big trout while enveloped by the spray of a waterfall coming off a glacier in the Rockies is essentially a myth. Though there are some exceptions, the water near the headwaters often lacks the minerals required for a strong food chain. A shortage of calcium and carbon means a shortage of algae and other green plants. A shortage of green plants means few insects. Few insects means few fish. In addition, the upper reaches of these streams often have gradients too steep to provide good habitat for trout, and because of the high elevation, some parts of the streams may freeze to the bottom in winter.

This is why the most productive portions of freestone streams are often some distance from their high-country sources, in the somewhat gentler landscape of the foothills. As the streams move away from their sources, they gain some of the critical ingredients that trout require. Vegetation from streamside trees and bushes falls into the water and decays. Animals defecate along the waterway. Both of these are sources of phosphorus and nitrogen, which stimulate aquatic plant growth. Warmer temperatures prevail at lower elevations, providing a longer growing season for the plants. The gradient is less steep in the foothills, and instead of flowing through a bed of rock, the stream may now flow through a bed of soil, which carries nutrients that wash into the water with the spring rains.

Of the three types of trout streams, the mountains have their greatest influence on freestoners. The mountains affect seasonal and day-to-day weather from the West Coast to the Great Plains. Weather determines the amount of snowpack, which controls the length, volume, and rate of spring runoff. Spring runoff influences the temperature, volume, and clarity of streams through the summer, and over the long term, it also controls erosion of the streambed. Temperature, volume, and stability of the water help determine the type and quality of habitat for aquatic insects and trout. Geology determines where the springs, spring creeks, and water tables are located, and the mountains directly determine the route that the water takes on its migration away from the Continental Divide.

The result of all this interconnectedness that originates with the Rockies is that the fishing on western freestone streams is much less predictable than the fishing on eastern streams. Eastern trips can often be successfully planned around the calendar, as in "the green drakes start to hatch on Penns Creek around May 20." This is pretty reliable information, for even in an unusual year, the hatches don't vary by more than a week or so. You're pretty safe booking the motel the same week each year. In many parts of the West, you'll hear that mid-June to mid-July is pale morning dun time in a normal year. However, there's a problem with the phrase "in a normal year." It means something different in the East than in the West. In the East, it means "if the season unfolds the way it usually does." In the West, it's more like an average of all the possibilities. For example, in a year of light snowpack, Montana's Yellowstone River can be in fine clear condition in mid-June. But after a winter of heavy snowpack, it may be high and dirty until late July. From one year to the next, there can be as much as six weeks' difference between times of similar conditions. But on average, the Yellowstone becomes fishable in early July.

For about ten consecutive years, my friend Jim Gilson came to Alberta to fish the Bow River in the last week of June. Some years the river was low, clear, weedy, and full of big fish rising to pale morning duns in skinny water. Other years the Bow was high, fast, and cloudy, and the only productive fishing was with sinking lines and big streamers and nymphs. On a couple other occasions in late June, the river was at the height of runoff—dirty and unfishable—and we were forced to look to other waters. The volatility of the weather and geography makes for very few "normal" years in the West. In the words of songwriter Bruce Cockburn, "The trouble with normal is it always gets worse." Blame the mountains.

Travelers planning a trip west to fish freestone streams should do their homework in advance to get an idea of what to expect. And even then, they shouldn't be surprised if conditions are different than what they anticipate. It's never a good idea to put all your eggs in one basket, nor to count their contents before they've hatched. Experienced western anglers usually plan trips with a primary destination in mind and at least a plan B and maybe even plans C and D ready as backups.

An important component in the life of a western freestone stream is spring runoff. When spring weather begins to melt the snow in the mountains, the high country drains like a sponge that's being squeezed, and the streambeds act as drainage routes for the surge of melting snow. Many freestone trout rivers have a two-stage runoff. Local runoff occurs when the snow immediately adjacent to the stream melts and drains directly into the water. The resulting discoloration occurs sometime between February and April, depending on elevation and latitude, and usually lasts only a few days. There is then a period of prerunoff fishing in low, clear water conditions. The main runoff comes a few weeks later, when a large volume of mountain snowmelt finally reaches the main river. The delay occurs because the warming and melting begins at low elevations and works its way up the system. So even when the foothills and plains are basking in summerlike conditions, the snowpack in the mountains may still be accumulating. Some mountain areas receive their heaviest precipitation as snow in the months of April and May. It also takes considerable time for the surge of snowmelt to travel all the way from the headwaters to the foothills, especially if the river passes through lakes or reservoirs along the way.

The snow begins to come down from the mountains in earnest when the nighttime air temperatures remain above freezing. It is then that the melting process can gain momentum without interruption. And when snow flurries become rain showers, the rain acts as a catalyst to the whole process, increasing the rate of melting.

During spring runoff, the increased volume and velocity of the water move and shift the gravel and rocks of the stream bottom. This abrasive action is called scouring and has several significant effects on the algae, weeds, and aquatic insects in the stream.

Scouring helps determine the types of plants and insects that can live there. Streams subject to frequent scouring are occupied by organisms capable of surviving it. The nymphs of some aquatic insects, like those of the little yellow stonefly *(Isoperla marmorata),* burrow down below the streambed during runoff, into what is called the hyporheic zone—the area beneath the surface of the substrate. They do this to avoid the dangers of scouring in the spring and to find water in the drought of late summer. The hyporheic zone is the bugs' version of a bomb shelter—a place of refuge when things get tough on the main floor.

Streams that are subject to frequent and extreme scouring usually have low populations of algae, plants, insects, and consequently trout, and are not often great trout streams. But even our best freestone streams occasionally experience extraordinarily severe conditions when Mother Nature flexes her muscles.

In June 1995 the one-in-one-hundred-year flood crashed into southern Alberta as the peak of spring runoff coincided with a rainfall of six to ten inches in twenty-four hours. Many of Alberta's trout streams, including the Oldman, Highwood, and Crowsnest Rivers, were significantly rearranged as flood levels peaked more than ten vertical feet above normal. In Montana, the Yellowstone River flooded with similar severity in the spring of 1996 and wreaked havoc on towns and farms in the Paradise Valley. This flood temporarily rerouted the Yellowstone River through the channel of Armstrong Spring Creek. Then, much to the dismay of the oddsmakers, in 1997 the Yellowstone underwent a second successive one-in-one-hundred-year flood.

As unpopular as they are with fishermen and landowners, spring runoffs and occasional floods are not detrimental to the life of a trout stream. The flushing action of runoff removes harmful materials from the sediment of the streambed and is healthy for the river, much in the same way that a periodic flush is healthy for the radiator of your car. Runoff helps keep spawning gravel clean so the trout can use it successfully. Spring runoff is also important for prompting the seasonal movements of trout. Spawning fish and recently hatched fry sometimes take their cues for migration from the increase in volume caused by runoff.

SPRING CREEKS

I had never fished dry flies in a snowstorm before. But I had never fished Armstrong's Spring Creek before. It was Easter weekend, and over lunch in the fishermen's shack, guide Al Gadoury made a suggestion: "Head for the upper pool about one o'clock. With this blustery weather, the *Baetis* flies will hatch and the fish should come up pretty well."

I got to the pool and waded into the tailout. I saw a rise and then noticed a couple of size 18 gray mayflies climbing up my waders. Within minutes, the pool was jammed with rising fish. Dozens of rainbows and

A fertile western spring creek.

browns hung beneath the surface, their spotted sides showing plainly as they churned and rolled to pick off the flies. Snouts and dorsal fins cut the water everywhere between my rod tip and the head of the pool, thirty yards away. I had expected some rising fish, but this was off the scale.

The fish rose; I cast; the fish ignored the fly. The fish rose and I cast again. And again. I changed the fly and cast again. They kept on rising. One of them bumped my leader while taking a natural. I thought I knew how to do this, but I was wrong. The fish were *right there,* they were feeding, and I couldn't get it done. I felt like I was being taunted.

After about twenty-five minutes of this, Gadoury came to check on me. He watched a minute and then said, "Try this." He handed me a #18 Gray No-Hackle and walked away. I tied on the fly and caught a trout on the second cast. Three casts later, I caught another. This was more like it. I had their number now. Then I threw at another fish, but it didn't take. Then another, and it didn't take either. Nor did any of the next four. The fish continued to feed hard. I tried for a brown rising beneath an overhanging willow branch. No good. Welcome to square one. It was the first time in twenty-five years of fly-fishing that I felt that the trout were daring me to catch them.

Eventually I learned that on this stream, different fish want different patterns, and only they know why. So even when you catch a couple of trout, it doesn't mean you've actually got things figured out. This trip was nearly fifteen years ago, and I've been back to Armstrong's a dozen times since, trying to get even. I catch fish but never enough to convince me that I really know what's going on. It's a humbling stream, but the things I've learned there serve me well nearly everywhere else I fish.

A spring creek is everything we want a trout stream to be. It has all the qualities that stimulate trout growth and none of those that inhibit it. Spring creeks produce high numbers of fast-growing fish that feed primarily on insects. As a result, these streams are regarded with an affection that borders on reverence by fly fishers around the world.

Spring creeks are the spoiled children of the trout stream family—born with silver spoons in their mouths, having everything they need and lacking nothing. If this metaphor seems a bit of a stretch, consider this: Spring creeks are born "grown up," appearing from beneath the ground as instant trout streams.

The water comes from underground collecting basins called aquifers. As it makes its way to the surface of the earth, the water is filtered through underground geological formations. Springs release water at constant volume and temperature every day of the year, and this is what makes spring creeks different from other trout streams. Constant volume insulates the stream from the harmful effects of erratic water level. Spring creeks don't swell during wet summers or shrink in dry ones. The banks and littoral zone, where the water meets the shore, remain stable.

Constant temperature gives these streams an advantage in both winter and summer. Many spring creeks remain free of ice in winter and as a result are not subject to problems caused by anchor ice, which forms on the bottoms of some freestone streams. Spring creeks are also immune to dissolved oxygen deficiencies that occur when trout water gets too warm in summer. In short, stable temperature lessens the amplitude in the sine waves of the seasons and keeps the water suitable for growth of aquatic life all the time. Many of the best western spring creeks have year-round temperatures near 50 degrees F, which is why insects hatch and trout rise throughout the year, even in winter.

Still another asset of spring creeks is their natural alkalinity and high calcium content, which promote growth of algae and other aquatic plants. These plants provide food and habitat for aquatic insects, which in turn feed the trout. The richness of the water is the reason that many of fly-fishingdom's heaviest insect hatches occur on spring creeks such as Idaho's Silver Creek.

A typical western spring creek rises in the fertile bottom of a large valley and flows a short distance through farmland before joining the river that created the valley. Because they are short and don't drain off the mountains, spring creeks are subject only to the brief local runoff that occurs when snow along the banks melts and drains into the stream. The lush vegetation along the shoreline insulates spring creeks from the effects of heavy rain. So when nearby freestone streams are battered and scoured by mountain runoff or heavy rain, these little gems bubble along clear, unaffected, and unfazed.

Because spring creeks begin in lowland areas, their gradients are gradual and their demeanors gentle. Some are narrow and lined with willows; others are wide and wide open. There are plenty of glittering riffles, slow glides, and long flats to attract fly fishers, but there is little water of high velocity, and no falls, rapids, or cascades. Also largely absent are the deep, mysterious pools that some fly fishers fantasize about. In many cases, the entire stream bottom can be viewed easily through polarized sunglasses. Don't be fooled, though, for even with all this shallow water, a good spring creek holds an amazing number of trout. The exceptional food supply sometimes means there are more fish than there are places for fish to live—but they get over it. Trout set up shop in a variety of unusual places—in shallow riffles, long flats, and seemingly insignificant depressions in the stream bottom.

In my fly fishing, I'm drawn to the shallowest water where I think I might find a fish. I set my personal record one bright April morning on Nelson's Spring Creek in Montana. In a tiny riffle off to the side of a main pool, a fish was set up and taking midges. The fish was nice, if not huge—about eighteen inches long. Because the water was less than four inches deep, fish had to lie about thirty degrees off vertical and rise diagonally. A productive spring creek gives the impression that the trout are everywhere—because they are.

Generally, spring creeks start out small and stay that way because they don't acquire additional tributaries on their short journeys to the main rivers. There are some sizable ones, though, like the Fall River in California. Some people also consider the Henry's Fork of the Snake in Idaho to be a giant spring creek because much of its water comes from giant springs in the river's upper reaches.

Spring creeks usually flow through fertile land that is used for farming or ranching. Many streams have been degraded through decades of overuse by cattle and neglect or abuse by landowners in the unenlightened past. But spring creeks have proven to be prime candidates for rehabilitation, and many are now returning to their full potential as trout streams. If the cattle are removed and kept out of the stream and a deeper, narrower channel is created, a spring creek will often do the rest of the healing on its own.

Some spring creeks, like Silver Creek in Idaho and Big Spring Creek in Montana, have sections that are open to public fishing. Many other streams are entirely private and are reserved for friends of the landowner or clients of guides, outfitters, and lodges. Some others, such as Armstrong's, Nelson's, DePuy's, and McCoy's in Montana, are managed by the landowners on a limited-entry, fee-fishing basis. In some cases, the rod fee goes toward maintenance of the fishery. This system, if not perfect, is a reasonable solution to the access problem in that it allows anyone the opportunity to fish but does not allow the creeks to be overrun by a few hundred grumpy anglers. The most popular of these streams require advance reservations, and prime season is usually booked full up to a year in advance. Though there is a daily limit on the number of anglers, the trout in these streams see a lot of traffic. Along with tailwaters, popular spring creeks are among the West's most heavily fished waters.

Spring creek trout are generally difficult to fool. There is a predominance of flat water and small insects, both of which stack the odds in the fish's favor. The angler's skill deficiencies are exposed in a hurry. The good caster who doesn't understand bugs runs into problems, as does the entomological genius who can converse with the trout in Latin but can't get his fly in front of them. But the wonderful thing about a spring creek is that while the fish are difficult to fool, they are also abundant, and a fisherman is able to spend most of his time casting to feeding fish rather than searching for feeding fish. Such numerous encounters with difficult fish improve skills immensely. It is no coincidence that a great many truly expert fly fishers have spring creek experience somewhere in their past, for these delicate little streams are "institutes of higher learning," and the trout that live in them are the most demanding of instructors.

So if a spring creek is a fishing classroom, what is the curriculum? What do these innocent little streams teach the fly fisher? They teach you first to be observant—of the water, the insects, and the fish. They teach you to look at the water, to look *into* the water, and to interpret carefully what you see. They teach you the importance of precise casting with light lines and long leaders. They teach you the need for gentleness in striking and playing big fish on tiny flies and light tippets. They might teach you that you need glasses to change those tiny flies. In all ways, spring creeks make it very clear that it is the fish, not the fishermen, who are in charge.

There is a distinctiveness to the appearance of a spring creek: Clear water slides silently over waving weed beds; watercress rests on the surface along the banks, with all plants showing the happy green of chlorophyll at work. Red-winged blackbirds bob and sing from cattails that crowd the edge of the water. Mallards scatter from slow pools as you approach. The scene often has mountains in the background and a red barn in the foreground. The stream looks and is intensely *alive,* and all those rings on the surface prove it.

TAILWATERS

Spring creeks are among the best fisheries created by Mother Nature, and tailwaters are man's accidental imitations of spring creeks. The simple definition of a tailwater is a river downstream of a dam, but not all dams create good fisheries. Generally, the best streams are downstream of deep reservoirs that are used for either water storage or electrical power production. Of the two, storage reservoirs usually produce the best tailwater fisheries.

Many storage dams discharge cold water to the river from deep in the reservoir, and this has profound effects on the fishery downstream. First, the water near the bottom of the reservoir changes temperature very little throughout the year, and consequently the temperature of the river immediately below the dam is also very constant. It doesn't get too warm in summer or too cold in winter. Second, these dams generally release water to the river at a constant rate, meaning the river downstream flows at a uniform volume, with fewer seasonal fluctuations than freestone rivers. Tailwaters generally aren't affected by runoff, and neither do they recede to

Holter Dam, creator of Montana's Missouri River tailwater fishery.

dangerously low levels in fall and winter. In addition, the water in the reservoir is enriched by nutrients present in the land before it was flooded, and these aid plant growth and insect life in the river below the dam. So trout streams below bottom-draw dams often have many of the same qualities that make spring creeks productive—stable flows, stable temperatures, and nutrient-rich water.

Some rivers downstream of power-producing dams are good fisheries and some aren't. Many of the good ones have a second reregulation dam a short distance downstream of the main dam, which restores stability in flow rates. The Afterbay Dam on the Bighorn River in Montana and Gray Reef on the North Platte in Wyoming are perfect examples. Without the benefit of a reregulation dam, power production usually causes frequent and severe fluctuations in river levels downstream, which is detrimental to the trout fishery. An exception is the Colorado River at Lees Ferry, where fluctuations in water level occur daily below the Glen Canyon Dam. Because this river is in a deep canyon, the bottom of the stream remains under water at any water level, and both trout and trout fishermen do well.

The tailwater phenomenon has created some great trout fisheries in places where none would ever occur naturally. Parts of rivers that would be too warm for trout have been transformed into trout streams by the cooling effects of bottom-draw dams. Good examples are the San Juan River, which flows through desert in New Mexico, and the Bighorn River, which weaves through the dry sagebrush country of southern Montana.

Productive tailwaters have some distinctions in terms of their insect life. Their rather narrow temperature ranges are suitable for fewer species of insects. But because of the richness of the water and the stable flows, those insects that thrive within that temperature range do very well. Put another way, tailwaters often have less diversity in species of insects but a much higher overall population of bugs.

Most of the best tailwaters have extremely high numbers of midges and small mayflies, especially blue-winged olives and pale morning duns. They usually have fewer stoneflies and large mayflies than freestone streams. Some tailwaters have good caddisfly hatches and some don't. Many have lots of scuds and aquatic worms. The unusually high volume of food is the reason tailwaters support great numbers of trout and also the reason they grow big trout. The fact that most of the food items are small is the reason tailwaters become "technical" trout streams, much like their spring creek counterparts, requiring small flies, long leaders, and plenty of finesse on the part of the angler.

Tailwaters are generally created on larger rivers, but there are some that could be classed as medium-size streams, such as the Frying Pan in Colorado and the Beaverhead in Montana. Along with these two, some of the best-known western tailwaters are the Bighorn and Missouri in Montana, the South Platte in Colorado, the San Juan in New Mexico, the Green in Utah, the Lower Sacramento in California, and the South Fork of the Snake in Idaho.

I'm reluctant to wade into the rather contentious issue of whether dams are good or bad for trout streams. Such discussions get complicated, passionate, and are usually without conclusion. Suffice it to say that on some rivers, like the San Juan and Green, fine fisheries have been created where there were previously no trout fisheries at all. In other cases, such as the Gunnison in Colorado and the Oldman in Alberta, dams have destroyed great wild trout fisheries by burying them under massive reservoirs. I will avoid altogether the temptation to launch a rant about the economic, environmental, cultural, and financial benefits and/or consequences of dams.

If you were to list the ten or twenty best big-river trout fisheries in the West, many of them would be tailwaters. The best of them are remarkable fisheries. They truly are giant artificial spring creeks. They hold huge numbers of fish, they have heavy hatches of bugs, and they have nearly endless fishing seasons. It's hard to hide lights this bright under a bushel, though, and tailwaters are also, hands-down, the busiest trout streams on the continent. Fishing among other anglers is the order of the day, and perhaps the only ingredient missing from the tailwater experience is solitude.

OTHER TYPES OF STREAMS

Some trout streams resist simple categorization, such as those that flow between lakes. In these cases, the quality of the stream is largely determined by the nature of the lake.

Other streams are difficult to classify because they're some sort of hybrid. Perhaps it's best if I just give some examples. The Madison River has as its two primary sources the Firehole and Gibbon Rivers, which join in Yellowstone Park to create the Madison. Both of these begin as freestone streams, but both receive the nutrient-rich outfall of numerous geysers and hot springs, which changes the chemistry of the rivers significantly and turns the Madison in Yellowstone Park at least partially into a type of spring creek, albeit one where the springs are hot, not cold.

Downstream, the Madison is joined by both freestone and spring-fed tributaries. It also flows through three reservoirs—one natural and two man-made. So the Madison is very hard to pigeonhole. Let's just call it one of the world's best trout streams.

Other streams are basically freestone in nature but receive an injection of nutrients from man-made sources. The Bow River in Alberta is the best-known example of this. Water treatment facilities from the city of Calgary release phosphates and nitrates into the river, which stimulate plant growth and help the Bow to produce some of the fastest-growing wild trout in North America.

CHAPTER 3

Fly Tackle for the West

Fly fishers love tackle. And they love to fish with it almost as much as they love to talk about it and tinker with it. A wide range of tackle is used by western fly fishers because there is a wide range of fishing available in the West. There is technical, fussy spring-creek fishing, where long leaders and tiny flies are inspected carefully by trout that know all the standard patterns by name. There is macho fishing for giant autumn brown trout, where the flies are about the same size as the fish anglers try to catch in the spring creeks. The great variety of fishing situations means that tackle should be chosen carefully.

RODS
If a single outfit is to be used for all western fishing, it must provide a good blend of finesse and power. In the past, many people chose a 7-weight or even an 8-weight as an all-around western rod. But today's 5-weight rods provide more finesse *and* more power than the 7-weights of twenty years ago, with the result that anglers are now able to address more types of fishing with lighter outfits. Today most people seeking versatility choose a 5- or 6-weight rod. I'm going to avoid the quagmire of adjectives for rod action and simply say that slightly stiffer rods are usually preferred because they make it easier to cast tight loops with high line speed, which is a benefit when the inevitable western breeze arrives.

   With the development of light, stiff graphite fly rods has also come a trend toward rods that do much of their flexing near the tip. These rods are very good for handling floating lines and small dry flies and are even better for making ninety-foot casts in the fly shop parking lot, which is unfortunately where most rods are tested. But for making short casts and for casting large flies, strike indicators, extra weight, and sinking or sinking-tip lines, rods that bend a little deeper into the butt section are usually better.

When selecting a rod, at least cast it and preferably fish with it before buying. Many fly shops have field-test programs that allow customers to "test drive" rods before making a decision.

If you decide to use more than one outfit, one should probably be a 3-, 4-, or 5-weight and the other a 6- or 7-weight. You generally get the most coverage by selecting outfits at least two line weights apart. These two outfits provide plenty of finesse and precision for delicate fishing and plenty of power when that's required.

In the days when fly rods were made of bamboo or fiberglass, the relationship between the length of the rod and the weight of the fly line was straightforward: Rods for light lines had to be short, and rods for heavy lines had to be longer. Today graphite fly rods can be designed in any length and line-weight combination imaginable. There are 9-foot rods for 3-weight lines, 9-foot rods for 12-weight lines, and 9-foot rods for every line weight in between. This doesn't change the fact that there are advantages and disadvantages with different rod lengths.

Short rods—say those less than 8 feet long—are great for close-range work because they're precise and accurate. They're also good for fishing small, overgrown streams that wind through a tunnel-like canopy of trees and brush. Short rods help keep the fly line within the tunnel so you don't have to climb the trees to retrieve your flies as often (or at least you don't have to climb so high). Short rods also keep the fly line close to the water, where the breeze is less powerful. The disadvantages to short rods appear when you need to make long casts and when the fly line must be manipulated after the cast, such as when mending or when short-line nymphing. Short rods make it more difficult to keep the backcasts off the water when you're wading deep. They are also awkward to use from a driftboat because they allow the fly line to interfere with the oars more often than the rower likes. Frequent tangles and strong words sometimes result.

Conversely, long rods—those over 9 feet—are good for long casts, for mending, and for controlling line. They are also helpful when wading deep or fishing from a driftboat. However, they are more tiring to fish with and are more difficult to use when short, accurate casts are required.

It's interesting that although modern rod manufacturers can freely mix and match rod length and line weight, the anglers' preferences for rod length have contracted over the last twenty years. There are still advocates of tiny rods and giant rods, but the vast majority of fly rods used for western stream fishing today are between 8 and 9 feet long. Rods in this range are comfortable for most people to cast and provide good versatility whatever line weight is used.

Western fishermen who mainly wade and fish smaller streams and who do all their work with a single outfit often prefer 8½-foot rods. Anglers who fish bigger water usually choose 9-footers. Those who use two outfits likely have 8½-foot rods for the lighter lines and 9-footers for the heavier lines. I've not mentioned two-handed Spey rods, which can be used effectively for trout in large rivers but are far more often used for steelhead and salmon.

REELS

The fly reel carries more prestige now than it used to. For a long time, it was considered just a place to store the fly line. The reel was the least costly part of the outfit and played second fiddle to the rod in its ability to impress companions. You could always get attention by nonchalantly mentioning the brand name of the rod you used, but nobody cared much about your reel. Today, though, fly reels rival rods in the charisma quotient. The variety of styles, sizes, and even colors available makes them much more fun to discuss and argue about.

It's not quite accurate to say a fly reel is just a place to store the line, but still, for trout fishing, the reel has the simplest job of the three components that make up the fly-fishing outfit. The reel must hold the line and backing, and must release it smoothly when either the fish or the fisherman pulls it out. Most importantly, when the line stops moving out, the spool must stop turning so you don't get what bait casters call a backlash and what my father called a "snarl."

The degree of sophistication and ingenuity with which a simple job is done is what gives a fine tool its charm. This applies to fly reels as well as pocketknives and shotguns. Fly reels can be made by stamping pieces out of sheet metal and screwing them together, by die-casting liquid aluminum in a mold, or by machining, which is the process of carving a solid block of aluminum into a fly reel. Life expectancy, reliability, precision, and cost increase from the former through the latter, to say nothing of that factor so often cited by fly shop owners—pride of ownership.

Most fly reels used today are single-action reels. This means that the spool and handle are directly connected to each other, with no clutch or gears between them. When the handle makes one revolution, the spool does too. The spool and handle turn one direction when line comes in and the opposite direction when line goes out.

Other types of reels are available but are not popular or widely used. Multiplying reels have a gear mechanism that causes the spool to turn more quickly than the handle, thereby allowing the operator to retrieve line more quickly. Perhaps the biggest fan of multipliers is Leigh Perkins, chairman of the Orvis Company. He's tried but has had a hard time persuading the fly-fishing public to embrace multipliers. Multipliers are usually a little heavier than comparable single-action reels, and the physics of the multiplication process puts the person cranking the handle at a slight mechanical disadvantage. Most multiplying reels take a bit more effort to crank, which seems to discourage some people from using them.

Antireverse reels are built so that the reel handle can turn in only one direction—the direction for retrieving line. When line is pulled off the reel, a clutch inside the reel allows the spool to turn while the handle remains stationary. This prevents the handle from spinning and bruising the angler's knuckles when a fish is running. Antireverse reels are not popular for trout fishing but are often used by saltwater anglers who must protect their hands, like musicians, surgeons, and safecrackers.

An automatic fly reel incorporates a spring mechanism that allows the fisherman to retrieve line by pulling up on a lever with the little finger of his rod hand. The objective is to allow line to be retrieved with one hand, and it works, but the trade-offs in weight, limited line capacity, and reliability are severe, and it's rare to see automatics in use today. They do serve a valuable purpose by allowing amputees to cast and retrieve with one hand.

The reel spool's resistance to turning is called *drag*. There are a number of ways drag is created, but two types are most popular. The first is the simple click drag or spring-and-pawl drag, where the teeth of a gearlike wheel on the inside of the reel's spool run against the point of a triangular pawl that's attached to the inside of the reel's frame. The contact between pawl and gear teeth creates both the resistance and the distinctive clicking sound a fly reel is supposed to make when the spool is turned. Some click-drag reels have drag adjustment knobs that allow for more or less drag by increasing or decreasing pressure on a spring that contacts the pawl. The range of adjustment possible on even the best click-drag reels is limited, due to the physics of how the drag is created.

The second type of mechanism is the disk drag, which has become popular in recent years. It is composed of two thin plates, or disks, which are faced with either cork or a smooth synthetic material. One disk turns and the other does not. The disks are drawn against one another, creating resistance. The advantage to a disk drag is that more drag and a greater range of drag adjustment are possible than with a spring-and-pawl system. There are many variations on the basic disk drag available today, including one in which the disk is squeezed by a caliper.

For all types of fishing, the drag must be set somewhere between the resistance required to prevent backlash and the resistance required to break

 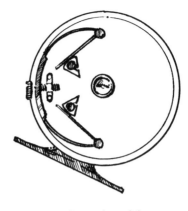

disk drag   spring-and-pawl drag

the leader when a fish runs. For trout fishing, this is simple. The drag is set
to prevent backlash and left there. If a big fish runs hard, the fisherman can
increase drag at any time by applying finger pressure to the external rim of
the reel spool or to the fly line itself.

The range of drag that is available with a disk-drag reel is rarely necessary for trout fishing, but anglers have never been known to let necessity,
or lack of it, inhibit their preferences. High-quality disk-drag systems are
now available on relatively low-priced fly reels, so most people feel that
there's no reason not to have it. If you were offered free air conditioning in
your new car, you'd probably take it, even if you lived in Siberia.

A factor that influences the cost of a fly reel is the quality of its finish.
The most scratch- and saltwater-resistant finishes are either anodized or
enameled and are expensive to apply. Such high-tech finishes are not essential on reels for trout fishing in fresh water, but they are nonetheless available
for those who appreciate the highest-quality equipment.

A recent trend in fly reels is the emergence of the large-arbor design. In
a large-arbor reel, there is space between the spindle and the spool, and the
spool is larger in diameter than that of a conventionally designed reel. The
obvious advantage is that the large arbor allows more line to be retrieved
with each revolution of the handle, but there are other advantages too. Line
comes off the reel in larger coils, which are less prone to tangling. In addition, the retrieve rate remains high even when there is very little line left
on the spool. As an example, one popular large-arbor reel boasts a retrieve
rate of 12 inches of line per revolution when the spool is full and 8 inches
per revolution when it's empty. Compare that with the retrieve rate of
a conventional reel for the same line—6 inches per revolution when full,

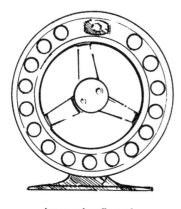

large-arbor fly reel   **conventional fly reel**

1 inch per revolution when empty. The fast retrieve rate is convenient for fighting fish—especially those that start by running away from you and then turn around and run toward you—and for quickly picking up slack line when fishing from a boat. The final advantage of large-arbor reels is that the drag remains relatively constant as line is removed from the spool. With a conventional reel, the drag increases noticeably as more and more line is pulled off the spool.

The disadvantages to large-arbor reels are, first, that they are usually somewhat more expensive than comparable conventional reels. Because of their larger size, most of them are machined, and this is a more costly process than die-casting. Second, they have a nontraditional look and feel. Some people have a hard time getting used to a reel that seems so large and looks as if it were designed by Darth Vader. Large-arbor reels are sometimes slightly heavier than comparable conventional reels, but excessive weight is avoided because of the air space between the spindle and the spool.

For trout fishing, the fly reel still has a simple job. If you are trying to reduce the cost of your outfit, get a less expensive reel and put the majority of your dollars into your rod and line.

FLY LINES

The most versatile fly line is a floating line, because it allows you to fish on the surface or under the surface. With sinking lines, you can only fish under the surface, because the line will pull a dry fly under. For most small to medium-size streams, a floating line is probably all you'll ever need. On larger western rivers, though, there is great benefit in using a sinking or sinking-tip line in certain situations.

Many people misunderstand what a sinking line can do for them. First of all, a sinking fly line is not the best tool for getting a fly deep quickly. The best way to do that is with a weighted fly and a long leader. It's in *keeping* a fly deep that a sinking line is an asset. Here's why: When you retrieve a sinking fly that's attached to a floating line, the fly immediately begins to move toward the surface. But when the same fly is attached to a sinking line, it stays deeper while it's retrieved.

But along with this advantage comes a disadvantage: Once it touches the water, a sinking line is within the grasp of the water, and you can't reposition it or make a second cast without retrieving all of the line. For this reason, most western fly fishers don't use full-sinking lines, but choose instead sinking-tips as their second lines. Sinking-tips have the advantage of sinking lines for fishing flies deeply and the advantage of floating lines for mending and recasting. They are especially good when fishing streamers from a driftboat, where a common approach is to make a cast, strip the fly five or six times, and then cast again. There are many different sinking-tip lines available, but the most popular are made with 10 to 15 feet of fast or extra-fast sinking line on the business end.

While sinking and sinking-tip lines are helpful for streamer fishing, their properties are of less benefit for dead-drift nymph fishing. The late nymphing guru Charles E. Brooks preferred a sinking line when fishing big stonefly nymphs in heavy water, but today most serious nymph fishers

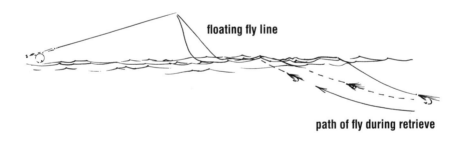

floating fly line

path of fly during retrieve

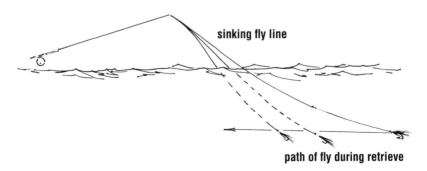

sinking fly line

path of fly during retrieve

A sinking fly line allows the fly to remain deep during the retrieve.

use floating lines and long leaders. These are easier to control and allow the use of strike indicators, which in recent years have become a standard piece of nymph-fishing equipment.

Floating lines are available in both weight-forward and double tapers. Most western fly fishers prefer weight-forwards because they take up less space on the reel, allowing more room for the backing they hope they need, and because they shoot a little farther when long casts are needed. Sinking and sinking-tip lines are usually available in weight-forward tapers only.

There are times and places in the West where a shooting taper is a useful tool. A shooting taper is a 30-foot fly line that's attached to a thin running line behind it. The running line is usually either very lightweight floating line or monofilament. A good caster can easily throw a shooting taper one hundred feet, because the front part of the line is much heavier than the running line behind it. This is helpful when fishing streamers in big rivers like the Missouri or Kootenai. Shooting heads are made in both floating and sinking versions.

A new invention that has a lot of merit is the multitip fly line. This is a floating fly line that comes with a number of different front ends, each with a different density. The standard version usually comes with a floating, slow-sinking, fast-sinking, and extrafast-sinking tip. The tip section is selected to suit the fishing method and is attached to the body of the line with a loop-to-loop connection. Multitip lines allow you to carry lines for a number of different purposes without the expense of separate spare spools and backing. The first multitip fly line I saw was a homemade job that Mark McAneely used for steelheading on Vancouver Island. They are now commercially available from a number of manufacturers. It remains to be seen to what degree they are embraced by trout fishermen.

Backing is necessary for western fishing. I know, I know, you can go years without ever hooking a fish that takes all your fly line away from you. But remember, when you need backing, you need it very badly, and if you don't have enough, you would probably offer your first child to get some more in a hurry.

A loop-to-loop connection.

LEADERS

There is no fly-fishing topic that has the potential for more discussion and less consensus than leaders. There are many types available—knotted, knotless, braided, furled, sinking, floating, poly—and no doubt more that are being invented as I write this. The most popular for general-purpose use are knotless tapered leaders. Don't rule out all the other types of leaders, but consider them special-purpose tools with which to address specific types of fishing. No matter what type of leader you use, it is important to match the diameter of the leader's tippet to the size of the fly. The easiest way to do this is to divide the hook size by four. This gives you a number that should equal the X designation for the diameter of the tippet. For example, this rule tells you that a size 12 fly needs a 3X tippet. It is a general rule only, and a tippet one size larger or one size smaller might be chosen because of the specific fishing conditions.

Most anglers carry a few spools of tippet material in varying diameters so they can make adjustments to the business end of their leaders. I usually start with a 9-foot, 3X leader and add tippet material if I need to. There are generally two types of tippet material used today: nylon and fluorocarbon. Fluorocarbon is more expensive than nylon but has some different properties. It is less visible in the water and more abrasion-resistant than nylon, and it has a specific gravity greater than water, which makes it sink slowly. It is significantly more expensive than nylon monofilament but is not as strong. It also does not deteriorate over time, which is good if it lives its whole life in your vest, but not so good if bits and pieces are littered in and around the trout streams. Many western fly fishers use nylon but carry some fluorocarbon for situations where its properties are helpful, such as when fishing very flat, clear water or streams with a lot of jagged rocks on the bottom.

WADERS

For many years, the most popular waders were made of neoprene, rubber, or lightweight nylon. But ever since the introduction of breathable waterproof rain jackets, fly fishers were waiting for that technology to be applied to waders. They wanted waders that not only would keep the river water out, but also would disperse the heat and dampness their active fly-fishing bodies created. It took a long time, but finally in the mid-nineties, breathable waders made their appearance. They arrived the way most new technology does—with great hoopla, high prices, and inconsistent quality. But fishermen still bought them in droves, attracted by the prospect of a better mousetrap.

Within the multilayer laminate of breathable waders is a waterproof breathable membrane that works like a microscopic screen. The membrane is porous, with the pores small enough to block passage of liquid molecules but large enough to allow passage of the much smaller vapor molecules.

Breathables allow vaporous moisture produced by the skin to pass through the waders, resulting in a cooler, more comfortable wader with no buildup of condensation inside. The fact that early versions sometimes leaked didn't hurt their popularity, for many fishermen found they were more comfortable in breathable waders that leaked than in nonbreathable waders that didn't.

Breathables are lightweight, flexible, nonstretchy waders. They provide no insulation, and when they first came along, many fly fishers thought they would be great for warm-weather use—which they are. But what caught most of us by surprise is how well breathables work in cold conditions when insulating layers are worn underneath them. The combination of synthetic fleece or pile inside breathable waders is a great cold-water system because it provides exceptional insulation while eliminating the dampness caused by condensation. I use breathables all season long, changing what I wear underneath to suit the conditions. On hot summer days, I wear a light pair of pants or even shorts underneath the waders, and for late-fall or early-spring fishing, I wear all the fleece and pile I can find. The best fabrics to wear under breathable waders are synthetics that wick moisture, such as polypropylene, fleece, and chlorofiber, and the worst are those that hold moisture, such as denim or any other type of cotton. In short, breathables are versatile; on their own, they are cool, but you can increase insulation by changing what you wear underneath them. The converse is not true of neoprene waders. They are warm, but you can't do anything to make them cooler.

Neoprenes are still the wader of choice for angling in the coldest conditions, such as winter steelheading or float-tubing in high-altitude lakes. Some of the best low-priced waders are the thin, tough, coated nylon ones made and marketed by a number of companies. While they don't breathe, they are compact and durable, which makes them great for backpack or horseback trips.

Most good-quality waders are available in both boot-foot and stocking-foot styles, and in chest-high or hip-high models. Stocking-foot waders allow you to select waders to fit your body and boots to fit your feet, rather than relying on the averaging that is used to size boot-foot waders. They also provide better support, because the wading shoes are laced up and can be adjusted for comfort. Boot-foot waders are much quicker to put on and take off, which is appealing for people who frequently fish for short periods of time, such as when an "emergency" hatch occurs on the way home from work.

For most western fishing, chest-high waders are preferred. This is not because wading chest-deep is often necessary, but because occasionally wading thigh-deep is possible. The term "hip waders" is a misnomer. They don't come up to anybody's hips, and they only allow wading in water about knee-deep. If that's as deep as you need to go, hip waders are great. But anytime I wear hip waders, I either wade an inch too deep or splash water up and over the top. Either way I wind up wet, asking myself why I wore waders in the first place.

Wading shoes and the feet of boot-foot waders are available with different types of soles to provide good traction in varying stream conditions. Felt soles are the most popular and are good on slippery rocks in the stream but not so great on muddy banks or grassy slopes alongside the stream. Studded soles are very good on the slipperiest of rocks in the water but are very bad on the floors of driftboats and even worse on inflatable rafts. Hard rubber soles provide good traction in gravel and mud but are the slipperiest on smooth, algae-covered rocks. Check what type the fly shops near your stream sell the most.

In the hottest weather of summer, some fly fishers like to wade wet, meaning without waders. Usually a pair of shorts and wading shoes are all that's needed. The advantage is that you are cooled by the water in the hottest part of the day. The drawback is that your legs are exposed to sun, mosquitoes, and the thorns and thistles of streamside vegetation. The system also becomes less attractive after the sun goes down and on those occasions when the weather changes unexpectedly.

I think a better idea for wet wading is to wear a pair of light, quick-drying pants made of a synthetic material like Supplex. These give you the coolness of direct contact with the water but don't expose your legs to all the nasty things mentioned above. Blue jeans are poor for wet wading because they hold water and increase your weight by what seems like fifty pounds.

Another wet-wading system seems to have come to North America from New Zealand. It is very practical but looks quite ridiculous. Lightweight long underwear, made of a wicking synthetic like polypropylene or chlorofiber, is worn underneath a pair of shorts. The underwear gives your legs adequate protection from wind, sun, bugs, and thorns and dries off very quickly once it's out of the water. The only drawback I can see is the abuse you take from your fishing partners. If you opt for this system, please give some thought to the color of the underwear you choose. Our sport is largely clothed in earthy, subtle hues, but one famous New Zealand guide can be spotted and identified at great distance because of the electric blue long johns he wears while guiding.

Some anglers and some fishing conditions require additional traction or stability beyond that offered by conventional wading gear. Traction devices that attach to wading shoes can make a difference on streams with smooth, round, algae-covered rocks, like the lower Madison or the Thompson in British Columbia. Wading staffs provide additional help, and some of them collapse to store in a holster that attaches to a wading belt.

VESTS

The fishing vest has been the standard means of carrying fly-fishing stuff for over sixty years. Simple ones with a modest number of pockets are relatively inexpensive. Elaborate ones made of highly technical fabrics with twenty-five or more pockets are much more costly. The main criteria for selecting a vest are capacity, weight, and durability. Vests are available in standard or short lengths, the short versions intended to keep fly boxes from dragging in the water when the wearer is wading deeper than he should be. The vest should be sized a little large, for it is almost always the outside garment and must often go on over a sweater or jacket.

In recent years, the chest pack has been introduced as an alternative to a vest. Some people prefer them because they are somewhat lighter and cooler, while still allowing anglers to carry more stuff than they really need.

ACCESSORIES

Fly fishing has become a highly accessorized pastime. An experienced instructor I know always tells his students, "If you like gadgets, you've come to the right sport." There is truth in this. To what degree you gadgetize the sport for your own pleasure is a personal decision. Even though I've made my living for many years by selling fly-fishing tackle, I'm still prepared to say that there are great gadgets and there are gadgets that are nearly useless. The great ones, like the magnetic net release, do an essential job, and do it well. The lousy ones usually employ an extensive instruction manual to teach you how to do something you didn't know needed to be done.

Essential Gadgets

Snips

This tool has either metal or ceramic cutting blades to trim the tag ends of knots. Most also have a small, protected point for clearing the eyes of flies.

Floatant

Most fishermen use a paste-type floatant, and some also like the powdered crystals that revive a fly after it's been slimed by a few fish. The crystals make dry flies float higher than you'd think possible, but their effect is less permanent than that of paste floatants, and they have to be reapplied fairly frequently. The crystals are great when you want to skitter a dry fly.

Forceps
Also called hemostats, these are useful for pinching the barbs on flies and for extracting flies from a fish's mouth and a fishing partner's neck.

Hook hone
Some hooks don't start out sharp enough, and none of them get sharper through use. This is one of the most important and overlooked fly-fishing tools.

Weight
It's often necessary to add weight to the leader to help get a streamer or nymph deeper. There are many types available, including split shot, lead strips, lead sleeves, weighted putty, and brass or tungsten beads. In some areas, lead is prohibited and a lead substitute like tungsten, tin, or bismuth must be used. In other places, including British Columbia, on waters managed as fly-fishing-only, the regulations prohibit the use of additional weight between the fly and fly line.

Fly boxes
Many anglers prefer compartment boxes for dry flies, because they don't crush hackles, and metal clip, foam, or fleece boxes for nymphs, wets, and streamers.

Strike indicators
Most anglers use strike indicators for at least some of their nymph fishing. Indicators made of stick-on foam, cork, brightly colored yarn, and small bits of bright-colored floating fly line are available.

Line dressing
New fly lines cast beautifully, and frequent use of line dressing keeps a line casting like new longer. Most anglers would be happier, and would probably catch more fish, if they used line dressing more often. Even lines that don't require dressing will benefit from an occasional wipe-down with a soft cloth.

Sunglasses
Eye protection is essential in a sport involving airborne projectiles. The most logical glasses for fly fishing are those with polarized lenses, which

reduce glare and allow you to see into the water better than standard lenses. Prescription polarized glasses are available, as are fishing glasses that incorporate bifocal magnifiers on the bottom parts of the lenses. These are very helpful when old eyes must try to thread tiny flies onto fine tippets.

Bug spray
Insect repellent is necessary at least part of the time no matter where you fish. Some are available in combination with sunscreen. If you choose a repellent with DEET as its main active ingredient, be careful not to get it on your fly line or anything else that's made of plastic, as DEET eats plastic. Apply it to the back of your hands, and transfer it from there to the rest of your exposed skin. Can somebody tell me why mosquito dope eats my plastic fly line but not the plastic bottle it comes in?

Sunscreen
This is an essential today because of the reduction of the ozone layer, the invasion of aliens, or whatever it is that makes it easier to get a sunburn than it used to be.

Camera
Take one if you want somebody to believe your stories.

Toilet paper
Don't leave home without it.

Optional Gadgets
Leader straightener
This is a piece of rubber that the leader is drawn through to remove the memory coils. It works well, but so do your thumb and finger, as long as you don't draw the leader through too quickly.

Landing net and net retriever
There are proponents of landing nets, and there are people who think they're unnecessary. I'm in the former group. I'm confident that I can get a fish in, get it under control, and release it more quickly if I use a net. I also believe that a net allows me to do this without bouncing the fish off of streamside rocks. A soft bag is essential to prevent the accidental scaling of a fish you intend to release. The net must be attached to your vest with some type of gadget. A popular one is the net retriever, which is like a giant zinger or a key retriever. Though they work well, many are heavy and don't extend quite as far as you want when you're reaching for a fish.

There are other types of gizmos that allow the net to release with a sharp pull. It's not the releasing that's the problem with these things; it's the re-attaching. Most of them require three hands. The best gadget for reattaching your net to your vest is the magnetic net release. One half of a powerful magnet stays on the handle of the net, and the other half attaches to the D-ring on the back of your vest. When you're finished using the net, you simply wave the handle of the net in the vicinity of the D-ring, and the two halves of the magnet find each other.

Thermometer
Water temperature is very important if you're a trout, and nearly as important if you're a trout fisherman. You can get an idea of what to expect from the fish by checking the water temperature before fishing. A thermometer also provides you with something critical to every fishing trip—a good excuse. If the fishing is not as good as it should be, you can always take the water temperature and then pronounce knowingly to your partner, "Well, no wonder—look at the water temperature."

Knot-tying tools
One of these will teach you how to tie an essential knot in just two short hours. Of course, if you took a half hour, you could learn to tie the knot without the tool. OK, that's a little harsh. Some tools are quite helpful for old eyes or unsteady hands.

Bear spray
Repels pests like bug spray does but is intended for larger pests.

Stomach pump
This somewhat controversial gadget allows you to find out what a fish was eating before you caught it. There are those who argue that once you've caught the fish, you know what it was eating or else you wouldn't have caught it. To which I reply, "So, the fish was eating natural size 6 Chartreuse, Rubber-Legged Chernobyl Ants?" This tool probably has a place in fly fishing but should only be used carefully and occasionally.

Cell phone
Not a chance.

CHAPTER 4

Western Casting
and Line Control

Fly fishing boils down to putting the fly in the right place, and then making it behave properly after it's there. Casting determines the former, and line control the latter. The importance of casting is obvious to most anglers, but line control is just as critical, for that's what affects the behavior of the fly while Mr. Trout is looking at it.

When talking about fly fishing, I sometimes find myself making comparisons with baseball. I suppose much of the time this doesn't make much sense, but one pretty good comparison is between casting and pitching, for success in both depends on accuracy. You won't strike out many hitters if your ninety-mile-per-hour fastball goes behind the batter into the dugout, and you won't catch many fish if you can cast a fly across the river but can't hit a picnic table at thirty feet. This is not a book about fly casting, but since the subject can't be avoided when discussing fly fishing, I'll tell you what I think about it here. I think fly casting is something people spend too much time talking about and too little time practicing. Tell me why people laugh out loud when they drive by a guy casting in a park but don't even snicker when they pass a busy driving range.

There are three sources of help if you want to become a better fly caster. In increasing order of preference, they are a book, a video or CD ROM, or a live human being. This, you may have noticed, is a book and is therefore the least effective way of teaching fly casting; hence my attempt at brevity. Our problem is that fly casting is made up of movements, while books are made up of words and still pictures. Even though I'm going to make a stab at it in a minute, learning to fly-cast from a book is a bit like studying ballet by correspondence.

Videotapes can be very helpful. Most of North America's top fly-casting gurus, including Lefty Kreh, Mel Krieger, Doug Swisher, Gary Borger, and Joan Wulff, have produced videos that show their methods and analyses of fly casting. From that list, you can reap the benefit of nearly two hundred years of fly-casting instruction. The drawback to videos is that while you can watch a great caster cast, the great caster can't watch you. This is why direct help from a qualified instructor is the best way to improve. The instructor can watch you cast and can immediately spot weaknesses or bad habits and suggest ways of correcting them. Most fly-fishing stores and clubs offer both basic and more advanced fly-casting instruction.

From here on in this book, I'll presume that the reader has a good grasp of fundamental fly casting and can perform a basic overhead cast with tight loops, can extend the cast by shooting line, and can make a basic roll cast. In this chapter we'll examine some of the specific techniques that have application in western fly fishing.

CASTING WEIGHT

Conventional fly casting is founded on the premise that the weight being cast is spread throughout the line, not concentrated at the end of the line. When we fish with heavily weighted flies or attach a couple of split shot to the leader, however, we really mess up this premise. Now there is weight in the line and at the end of the line, and the outfit doesn't behave the same way. In the West, there are many situations where heavy flies or additional weight on the leader are necessary, and for reasons of both safety and proficiency, it's important to be able to manage the extra weight.

First, when casting weight, a short leader is easier to use than a long one, because it is less prone to tangles. It's rarely necessary to use a leader over 9 or 10 feet long with weighted flies, and when a sinking fly line is used, the leader is often only half that long.

Second, you must open up the casting loop by moving the rod through an exaggerated arc. You must apply power throughout the casting stroke rather than focusing it at one point. This makes the rod bend deeply into the butt. The proper stroke for casting weight is a long, sweeping, accelerating, arcing motion. It is very nearly the opposite of the short, concentrated flick of the rod tip that is used for conventional casting without weight.

Third, you must wait until the line has straightened out behind you on the backcast before you begin the forward cast. This is even more critical when casting weight than when casting conventionally. You will feel a *thunk* as the line comes tight on the backcast. If you don't feel it, you haven't waited long enough, and problems will begin shortly.

Fourth, you mustn't underpower the forward cast. Many people are timid about casting weight because they think it might hurt when a #4 beadhead stonefly nymph hits them on the back of the head. Well, they're right, it will hurt a lot. But it will happen only if the fly travels through the air at head height. You need to keep the fly high above your head during the forward cast. To make this happen, the fly must travel fast enough to overcome the downward (meaning toward your head) pull of gravity. If a powerful forward cast with an open loop is used, the fly will stay high as it goes over your head. But if the forward cast is timid and underpowered, the fly will begin to fall almost immediately and will be much more likely to hit you.

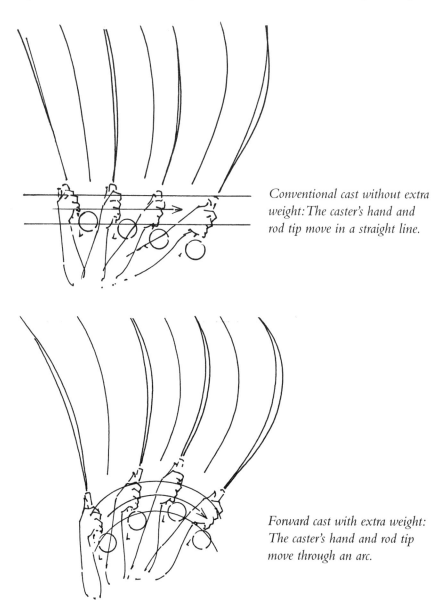

Conventional cast without extra weight: The caster's hand and rod tip move in a straight line.

Forward cast with extra weight: The caster's hand and rod tip move through an arc.

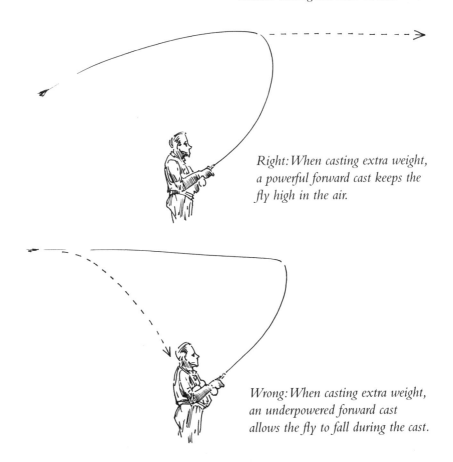

Right: When casting extra weight, a powerful forward cast keeps the fly high in the air.

Wrong: When casting extra weight, an underpowered forward cast allows the fly to fall during the cast.

Fifth, you should make the backcast somewhat off to the side of your body and the forward cast more overhead. This will smooth out the cast and reduce the likelihood of tangles. This is sometimes called a Belgian cast, which is a good term to toss out when you need to impress someone who can't figure out why you cast so funny.

Sixth, reduce or eliminate false casting. This rule should be applied to all fly casting because of its connection to the adage "you can't catch a fish with your fly in the air." When casting weight, the rule applies because of the safety factor: The more false casts you make, the more likely you'll mess one up and whack yourself on the head. When there's a lot of extra weight in the fly or on the leader, you should use the water haul. This is done by letting the fly and line land briefly on the water on both the forward cast and backcast, and then using the surface tension of the water to help load the rod for the next cast. It looks terrible, but it is safe and effective in places where heavy weight is required.

THE DOUBLE HAUL

The double haul is a technique devised by Portland angler Maurice Abraham in the early 1930s. Abraham showed it to fellow Oregonian Marvin Hedge, who introduced it to the tournament casting world at an international tournament in St. Louis in 1934. Using the double haul, Hedge beat the previous distance record by twenty-two feet, and since then the phrase has been a part of the fly-casting vocabulary.

The double haul's original purpose was to increase distance, but because it achieves this by increasing line speed, it is useful whenever high line speed is required, as when casting into wind or when shooting a lot of line on the forward cast. It helps limit the number of false casts, which is especially beneficial when fishing from a driftboat. The principle of the double haul is pretty simple; the execution takes some persistent practice.

A *haul* is simply a tug on the fly line with your line hand that occurs at the same moment the power is applied with the rod hand. The haul increases the line's speed because it moves the line through the rod at the same time the rod is already moving the line through the air. The line receives velocity from two sources simultaneously—the rod and the line hand—and the two velocities are compounded. You get the same effect if you run down the aisle of a moving train. Your actual velocity is the sum of the speed you're running plus the speed at which the train is moving. The result is that you are moving faster than the train. Likewise, when the double haul is used, the line moves faster than the rod.

Nearly everybody makes a single haul on the backcast. It happens by itself because the rod hand and the line hand naturally move away from one another during the backcast. To execute a double haul, you must make a second haul during the forward cast. For this to happen, the two hands must be near one another when the forward cast begins. This is the tricky part, because after making a haul on the backcast, the hands are quite far apart. So the line hand must move up toward the rod hand during the pause between forward cast and backcast. And as the line hand moves up, the slack created between the hands must move out through the rod (this bit of line shoots on the backcast the same way line shoots on the forward cast). Then, just as the power is applied on the forward cast, the line hand tugs or hauls on the line. This is a little like watching two football games at once on TV, and it takes a while to learn. The double haul is best practiced on a lawn, not a stream, and is best broken down into small steps. It can be used when false casting and when shooting line on the final delivery.

Many good casters double haul all the time. It helps keep slack out of the line, maintains line speed, and reduces the effort required of the casting arm.

It's important to realize that the double haul won't help a bit unless all other components of the cast are sound. You must cast tight loops with a proper application of power, pausing properly between forward cast and backcast. If any of these elements are weak, the double haul is, in the words of Lefty Kreh, "just a way of throwing your mistakes farther."

CASTING IN THE WIND
Nothing handicaps fly fishers and diminishes our enjoyment of the sport as much as wind. Unfortunately, the West is famous for wind, and it always seems to blow from the worst possible direction and to increase its velocity at the worst possible time, such as the same moment a giant brown trout starts rising in a difficult spot. You have two choices: You can wait for a day or a time when the wind isn't blowing (be sure you have a deck of cards with you), or you can take the advice of the Eagles and "get over it."

It will sound like we're talking about airplanes here, but the application of two principles of physics will help when casting into a strong wind: aerodynamics and velocity. In English, this means you must form a tight loop with the line, and then make it go fast. For many people, however, the two don't occur together. Most casters try to make the line go faster by throwing harder, which usually creates wider casting loops. This is counterproductive, because wide loops expose more fly line to the wind and slow everything down. Casting a wide loop into a wind is like picking up a sheet of plywood and trying to run into the wind with it broadside. Casting a tight loop is like turning the plywood on end. It reduces air resistance. A tight loop is aerodynamically efficient, and a wide loop is just the opposite.

The way to cast tight loops is to make sure the rod tip travels in a straight line rather than an arc. The way to increase line speed is by using the double haul in combination with a long casting stroke.

To cast a tight loop, the rod tip must move in a straight line.

Delivering a fly to the water into a strong headwind is a tricky business. The cast must be directed low so the line and fly have a short distance to fall once the line is straight. Yet if you direct it the slightest bit too low, it will crash into the water and probably spook the fish.

There's another technique that can help deliver a fly into a strong headwind. I guess if you wanted to be cute, you could call it the "Don't shoot!" method. To do it, you use a double haul, but you don't shoot line on the final delivery the way you normally would. Shooting line on the delivery causes the line to slow down gradually as the loop unrolls, which under normal circumstances achieves the desirable gentle touchdown of the fly. In a headwind, however, the fly and leader blow back toward you if you shoot line on the delivery. If you don't shoot, the line will maintain its high speed right until the moment it is straight. This was shown to me by New Zealand guide Bob Vaile as a good method to use in the wind and to help straighten out the 15- to 18-foot leaders they often use there.

A variation of this is favored by Montana guide Neale Streeks. He adds a third haul with the line hand, just as the leader is unrolling, to further increase line speed at the final moment of the cast.

The wind that affects fly casting least comes toward you from your non-casting side. In other words, if you're right-handed, the breeze that's easiest to manage comes straight from your left. Line tangles or collisions with your body are rare, because the wind blows the line away from your body. This off-side breeze will affect your accuracy somewhat, though, and you'll have to allow for the sideways drift of your fly and line during the cast.

A breeze that comes from your casting-arm side causes problems because the wind blows the line *into* your body. To manage this, simply tilt the rod tip sideways slightly, and allow the wind to take the line to the other side of your body while keeping your casting arm in its normal position. If you're a right-handed caster, you keep your hand and arm to the right of your body but point the rod tip slightly to the left. The line will move safely back and forth to the left of your body.

The worst winds are gusty and inconsistent. It's hard to fight something that isn't there all the time. The breeze blows for a while, you crank up the velocity of your cast, and then, just as you punch your delivery out at Mach 3, the breeze stops for a moment. Your fly crashes into the water, and the wakes of fleeing trout appear throughout the pool. I have no particular advice for handling gusty winds except possibly retirement to the nearest bar.

THE REACH CAST

The reach cast has probably been used for a few hundred years by fly fishermen who didn't realize they were doing it. The first to name it and draw

When the wind blows from the right, a right-handed caster tilts the rod tip to the left, while keeping his casting hand to the right of his body.

attention to its importance were Doug Swisher and Carl Richards, in their 1975 book *Fly Fishing Strategy.* I would like to formally add my agreement with the assessment of so many others that it is the single most useful cast in fly fishing. It is sometimes called a reach mend by Gary Borger and other instructors.

The reach cast allows you to use the full length of your rod and arm to change the angle at which the fly line travels to the target. The line can be cast so that it goes straight from you to the target, or from a point ten or twelve feet beside you to the target. You can place the line on the water in the most advantageous position to get a good drift of the fly. It's like being able to change where you're standing, even when you can't move.

The reach cast is based on the following principal: Once the rod has stopped on the forward cast, the destination of the fly is established and can't be changed. What the rod does after this moment affects the line's position but not the fly's destination. During the time it takes for the line to finish straightening and fall to the water, the rod can be moved to either side of your body to position the fly line in the best place.

Like the double haul, this is a cast that is best learned in the backyard. To do it, make a standard delivery cast. Just as the rod stops, extend your arm and reach smoothly to the right or left with the rod. When it's done, your arm should be extended and pointing to the right or the left, and the line should go straight from the rod tip to the fly. If the line lands in a curve, it means you've started the reaching movement too late. You should shoot a bit of line with the reach cast so the fly doesn't land short of the target.

An upstream reach is the fundamental tool to achieve a drag-free drift when you're upstream of the fish (see chapter 6). It's especially good when fishing dry flies from a driftboat. It can also be used to place the line in water of a more preferable current speed when you're fishing straight across to a fish rising in a band of slower water near the bank.

In some situations, a conventional delivery makes the fly land in a good place but the line land in a bad place. A good example is when you're fishing directly upstream to a rising fish. Even if you make a perfect cast so that the fly lands four feet upstream of the fish, the bad news is that four feet of leader must drift right over the fish's head before the fly does. With a reach cast, you can put the fly in the same spot while keeping the line and leader off to the side of the fish.

A variation of the reach cast can be used to attain a dead drift when fishing directly downstream, as you occasionally need to do. In this instance, the reach is directly back toward you. While the line is falling to the water, the rod moves slowly up and back toward you, finishing in the same position it started the forward cast from. After the cast, as the fly drifts downstream,

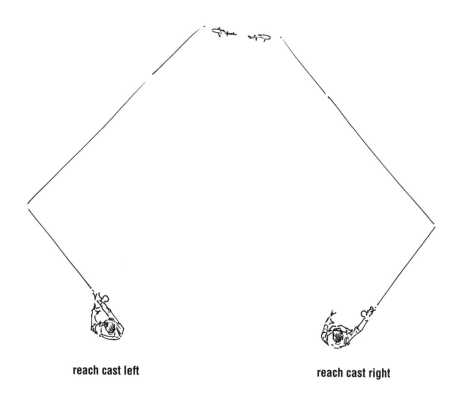

reach cast left   **reach cast right**

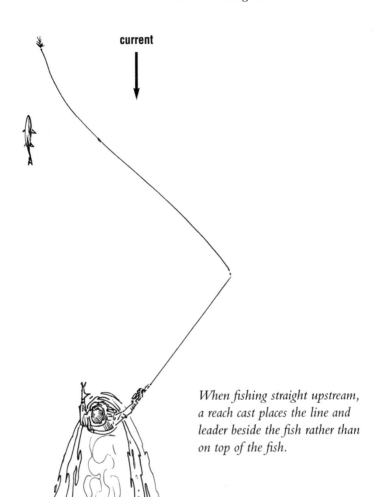

current

When fishing straight upstream, a reach cast places the line and leader beside the fish rather than on top of the fish.

the rod is lowered to pay out slack at the same rate the fly drifts. This is called a parachute cast or parachute mend by some fly fishers.

SLACK-LINE CASTS
In some situations, a straight-line delivery leads to immediate drag. An example is when fishing in an area where there are bands of current moving at different speeds. Here, one solution is to intentionally cast with slack in the line and leader. The theory is that the current has to pull the slack

out of the system before the fly will drag. Between the moment the fly lands and the moment the slack is all gone, there is a "period of grace" when the fly drifts naturally. The fly is supposed to make its appearance in the trout's window of vision during this period. This is a pretty good theory, and it even works in practice—when everything goes right.

What's needed are some ways of making accurate casts that leave slack in the system. The first of these is called an S-cast, or serpentine cast. It uses the same principle as the reach cast but requires a different rod manipulation. After the rod stops on the final delivery, the rod tip is wiggled side to side such that the line falls to the water in a series of curves. This is an easy cast to make, but it's not the most effective slack-line cast. It puts slack in the fly line, but what's more effective is a cast that puts the slack closer to the fly, in the leader.

A good way to put slack in the leader is with something magazine writers call a pile cast, dump cast, and other assorted names depending on who has invented it this time. When done properly, the fly line lands straight but the leader lands crooked. A good pile cast can put the fly and an entire 12-foot leader inside a hula hoop. There are at least two ways to make this cast. The first is by intentionally making a wide, arcing stroke on the final forward cast. This opens up the loop and prevents the leader from straightening out. You could also call this a beginner's cast, because it is the same cast that new fly fishers often make when they're trying to deliver the fly to the water.

A variation on this, described and demonstrated by Gary Borger in his books and casting videos, is done by making a standard, tight-loop delivery that is angled upward about thirty degrees above the water. As the line straightens, the rod tip is pulled smoothly down until it touches the surface of the water. This brings the fly and leader back toward the angler and allows the leader to land with plenty of slack.

The drawback to both these casts is that they finish high above the water and the fly and leader have a long way to fall, thereby exposing themselves to the breeze for quite a long time. They are difficult casts to make with accuracy when the wind is blowing.

A cast that overcomes this problem to some degree is what I call the tug cast. A normal, tight loop delivery is made low to the water. Just as the line and leader are straight, the line hand tugs quickly back, making the line and leader jump back toward the angler before they land on the water. This is a lot like Neale Streeks's triple haul. It puts a bit of slack in the system, with most of it in the leader. This doesn't create nearly as much slack as the pile cast, but when the wind is up, it's sometimes the only choice.

CURVE CASTS

Let me get this out of the way right at the start. Curve casts are of the most use to people who give indoor casting demonstrations at fishing shows. They are flashy and impressive but have rather limited applications in real fishing conditions. Most of what you want to achieve with a curve cast can usually be achieved more easily with a reach cast. There are, however, a few occasions when it is good to be able to throw a curve. You never know when a talent scout for one of the big fishing shows might be watching.

In theory, curve casts allow you to cast around obstacles like big rocks or overhanging branches and to make fly-first presentations to rising trout. You can make the line curve in one of two directions. For a right-handed caster, a cast that makes the line curve to the left is called a positive curve, and one that makes it curve to the right is called a negative curve. The positive curve can be made a number of ways, but the simplest is to make a sidearm cast with extra velocity, and then stop the line abruptly with the rod as the line is straightening out. Don't shoot any line. The fly will carry on past straight, and the result is a curve to the left (for a right-handed caster). The positive curve is the easiest and most useful of the two curve casts, and with practice, good casters can develop the consistency and accuracy that real fishing situations require. It is most easily done when using a relatively short leader and a nymph, streamer, or small dry fly. Large, fluffy drys are too wind-resistant and fall to the water before they make it around the corner.

A negative curve cast is much more difficult. You can do it with a backhanded sidearm cast, using the same principle as for the positive curve, but for most folks that turns out to be a bit impractical. Another way is to roll your wrist during the forward cast. To make a negative curve, a right-handed caster makes an overhead cast and rolls the wrist counterclockwise while applying the power. This method can produce a slight curve in the line, but only experts and demonstration casters can make anything approaching a right-angle negative curve. It's very difficult to do consistently and accurately, and I know of few anglers who use it much. It's probably easier to learn to throw a positive curve with your other hand.

THE TUCK CAST

The tuck cast was devised by George Harvey of Pennsylvania and is a very useful cast for nymph fishing. It really is nothing more than a positive curve cast directed downward at the water. A tuck cast makes the fly enter the water before the line and leader, and places slack right above the fly. This combination allows the fly to get to the bottom more quickly than

A tuck cast is a positive curve directed down at the water.

with a standard delivery. It is easiest with weighted flies, which is another reason it's become a standard cast in nymph fishing.

MENDING

All the techniques described so far have been part of the cast, because they are adjustments that are made before the line hits the water. When an adjustment is made after the line has landed, it is called a mend. A mend is made by simply flipping the rod tip to adjust the position of the line on the water.

Mends have application in dry-fly, nymph, streamer, and wet-fly fishing. For dry-fly fishing, they are used to help achieve a drag-free drift. A mend in an upstream direction is the one most often required. This puts an upstream loop in the line that the current must remove before drag can occur. In general, mends are made to compensate in advance for the bad things the current will do to the drift of the fly.

There are benefits and drawbacks to mending. The benefit is that a mend is somewhat easier to make than a reach cast or slack cast. One of the drawbacks is that a mend usually removes slack from the leader. That's bad because a bit of slack in the leader is usually desirable in dry-fly fishing. A second drawback is that the fly sometimes jerks suddenly across the water the moment the mend is made. For this reason, any mends that will be required should be made as soon as the line lands and well before the fly gets to the fish's position. If you wait until drag is just about to set in before making the mend, the fly will certainly jerk violently right in front of the fish's nose. The fish won't like that. Make the mend well before you need it.

In nymph fishing, mends are also used to achieve a drag-free drift. The difference is that drag is a three-dimensional issue in nymph fishing, while only two-dimensional in dry-fly fishing. In nymph fishing, the mend is made in an upstream direction anytime the line or leader starts to drift faster than the fly.

Mending has good use in streamer and wet-fly fishing too. Whenever the fly is cast across and downstream and fished on a tight line, mending is used to control both the speed and depth of the fly's movement. An upstream

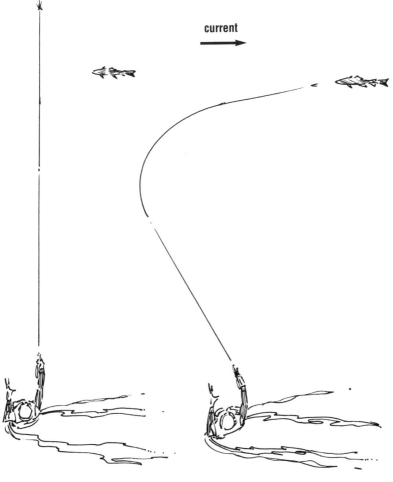

Position of the line before mending.   *Position of the line after mending.*

mend, made right after the fly lands, slows the drift of the fly and allows it to go deeper. A downstream mend does the opposite. A number of mends can be made in succession to maintain the desired effect through the drift.

A special type of mend was developed by Doug Swisher and is particularly helpful for streamer and nymph fishing. Called the stack mend, it is described and demonstrated clearly on Swisher's video *Advanced Strategies for Selective Trout*. A stack mend transfers slack line from a point near the rod to a point near the fly. Its sole purpose is to allow the fly to sink quickly. To make a stack mend, the fly is cast beyond the target. As soon as the fly lands, the rod is drawn up and back into the position to start a roll cast. Then a short, sharp roll cast is made, but it is directed low and right at the spot where the fly landed on the water. The roll cast does not complete itself and pull the fly out of the water, but instead dies early, depositing a loop of slack line right on top of the fly. Several stack mends can be made in succession to allow the fly to sink even deeper. This is the best method I know for getting a fly near the bottom quickly. It works best with a floating line and 9- or 10-foot leader.

RETRIEVING

Retrieving fly line is a pretty simple part of the game, yet there are still some mistakes that can be made. In general, if you are retrieving line, you are doing it either to strip away slack that accumulates as the fly drifts toward you or to make the fly swim through the water in a manner that imitates a natural food item. In either case, the most effective way to retrieve is with the rod tip held low and the line coming over the first or second finger of the rod hand. The line hand strips line from *behind* the rod hand, not in front of it, to maintain complete control throughout the retrieve.

When retrieving to impart action to a streamer or wet fly, the low rod allows a direct connection from the stripping hand to the fly so that the fly moves every time a strip is made. An exception to the low-rod rule occurs in short-line nymph fishing, when the rod is held high to keep as little fly line on the water as possible, making it easier to get a drag-free drift of the nymph.

STRIKING

Striking is the action taken by the angler to set the hook in the fish's mouth. It's a necessary part of most fly-fishing methods, but I've always had a little trouble with the word *strike*. It implies something pretty violent, which it should rarely be. When fishing with nymphs, the strike must be quick so that the hook bites the fish before the fish realizes its mistake and spits the fly out. But the striking motion must also be short, so as not to break the leader or throw a little fish into the trees behind you. It is done with a short, sharp move of the rod tip. A good way to practice is to try to strike without taking the fly out of the water. Then, if there is no fish attached, you can continue to fish out the cast instead of having to start over with another cast.

With dry flies, some on-the-job analysis is required. In general, large fish take dry flies slowly, and small fish take them quickly. If you strike too fast when a big fish takes your dry, you'll probably pull the fly away from him. Conversely, if you strike too slowly with a small fish, it may spit the fly out before you tighten up.

If the fish is already feeding at the surface, you might know its size, in which case you can plan your strike accordingly. When a big fish comes up for your dry, wait until it has opened its mouth, closed its mouth, and turned back down, before simply tightening up gently with the rod tip. In New Zealand, where all trout are big, the guides tell their clients to say, "God save the Queen" before setting the hook on a fish that's taken a dry fly. But often you won't know the size of the fish until later. I'd rather miss a little fish by striking too slowly than miss a big fish by striking too fast, so I err on the slow side.

A trout that takes your streamer thinks it's committing a murder. Consequently, the take is often violent, and because it usually occurs on a tight line, a strike from the angler is not always necessary. Often the fly is swinging downstream and suddenly a fish is on. Other times, though, the take can seem subtle, probably because the trout is moving toward the angler when it takes the fly, thereby pushing slack into the leader and preventing the angler from feeling a violent hit. In these cases, the angler must strike. The most common strike is the same one used with nymph fishing or with spin- or bait-casting tackle—the rod tip is elevated quickly to drive the hook into the fish's mouth. The problem with this is that if it's unsuccessful, the fly comes out of the water and the jig's up, at least for that cast. It's sometimes better to strike the way saltwater anglers do, by keeping the rod low and tugging on the line with the line hand. If the fish misses, at least the fly is still in the water, where the fish can make another try for it. This is hard to learn, and stout leaders must be used to prevent breakoffs when a big fish gets ahold of the fly.

CHAPTER 5

Reading Western Streams

Inexperienced fly fishers sometimes presume that fish are distributed evenly throughout all parts of a stream. That is never the case. There are always sections of the stream that hold fish and others that don't. Reading water is the ability to look at a stream and correctly distinguish the former from the latter.

It takes time and experience to learn where fish concentrate in a stream, but understanding some fundamental principles will help. One of these is hydrology, which the dictionary describes as "a science dealing with the properties, distribution and circulation of water." For our purposes, hydrology explains the way water behaves when it's flowing. Moving water is simultaneously subject to three influences that determine its behavior: gravity, friction, and inertia.

Gravity makes water flow downhill. The steepness of the incline, called the *gradient* of the stream, determines the speed with which the water flows. The headwater portions of mountain streams flow through tilted country and have steep gradients and high velocity. In contrast, prairie streams and spring creeks have gentle gradients and lower velocity.

Counteracting the unrelenting pull of gravity is friction between the water and the streambed. Wherever the water meets the earth, the water is forced to slow down. This is why the water near the bottom and the banks of a stream flows more slowly than the water in the middle of the stream. The most extreme evidence of friction between water and land is erosion. Over time, the abrasive force of flowing water digs holes into the bottom and banks of the stream, thereby influencing its depth.

Inertia is the force that makes a moving object keep moving, and keep moving in a straight line. It is the most overlooked of the three properties that determine the character of a trout stream. Because of inertia, water flows in straight lines, changing direction only when it has to. The main current in a creek or river flows straight until it hits a bend in the stream-bank, then turns and follows that bank along the outside of the bend. When the bank turns back in the opposite direction, the water does not follow it immediately but continues in a straight line. It flows straight until it hits the opposite bank, and then follows that bank and repeats the process. So even though the streambed winds in a series of smooth S-curves, within the streambed the water zigzags back and forth from one bank to the other in a series of straight lines.

In combination, it is these three horsemen of gravity, friction, and iner-tia that give flowing water the changeable character that concentrates cur-rent, food, and ultimately trout in certain parts of streams.

The second principal of reading water is familiarity with the trout's basic requirements for survival. These are shelter from heavy current, safety from predators, and access to food. The manner in which the stream provides

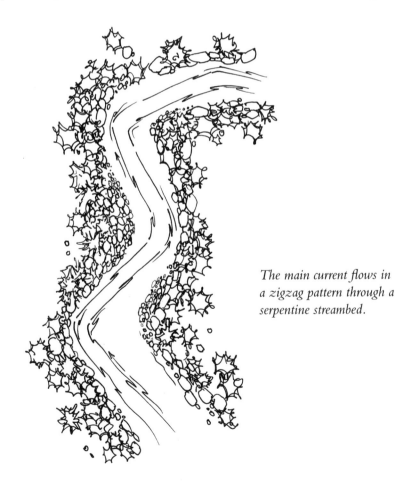

The main current flows in a zigzag pattern through a serpentine streambed.

these requirements determines where the trout will be. A location where the fish have the first two—shelter from current and safety from predators—is called holding water. This is the place trout are found when they are just hanging around and doing nothing in particular. Think of holding water as the fish's homes, sometimes called lies or even fish-houses.

Feeding water is the restaurant trout go to for a serious pig-out. When food becomes extremely abundant, as it does during a heavy hatch, an egg-laying flight, or a migration of nymphs, trout move to places where this food is concentrated by the flow of the stream and can be obtained quickly and easily. This allows them to live within the bounds of their immutable feeding law: The calories gained from food eaten must be greater than the calories expended to eat it. While they're in feeding water, feeding temporarily takes priority over the otherwise dominant instincts for safety and current relief. Trout go to feeding water to chow down while the food is abundant, after which they move back to the safety of their holding water. It's the "get in, get fed, and get out" approach that fast-food restaurants like their customers to use.

This is not to say that fish never eat while they're in their holding water. If food finds its way into a trout's living room, it will usually be eaten. So although fish are easiest to catch when they're in feeding water and the feeding mode, they spend far more time in holding water. We try to catch them in both places.

Trout like feeding water best if there is holding water nearby so they can get to safety quickly if trouble arrives, but there is often some distance between the two, especially in big rivers. If there is too much distance between shallow feeding water and the safety of holding water, the feeding water will be used mainly at night.

A spot in a stream where holding water and feeding water merge—that is, where the trout's requirements of safety, shelter from current, and easy access to food are all met in a single location—is called a prime lie. If fish can feed easily and often, without exposing themselves to predators, they have no reason to move from their holding water, and they don't. To the fish, this is like having room service. Why go out to eat when the food is delivered right to your door? And who do you suppose lives here, in Trout-ville's most affluent neighborhoods? The wealthiest (read: biggest) fish in the stream.

Trout streams will always remain a bit mysterious. All their secrets are not apparent to fishermen. One way they fool us is in the way the surface of a stream can disguise its velocity. It's easy to presume that all broken water is fast and all smooth water is slow. This is not true. A place where two currents merge, such as downstream of an island, may have a very bouncy, choppy surface but low velocity. Conversely, in the tailouts of pools, the water is often smooth on top but moving quite quickly. Reading water is a skill that develops with time and experience. Though the information that follows will help, there's nothing to compare to on-the-water training.

HOLDING WATER

The places described below are holding areas for trout in streams of any size.

Broken Water

If the surface of the water is broken, predators can't see in from above. The fish seem to know this and exhibit a greater sense of security in these places. A broken surface also indicates an uneven, rocky bottom, which provides small areas of current relief for the trout. Many anglers are attracted to areas of smooth water, but all other things being equal, fish are more willing to feed, and are easier to catch, in holding water with a broken surface than in holding water that is smooth on top.

Pools

It's a good idea to watch other anglers fish. I do it because I often learn things, even if the stream is one I think I already know well. It's best if you can watch without the other guy knowing you're there, even though you'll probably feel a little sneaky doing it. I've learned some neat tricks this way, but my spying has also shown me that about 80 percent of anglers just fish in the major pools.

Pools are the deepest and slowest-moving parts of the stream. They are not the only places to find fish, but they are the most obvious and as such are the first places most anglers cast. They are the places you'd choose to go swimming on a hot day if you weren't so busy fishing. The upstream end of a pool, where the depth begins to increase, is the head, and the area at the downstream end of a pool, where the water begins to get quicker and shallower, is the tail or tailout. The shallow, dancing water between pools is called a riffle. Gravelly riffles are very important parts of a trout stream, because they are ideal habitat for many aquatic insects.

If you climb a high bank and look down into a trout stream, you'll see fish in the deepest parts of the pools nearly all the time, but knowing they're there won't necessarily help you catch them. The residents of deep pools often lack the motivation fishermen like to see in trout, and they often just lie on the bottom, seemingly asleep and uninterested in everything, including food. You can catch fish from the depths of the pools, but it's usually an uphill battle. Persistence with sunken flies is usually the best approach. In big rivers, the only effective way to fish the deepest parts of pools is with sinking lines and streamers or nymphs.

A pool in a freestone stream. The head of the pool is in the center of the picture, where the water begins to deepen. The water is flowing left to right.

The good news is that within most pools is a prime lie. It is located along the edge of the current just downstream of the head of the pool. Gary Borger calls this "the eye of the pool," and the best ones are formed on the insides of corners. There is usually broken water on the surface, which provides overhead cover, and a depression, or bucket, on the bottom. Fish lie in the depression, along the edge of the current where they have easy access to the food that arrives at the head of the pool. These are great spots in streams of all sizes, as long as the water is deep enough to make the fish feel safe. The eye is the premium holding spot in the pool, and in almost every case the premium spot is occupied by a premium fish. They can be fished with any type of fly but are best suited for nymphs and dry flies.

Undercut Banks
When streams flow through beds of earth rather than rock or gravel, they create undercut banks, which are some of the best places for big trout. Undercuts develop on the outsides of bends where the current pushes hard against the streambank, and these holes often extend a surprising distance back beneath the bank. Fish in these places are out of sight of most predators—especially those that come from above, like birds and fishermen—

An undercut bank can hold fish, even if the water is fairly shallow.

and they also have relief from current because they're right next to the bank, which slows the water. In addition, the main current brings food right by their noses. Undercut banks are among the best examples of prime lies and are greatly favored by brown trout. They are often found in meadow sections of streams and are good places to fish with grasshoppers in late summer, or with floating mouse patterns after dark, if you have a strong heart. They are more important in small streams than in big rivers.

Converging Currents

Wherever two distinct currents join, an important effect is created. The two currents cancel each other out to some degree, and the velocity along the seam where the two currents meet is much lower than that of either current before they met. A fish lying on that seam can maintain its position with little effort, taking advantage of the reduced velocity while food passes by on both sides. If the water is more than two feet deep, these are among the best of prime lies. They can be fished with any type of fly.

Rocks and Boulder Gardens

Big rocks—either singly or in numbers, protruding above the surface or not—interrupt the flow of the stream and create great character in a river. Each rock is a miniature island. Behind each rock is a small area of lesser current, and just downstream of that is a miniature point of converging

Large rocks provide character and holding water in trout streams.

Fish often lie beneath overhead cover.

currents. Large boulder gardens in fast water create what is called pocket water. This water can be confusing to read until you mentally break the large area into small pieces, looking for small bits of quiet water—the soft spots—amongst the turbulence. A fish doesn't need a large area of relief from current; it simply needs an area of quiet water as big as it is. If the depth in such places is adequate, boulders can create prime lies in both small and large streams.

This water is tricky to fish. Because of the many different current speeds, it's hard to control the behavior of the line and the fly. The best solution is to approach very close to the pocket and to hold the rod tip high after you've cast to keep most of the fly line off the water. Pocket water can be fished with any type of fly, but perhaps the most reliable are weighted nymphs and large, buoyant dry flies. Some pocket water on big rivers can only be fished from a boat, in which case teamwork between the rower and caster is essential.

Overhead Cover
Overhead cover is created by things that extend into or hang out over the edge of the stream. These can be standing or fallen trees, tree roots, bank-side willows, or overhanging grass, but they can also be floating patches of weeds, foam, or scum. Fish often lie beneath them.

It's hard to fish many of these places with sunken flies because of one of fly fishing's numerous Catch-22s: If you place your fly close enough to the debris for the fish to be interested in eating it, the fly will hang up in a branch before the fish gets it, but if you keep your fly a safe distance from the debris, the fish won't be interested in it. Often the solution is to use a dry fly. You can let it drift very close to the debris, knowing it will bounce safely away from most of the branches.

Logjams

A special type of fish-house exists where piles of deadfall collect in the river. Logjams provide trout with both cover and current relief. If there is a strong flow of water coming by or through the logs, they are also prime lies. Some species of stoneflies crawl out on logjams to emerge, and consequently good dry-fly fishing sometimes occurs in these neighborhoods when the adult flies return to the water to lay eggs. Like bankside overhead cover, logjams are difficult places to fish and are most appreciated by people who earn their living selling flies.

Beaver Lodges

On many western streams, beaver lodges provide holding areas for trout. In addition to the obvious overhead safety provided by the sticks and branches

The deep water near a beaver lodge often holds big trout.

of the lodge, the beavers usually dig a deep trough on the stream bottom that extends out from the entrance of the lodge. This deeper water is often a holding lie for big trout, especially browns.

Weed Beds

Weed beds provide trout with everything they need. They hide the fish from predators, slow the current to a comfortable speed, house insects that the fish eat, and even inject oxygen into the water during the day through photosynthesis. That's the good news. The bad news is that weed beds are difficult places to fish. If they're thick, weeds can make it impossible to use anything but dry flies and the occasional small nymph, drifted carefully through the channels. When the weeds extend near the surface, they create great variety in current speeds, which makes it very difficult to get a drag-free drift. The best example of this might be the famous Harriman State Park section of the Henry's Fork of the Snake in Idaho. By midsummer the weeds reach within a foot of the surface, and the river, though smooth at first glance, is really constantly shifting and writhing.

FEEDING WATER

In general, feeding water is much harder to identify than holding water, unless the fish help by showing it to us. This is because some of the places trout use for feeding look just like other places they don't use. The proper combination of current speed, direction, and depth that creates good feeding water is often not apparent to us poor humans. Often the only time you can be sure you're looking at feeding water is when you see fish feeding in it. I guess you have to be a trout to understand. The places described below are feeding areas in streams of all sizes.

Heads of Pools

These are easy to recognize and are important feeding spots in both small and large streams. The head of a pool is the area where the water first begins to deepen as it enters the pool. It is near the eye of the pool, but it is not the same as the eye. The eye is located along the edge of the current in water two feet deep or deeper, while the head of the pool extends across the full width of the stream and is much shallower.

It is the riffle upstream that makes the heads of pools such good feeding areas, for reasons of both biology and physics. Riffles are shallow, and sunlight easily penetrates to the stream bottom, where it promotes growth of plants that support insect life. Because the surface of the water is broken and the current is quick, riffles are areas of high oxygen content. And there is usually gravel on the bottom, which is good habitat for many aquatic

The angler has hooked a trout that was feeding near the head of the pool.

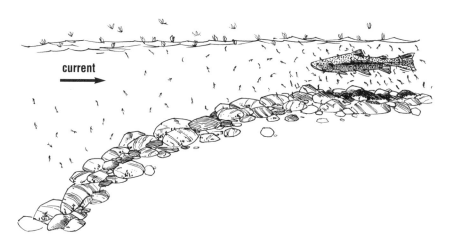

A riffle is a vertical constriction in the stream. Food is concentrated in a small area where fish can get it easily.

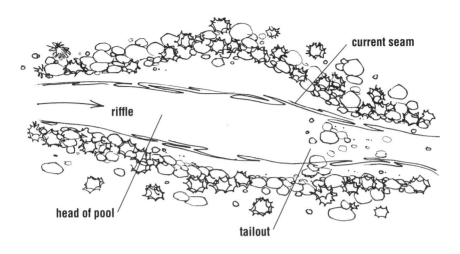

A typical pool.

insects. Because of their biology, riffles are areas of extremely dense and diverse aquatic insect life. Most hatching activity begins in riffles, and feeding fish work their way up to the head of the pool from the deeper holding water below, seeking the mother lode of emerging insects.

Considering physics, it is necessary to understand "the law of the riffle." The riffle between pools is a vertical constriction of the water column, which concentrates drifting food into a smaller space. All the food that was spread through several feet of water in the pool above is concentrated into just a few inches of water in the riffle. In a riffle, the nymphs on the bottom and the adult flies on the surface are only a few inches away from each other, and a trout can watch both simultaneously. So a fish lying at the head of the pool is positioned immediately downstream of the most productive part of the stream, in the place where food is most concentrated. It can pick off drifting nymphs, swimming emergers, and adult insects with equal ease and minimal expenditure of energy.

The heads of pools are best fished in the early stages of a heavy hatch. If you see a lot of adult insects in the surface but few fish rising, the fish might be feeding heavily on nymphs that are swimming to the surface to emerge. A good plan in this case is to fish a nymph at the head of the pool. I especially like doing this in late summer and autumn, when little *Baetis* mayflies begin to emerge in the afternoon. If the day is cloudy, overcast, or better yet, drizzly, the hatch will be intense, and the fish will concentrate at the heads of pools when the emergence begins. In my experience, the heavier the hatch, the farther up into the head the fish will feed, sometimes actually taking up stations in the shallowest part of the riffle above the pool.

After a few days of repetitive insect activity, trout get tuned in to the insects' routine and move into riffles prior to the hatch, lining up for the excitement they believe is soon to come, much the way we line up to get into a concert or football game.

Back Eddies and Stagnant Backwaters

On many western streams, numerous wide, baylike areas are attached to the main river channels. Some of these are still, and some are slowly revolving back eddies. There are a number of big ones on the Missouri River below Holter Dam in Montana and on other streams throughout the West.

Flies drift into these places during good hatches, and once there, the bugs stay there, either simply collecting randomly throughout the stillwater or going round and round in the eddy. These are often places where fish actively feed long after the hatch is over, simply because of the great number of bugs that accumulate there. On hot August days on the Missouri, the spinner fall of tiny *Tricorythodes* mayflies starts early in the morning and finally ends about noon. Most fly fishers then retire to the bars in the towns of Wolf Creek and Craig to cool off, but the fanatics head for these backwaters instead to continue their dry-fly fishing through the afternoon.

Trout feed in both the foam-covered eddy and the stagnant backwater bay in the foreground.

These places are often the least esthetically attractive parts of trout streams, but there's no denying their productivity. They often have silty, weedy bottoms and scummy foam collecting on the surface. I came upon such a place in the Crowsnest River one September afternoon. My companion and I were on a high bank, looking down into a foamy back eddy. It's not uncommon to see a few fish cruising these areas, rising now and again and picking up leftovers from the previous evening's hatch. This time, though, about two dozen big rainbows were cruising through the foam, occasionally bumping it from below, at times eating something stuck in the foam, and frequently slicing the foam with dorsals and tails as they took something lurking underneath. We couldn't figure out what to do with these fish. Our dry flies got stuck on the foam where the fish couldn't see them. Our nymphs dropped through, but it was impossible to know what happened to them once they did. After messing around with the fish for a while, our solution was to move up the river to a more conventional piece of water.

If the water in these places is still, the fish feed by cruising, just as they do in any type of stillwater. If the fish are visible, small nymphs and dry spinners or emerger patterns can be cast into their paths. If they aren't visible, things get much more difficult. The fly must be cast and left on the water until a fish finds it or the fisherman runs out of patience. An occasional slight twitch of either a dry or a nymph can sometimes attract a nearby fish's attention.

If there is current in the bay, the fish will take up a position facing into it. Since these are often large eddies where the current flows "backward," you must choose your position carefully. Fish feeding in the reverse current will face downstream relative to the rest of the river. Many times I've experienced the sinking realization that the fish stopped rising because I walked right into their field of view.

Shallow Banks

As a river turns a corner, the main current pushes across to the far bank. From there down, the strongest current and deepest water are along the outside of the bend, and good holding water is often located along the deep bank. But good trout will also feed downstream of a bend on the opposite, or shallow, side of the river during a good hatch. There is usually little character to this water, and you don't find fish in it unless they are feeding. In fact, you'll often find them by spooking them as you hurry along the bank, anxious to get to the next good spot. The next time this happens, remember the place and return to it later with more caution. The problem with these shallow banks is that most streams have many of them, but the fish only use a few of them.

Tailouts

The tailout of a pool is the point where the water starts to get shallower and faster before breaking into the next riffle. This is where the vertical constriction of flow and the resultant concentration of food begins. In gravelly streams, there is frequently a small depression in the tailout that is a favorite feeding spot for trout. But that's not necessarily good news. Fish in tailouts are often difficult to approach, as the water is usually fairly shallow and very smooth on top. It is tricky to fish into a tailout from downstream, because the water moves more quickly in the riffle below than in the tailout itself. The quick current in the riffle pulls the fly line away from the fly in the tailout, and that dastardly villain—drag—is the usual result. It is often best to fish tailouts from upstream, being careful to stay off to the side and a good distance away from the fish to remain out of sight. Dry flies or nymphs are the usual choices for fish feeding in tailouts.

Slow Flats

In streams with gentle gradient, there are often long, slow stretches of water with uniform velocity, depth, and direction. Spring creeks have much water like this, and on these streams, fish will feed in the flats anytime there is insect activity. On less productive freestone streams, the flats are usually void of activity until late in the day when the sun is off the water. In order for a flat to be a good feeding area, there must be good holding water nearby.

Unexplainable Feeding Water

This is the category into which I place water that seems to be used by fish for no reason at all. There probably *is* a reason; it's just not one we have come to understand, and the fish aren't talking. I've found fish in some odd places, including very fast, slick, shallow water; in the very lip of a small waterfall; and facing backward in a small bay along the bank of the stream. I saw most of these fish when I spooked them. When this happens to you, simply file it away in your memory and check these places the next time you fish the stream. (But trust me—the fish usually aren't there the next time.)

READING BIG RIVERS

We must differentiate between small and large trout streams, because finding the trout is a different task in each. There are no standard dimensions for small and large streams, but I'll take a stab at it here. Let's consider a trout stream to be large if it can't be easily crossed on foot. Well-known

Big water with good character. The current seam provides contrast in speed, depth, and surface type. Trout hold along the seam. The water is flowing toward the camera.

examples of big rivers are the Bighorn, Deschutes, Missouri, Bow, Yellowstone, Snake, Elk, Henry's Fork, South Fork of the Snake, Kootenai, Spokane, and Green. Qualifying as small streams are most spring creeks and freestone streams, such as the Frying Pan, Upper Gibbon, and Upper Gallatin. Some streams are hard to categorize, like the Beaverhead, which is narrow but fairly fast and deep, and others that would qualify as large rivers in early summer and small streams later on when the water level has receded. We could also use the new-age definition: If the stream feels like a big river, it is a big river.

The ingredients that create good trout water are the same in all sizes of streams, but the good water is harder to identify on big rivers. On small streams, finding fish is simply a matter of finding water deep enough for fish to hide in. On big rivers, though, deep water is everywhere, and the immense magnitude of the playing field intimidates many anglers.

Small streams are easier to understand because all the pieces of the puzzle lie close to one another. You can see everything that's happening in the stream with a single glance. The riffles, pools, and flats are well defined, and the differences in depth, speed, and direction of current are readily apparent. Reading a small stream is like looking at a single plate of food on a table. All the information you require is immediately available. But it's not so simple on a big river. Not only is it hard to tell where one pool ends and another begins, but the distance between pools is great, and there are long stretches of water where nothing changes. Many anglers' first response to a big river is to think, "There's a lot of water out there; I'd better try to cover it all." This thought is followed by much deep wading and long casting but precious little fish catching. Such behavior is based on a premise that the deeper you wade and the farther you cast, the more fish you will catch. It is a corollary of the theory about fences and greener grass, and it is rarely true.

To return to our food analogy, reading a big river is like figuring out what to do at a giant buffet. It requires some thought. You know there's some great stuff somewhere on the table, but you can only see what's right in front of you. If you want to find the pecan pie that you suspect is out there, you have to negotiate your way past the sour pickles, cold cauliflower, and brussel sprouts first.

To find fish in big water, you must look for water with *character*. Character is variation in the components of depth, current speed, current direction, bottom type, and surface type. Look for places where these variations meet one another. These places are seams. The more seams there are, the more character the water has and the more likely it is to hold fish. Conversely, if the speed, depth, and direction are fairly constant—that is, if there is little or no character to the water—it is probably poor holding water. Perhaps the most important, yet most difficult, aspect of reading big rivers is learning to bypass the water without character. If making the most of a big buffet is knowing what food not to eat, then making the most of a big trout stream is knowing what water not to fish.

Thankfully, on big western rivers most of the character is located close to the banks. Friction between the water and the bank slows the water there, and irregularities along the edge—rocks, gravel bars, bushes, trees, and fallen logs—provide cover as well as contrasts in speed and depth.

Midstream features, such as gravel bars, boulders, bottom depressions, and weed beds, also provide character and should be fished when it's possible to wade or cast to them easily and safely, or when you're fishing from a boat. But if you're wading and there's a good spot in the middle of the river that you can't fish safely, it's best to forget about it.

Big River Holding Water
Broken water
In general, the easiest water to read on a big river is broken water. Broken water indicates large rocks on the stream bottom, and fish will hold in the quiet water behind the rocks. Long stretches of medium-speed, medium-

depth broken water are called runs and often hold a lot of fish. At first glance this water might appear uniform, but there is usually character there if you look closely. Watch for subtle variations in depth and speed, and concentrate your efforts in the soft spots where the fish can hold with little effort. Dry flies will work in broken water and runs less than two feet deep, while deeper water is usually best fished with nymphs and streamers.

Deep pools

As in smaller streams, deep pools in big rivers usually hold trout. They are even harder to fish on big rivers, though, because they are bigger and deeper. They are especially good places to find fish in winter, and some of the best off-season fishing is enjoyed by fishermen who thoroughly scour the deep pools with streamers and nymphs on fast-sinking fly lines. These methods also work in the summer, but many anglers, myself included, prefer to fish shallower holding water.

Points and deflections

One of the best places to find fish in a big river is where water flows past a point. A point or deflection can be a spit of gravel, a fallen tree, a pile of boulders, or a single rock. The only requirement is that it project from the

As the river enters a corner, a strong seam is created where the water flows past a point (upper left). The water is flowing towards the camera.

bank into the river and constrict flow in some manner. Contrasting current speeds are always produced when water flows past a point. A triangular piece of slower water forms downstream of the point, and the seam where the slow water meets the fast is where the fish usually lie, so long as the depth is adequate (at least eighteen inches).

Another type of point is created each time the river turns a corner. The water flows past a point on the inside of the bend, creating a huge triangle and a long current seam. This current seam is a great place to find fish, and

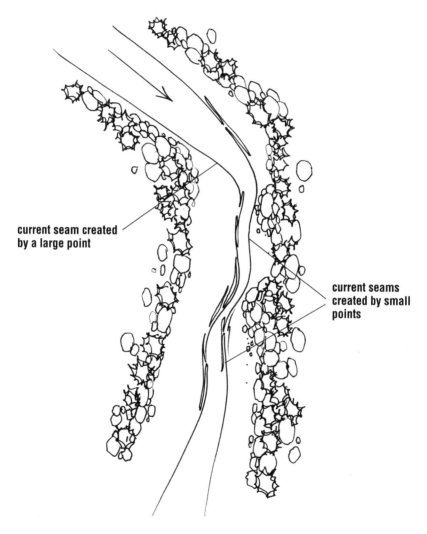

current seam created
by a large point

current seams
created by small
points

Current seams on a big river.

A vertical deflection.

at the top of the triangle is the eye of the pool, which is just as important in big rivers as in smaller streams. Such corners also create strong flows along the outside bank, and there you should look for small points that produce the same effect in miniature.

Points and deflections also project up from the stream bottom. An example is when water flows over a shallow gravel bar. The effect simply happens vertically, rather than horizontally. The current seam and triangle of slower water are under the surface, downstream of the gravel bar.

On many western rivers, small rocky points extend out from the bank and continue under the water, producing a vertical and horizontal point simultaneously. The water at the bank is deflected out and around the point, and the water a few feet out from the bank is deflected up and over the point. This double-whammy point produces a prime lie.

The type of deflection usually dictates the most logical fishing method. Large ones at the heads of big corner pools are ideal places to fish streamers down and across. Smaller deflections are good places to cast nymphs or dry flies upstream.

Depressions, slots, and holes
Variations in water depth often appear as depressions and deep slots, and these deeper areas, which are often in or around riffles, are places to find fish. Look for the darker blue or green color that means deeper water. The depth change need not be dramatic for fish to hold in a depression. If the riffle is eighteen inches deep and the depression twenty-four, that's enough. Such depressions are usually more abundant in early season on rivers that freeze in winter. When ice breaks up, it shifts and disturbs the gravel, forming new depressions and slots in the river bottom. These are often terrific places to fish nymphs or large dry flies if the fish are looking up.

Midriver slots and depressions become especially important in late season when low water or fishing pressure pushes the fish away from the banks. Knowledgeable guides often concentrate on the banks of their big rivers early in the season and focus on the green holes and depressions off the banks later in the season.

Side channels

Fishermen who have trouble reading big water should initially concentrate on parts of the river that are broken up by islands. Smaller side channels are easier to read and easier to fish than the main channel of a big river. Treat them like you would a small stream.

Below islands

The places where currents rejoin below islands are very good holding areas in big rivers. It's easy to understand why these spots are prime lies when you're fishing from a boat. If you position the boat directly downstream of the island, you'll see that the current moves swiftly by on both sides of you but the boat remains nearly stationary. Fish notice this too and stack up below islands, taking advantage of the gentle current and the fact that there are not one but two conveyor belts carrying food past their station. In big rivers, especially, the current seam often extends downstream some distance

The area where two currents converge below an island is often a prime lie in a big river. Look for the area of "slow chop," which may extend some distance below the island. The water is flowing toward the camera.

below the end of the island—sometimes as much as several hundred yards. This often produces a type of water I think of as slow chop. I've heard guides describe it as dancing water. It is water with a lot of vertical movement on the surface but quite low velocity. This kind of water is good with any type of fly, including drys. If the surface is especially turbulent, the area is best fished with sunken flies.

Big River Feeding Water

All of the feeding spots previously described are good in streams of all sizes, but some are particularly important in big rivers.

Heads of pools

Some of the most consistent places to find feeding trout in big rivers during summer are at heads of pools. Prior to and in the early stages of heavy hatches, the fish work their way up into the shallow heads of pools from the deeper water below. Nymphs and drys are the best choices here.

Shallow tailouts

In big rivers, fish often feed in the shallow tailouts of pools. These are places where the river gathers itself, hesitates, and seems to take a breath before falling into the next riffle. Sometimes there are small bays in such places, and often side channels leave the main rivers here. The fish usually feed near the banks, and you can see them if you wear polarized glasses and approach carefully from downstream or from a high bank. These fish are often touchy and easily spooked, and they are candidates for small nymphs or small dry flies if they are rising. These tailouts are often at their best at dusk.

Small deflections

If there's a good hatch in progress, watch the area beside and downstream of small deflections along the banks of the river, in areas of medium current speed. Fish move in from the deeper water farther out in the river. If the hatch is strong, the fish will feed in twelve inches of water or less. These miniature points cause a concentration of insects, and the fish set up there to pick them off. Fish use these deflections on both the deep and shallow sides of the river.

Shallow banks

Shallow inside banks, located downstream of big corner pools, are often great feeding areas on big rivers. Many prime dry-fly spots are in these kinds of places on both Montana's Bighorn River and Alberta's Bow. The

A shallow bay in the tailout of a big river. Fish will often feed on the surface here. The angler is fishing the riffle at the head of the next pool. The water is flowing away from the camera.

bad news is that unless the fish are there to confirm it, these are perhaps the most difficult places to identify as feeding water.

Slow flats
The long, slow, uniform sections of big rivers are difficult to read and are often best ignored unless there are a lot of flies on the water. During a good hatch, fish will appear in these places to feed. They are generally best late in the evening.

APPLIED WATER READING
If reading water is the ability to look at a stream and predict where the fish will be, *understanding* water is the ability to choose a fishing method that suits a particular spot. This is often what separates average fly fishers from exceptional ones. Let's go fishing.

It's mid-August and we'll be walking and fishing one bank of a big western river. Our first obligation is to stop at the ranch house to gain permission to cross the land along the river. We chat with the rancher for a few minutes on his doorstep, and he gives us his assessment of the summer from an agricultural perspective. These visits are important and should never be hurried. After the fishing season is over, we must remember to stop by again with a gift and thank-you card.

We arrive at the water about 8:30 A.M., and after our waders are on and rods are strung, we check for insect activity. At this time of year, we can expect a spinner fall of *Tricorythodes* mayflies about midmorning. Today the spinners are still swarming quite high in the air, which tells us that we have perhaps an hour until they come down to the water to lay eggs.

Just downstream of the spot where we reach the water, a small side channel breaks away from the main river. In spring it's big enough to float through in a driftboat, but now, in the low-water conditions of late summer, it is less than ten feet wide and just a few inches deep where it leaves the river. But before it goes thirty yards, it widens and deepens and almost stops flowing. It is not a particularly attractive spot. The bottom is silty, and weeds and scum lie in the dead water along the edges. It's hard to wade because of the depth and the soft bottom. Tall backcast-catching grass grows on the island. In the little bays along the shore are thousands of empty caddis pupa skins. This is evidence that caddisflies hatched through the night—and more than a subtle implication that we should have been fishing then.

Circling wide around the area, we approach it from downstream. At first there seems to be nothing happening. We cautiously move up a few steps. Then, just beside the tiny riffle that dumps into the deeper water, something subtly breaks the surface. We watch longer and it happens again, but not in the same place. Looking at the surface, we see that dead and battered caddisflies have collected in the stillwater next to the riffle, along with other assorted bugs—a few ants, the odd beetle, some day-old Trico spinners, and a few half-drowned grasshoppers. We sneak up closer, and then we see two big rainbows cruising around picking up leftovers. Their pink sides give them away and they weave back and forth, sometimes in water just a few inches deep, occasionally tipping up to take a fly with an audible *tap*. These fish have probably been in this scummy water all night, content to feed undisturbed on what a friend calls "the junk hatch." We can actually see the fish only part of the time, and when they turn and swim in our direction, we freeze and try to make ourselves look like trees. These fish are difficult to catch because they are cruising. We must cast either very quickly after the rise or when we can see them in the water. Either way there is some risk of lining the fish and scaring them.

We hook one of these fish on a spent caddis pattern; it jumps once and the fly lets go. We watch the smoke trail and wake of the other fish, which is now spooked, as it rockets down the channel to deep water.

Back at the main river, we hold our hands up to block the sun and see a big column of Trico spinners glistening above the water as they dance gracefully up and down through the morning air. The warmth we feel tells us that the spinner fall is imminent. We move upstream a hundred yards to the tailout of a big pool. The water along our bank flows gently into a little bay just before it gathers and breaks into the next riffle. It is an innocent-looking spot—nowhere more than eighteen inches deep—and would normally not warrant even a single cast, but for some reason fish feed here when there are flies on the water. The spinners are still swarming, but they are much closer to the surface now. We change to 12-foot, 6X leaders and tie on #18 Trico Spinner patterns. These are a little bigger than the real flies, but sometimes that seems to get the fish's attention. Besides, we have a much better chance of holding a big fish with a #18 than with a #20 or #22.

After about fifteen minutes, the flies come to the water. At first nothing happens, but then there is a rise and a moment later another. Then two simultaneously. In the next ten minutes, four or five fish appear mysteriously in the little cove and begin feeding. These fish don't cruise, because the spinners are abundant. They simply sit in one spot and bob up and down, sipping and slurping on Tricos.

One of the fish is hooked and runs out through the group. The remaining fish briefly scatter, but within thirty seconds they are back at it. The spinners are thick on the water, and the fish simply want to be there and are single-mindedly focused on feeding. We catch a second fish, spook two more with bad casts, and then it seems to be over.

When the brief spinner fall ends, we change our tackle to fish the next half mile of classic bank water. We shorten our leaders to 9 feet, with 3X tippets. With these, we can fish nymphs into the pockets along the bank or throw hoppers into the same kinds of places a little later when the sun warms the grass and gets the real hoppers moving. If we're feeling especially sneaky, we might fish a hopper with a small beadhead nymph beneath it on a dropper. This hopper-dropper method is an especially good way of "buffet-style" fishing in parts of the West where it's legal to fish with more than one fly.

This bank is nearly half a mile long and has plenty of fish, but we can't just flail away at all of the water. It would take forever to cover it all, so we concentrate on the best spots. The water near the bank is from one to three feet deep, and we look for small interruptions in the flow caused by rocks or irregularities in the streambank. These are small points or deflections. There are also some weed beds in the slower sections, and we work our flies along the edges of these when possible. We probably won't get wet above the knees, and 90 percent of our casts will be to within six feet of the bank.

It is a couple hours before we finish with this water and arrive at the head of the giant pool we have been fishing since the spinner fall began. At the head of this pool is an island. Where the two currents rejoin below the island is a deep, choppy slot that is a perfect place to fish a streamer. We put on sinking-tip lines and short 1X leaders, and get into a position to swing big Woolly Buggers into the chop with down-and-across presentations. The water is midthigh- to waist-deep, so a weighted fly must be used. It takes about a half hour to work this slot, and we fish it thoroughly, proceeding from the top down.

When we are through here, we have a choice. We can cross to the island and work up the outside—the wide side—or we can fish the small channel between the bank and the island. Let's fish the small channel now and the main river on the way back.

Most of the small channel is very shallow and clogged with weeds. But near the top there is a small gravel bar that showed up a few years ago courtesy of the ice in spring breakup. The gravel deflects and funnels the water, and as the water slows and spreads out, it forms what I call a deep riffle. It could be thought of as a small pool. The water is knee- to thigh-deep with a broken surface. It is just the right depth to keep fish hidden and just the right speed for us to fish comfortably. This is another innocent-looking spot, but it is the only place in this channel with enough depth to provide trout with cover. A friend of mine once took fourteen trout here without moving his feet. It's a great place to fish a nymph with an indicator. Earlier in the summer, a big stonefly nymph would be a good choice, but the low, clear conditions of August point us in a more subtle direction. A Flashback Pheasant Tail or an A. P. Nymph drifted below a small yarn strike indicator is a good choice.

After fishing the little nymph spot, we continue to the top of the island. It's now midday, so we sit down on a fallen log to eat our soggy sandwiches and watch for rises in the tailout where the side channel leaves the main river. In midday the fish are less likely to actively feed on the surface, but against the far bank a single fish begins to rise. We're not sure quite what it's eating, though it could be terrestrials, because the fish is close to the grass that lines the bank in this spot. After it's risen three times, we bolt the rest of the sandwiches and wade into the water. A small beetle fools this rainbow, but it's the only fish that seems interested in feeding in the bright August sun.

When we've finished lunch, we start back down to the truck. We'll fish our way back along the outside of the island. At the top of the island is a typical large point where the river starts to take a corner. The water deflects off the tip of the island, producing a long seam between fast water and slow.

We put the sinking-tip lines on again and work our way down the run, casting across and letting the current swing streamers from the fast water into the seam straight below us.

On the way back, we may poke our noses in here and there to look for rising fish. Or maybe we'll have another sandwich and a nap under a tree and hang around for the caddis activity that should occur near dark.

By the time we open the tailgate and start taking down tackle, it's late, we're tired, and we have quite thoroughly covered about a mile of river. We have also fished more types of water with more methods than many fishermen would use in a whole season.

Experienced fishermen pick away at the edges of a big river and find little need for deep wading or long casting. Successful anglers understand that big rivers don't necessarily mean big fishing, even though they hope they do mean big fish.

CHAPTER 6

Western Methods
for the Wading Angler

DRY-FLY FISHING

It truly is the fly fisher's finest hour when trout are drawn to the surface by a hatch of insects. To find a fish feeding happily on the surface, then to sneak into position and deliver a dry fly that the trout takes with confidence, is to experience a satisfying confirmation of both physical skill and intellectual understanding. But it's more than that. The moment a feeding trout pushes its snout through the oily surface of the stream, it leaves its world and enters ours. For me it's a rush equaled only by the flush of game birds in front of a pointing bird dog. In both cases, time slows down and the moment is both excruciatingly intense and perfectly sublime. It's probably a little extreme to put it this way, but for many of us, fishing with other methods is little more than a way to pass the time while we're waiting for the trout to rise.

That's the subjective side. Objectively, it's a little harder to explain why dry-fly fishing has been elevated above other methods in the minds of fly fishers. We're told that trout do the majority of their feeding beneath the surface, and that would seem to make it logical to do the majority of our fishing in the same place. We know we'd probably catch more fish if we fished under the surface most of the time. Well, it doesn't work like that—at least, not for most folks. There are some who prefer to fish with sinking flies, but they are a small club.

I think it's because dry-fly fishing is entirely visual that it is so often preferred above other methods. Rightly or wrongly, humans value vision above the other senses, and because of this, events we see with our own eyes are most deeply imprinted in our brains and memories. So while nymph and streamer fishing may often be more logical, dry-fly fishing is regarded as more entertaining

Unlike sunken-fly methods, however, dry-fly fishing is not available to us all the time. The main limiting factors are water temperature and depth.

If the water is too cold (below 45 degrees F, say), too warm (above about 70 degrees F), or too deep (more than three or four feet), trout will be reluctant to take food off the top no matter how many bugs are up there. But when the temperature and depth are in the right range, we can reach hopefully for the dry-fly box.

Most tackle choices for western fly fishing boil down to a decision in favor of either specialization or versatility. The dry-fly specialist will probably choose a 9-foot rod for a #5 or #6 line if he fishes big water, and something a little lighter if he's on smaller water—probably an 8½-foot rod for a #3 or #4 line.

Some fly-fishing books and magazines imply that different reels are required for dry-fly, nymph, and streamer fishing. In truth, all western fishing can be addressed with a reel that holds the fly line you've chosen and fifty to one hundred yards of backing. For dry-fly fishing, the line should be a floating, weight-forward or double-taper. The most common leaders are 9 to 12 feet long, with the tippet diameter matched to the fly size (see chapter 3).

To paraphrase Patrick McManus's friend Rancid Crabtree, the two best times to fish dry flies are when the trout are rising and when they ain't. The obvious time to use dry flies is when the trout are already rising to natural insects, but dry flies are not limited to those times. Trout that aren't rising can also often be caught on dry flies. My theory is that there are times when conditions are right and the fish are willing, but there just aren't any bugs up there to eat. The fish are all dressed up but there's no place to go.

Whether fish are rising or not, the mechanics of fishing dry flies are the same. In each case there is a target—either a fish you see feeding or a place where your water-reading skills suggest a fish should be holding. After that, the game boils down to choosing the right fly, getting it to the target, and then making it behave properly, which most often means having the fly drift naturally, without drag. Drag is the unnatural movement of a fly that occurs because it's attached to a leader. A dragging dry fly skates across the surface, announcing to the fish below that it is a fraud. A fly drifting without drag behaves as if there is no leader attached. Much of our strategy in dry-fly fishing is chosen for this purpose, beginning with where we stand. If you choose your casting position carefully, it might be easy to get a drag-free drift. But not always. Current speed varies throughout a stream, and when the fly is moving at a different speed than the fly line or leader, drag will occur. In fact, when an angler says a river is difficult, it often means that the currents in it make it difficult to get a drag-free drift of the fly.

The Upstream Dry-Fly Method

The most common method for fishing dry flies is to approach from downstream and cast the fly upstream or up and across so it lands a few feet above the target and drifts over it without drag. The slack that accumulates as the fly drifts toward you is stripped away smoothly with the line hand so you can set the hook easily by raising the rod tip when the fish takes your fly. It's a method that came to us from the chalkstreams of Great Britain, where on some streams it is still the only method allowed, and it works well in North American streams, both east and west.

It's important to remember that a fish that's rising steadily in moving water is essentially a stationary target. It holds in one place, facing into the current, and moves to the surface to pick off the bugs that are about to drift over it. The fish may move around a bit, depending on the density of the hatch, but it's usually safe to try to have your fly drift over the exact spot where you last saw it.

Though there are exceptions, which will be addressed later, casting at a slight angle to the target (up and across the stream) is often better than casting straight upstream. Because the leader and tippet land beside the fish rather than right on top of the fish, chances of frightening or alerting it are reduced.

Even when you're fishing upstream, the variation in current speeds will still create drag at times, and you may have to get creative to achieve the natural drift you want. If drag is a problem, first try standing in a slightly different spot, and if that doesn't work, be ready to use the reach casts, slack casts, and mends described in chapter 4.

The upstream method will always be one of the most important dry-fly methods, but in the West, circumstances have prompted the development of some additional ways of presenting dry flies. The versatile angler is capable of making good presentations in any direction. Master fly-fishing technician Doug Swisher of Hamilton, Montana, calls this "fishing the clock," which means being comfortable fishing from positions below, above, and across from the target, and anywhere in between. The main tool that allows this is the reach cast.

The Across-Stream Dry-Fly Method

When fish are feeding in midriver, or when you want to cast to a spot that can't be approached from below, it's possible to fish drys nearly straight across-stream. There are both benefits and drawbacks to this. On the positive side, the leader doesn't drift over the fish and spook it (unless you cast too far). On the negative side, the current often flows at several different speeds between you and the fish, which make it difficult to achieve a drag-free drift.

When fishing across-stream to a rising fish, it's advisable to make your first cast a bit short of the fish as a kind of test to see how the currents will affect the drift of your fly. This is like looking at a preliminary target in trap, skeet, or sporting clays before shooting the first time. It's always better to find out what kind of drag problem there will be *before* you put a cast over the fish. Once you know the nature of the problem, you'll know how to address it. The most common difficulty is that the water between you and the fish flows faster than the water the fish is in. A standard straight-line delivery allows the fly to drag almost immediately. An upstream reach cast can be used to compensate, because it places the line and leader on the water upstream of the fly, and this usually buys a few extra seconds of drag-free drift.

Other times there are strips of current flowing at different speeds between you and the fish, in which case a slack-line cast is the best solution.

Ideally, the fly should drift right to the fish or to within a few inches of the fish on the near side. If the fly passes by on the far side of the fish, the tippet will go over it, and Mr. Trout might suddenly become a skeptic.

The Downstream Dry-Fly Method

In terms of big-picture history, western spring creeks are the new kids on the block. They don't have the long, rich tradition that's associated with similar waters in the eastern United States and the United Kingdom, but they have inspired the development of a number of important and distinctly western fly-fishing methods. Perhaps most significant is the downstream dry-fly method, which is great for fishing to trout rising in slow, flat water or for fishing underneath bankside vegetation.

When using the conventional upstream method, the tippet drifts over the fish before the fly does. This isn't a problem on water that is riffled or less than completely clear. But in flat, clear water, there is nothing to hide or disguise the tippet, and the advantage is strongly with the fish. You show it the "string" before you show it the food that's attached to the string. With a bit of experience, trout learn that the sight of monofilament means "don't eat this." The downstream dry-fly method eliminates this problem by ensuring that the fish sees the fly before it sees the tippet.

To do it, you must get into position forty to fifty feet up and across from the rising fish. You must stay far enough from the fish to be out of its sight, and your wading must not send dirty water down to the fish, which would spook it. The fly is cast to a spot a few feet upstream of the fish with an upstream reach cast. As the fly begins to drift, the rod tip is moved down-

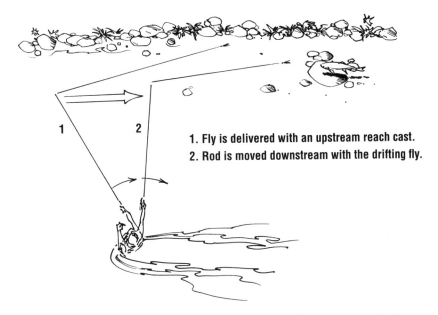

1. Fly is delivered with an upstream reach cast.
2. Rod is moved downstream with the drifting fly.

With the downstream dry-fly method, the fish sees the fly before it sees the leader.

stream at the same rate as the current, which allows the fly to drift drag-free into the fish's window of vision and, with luck, into its mouth. A variation is to intentionally cast the fly onto the water beyond the fish's lane, then drag it back toward you by raising the rod tip and moving it upstream a few feet. When the fly is lined up in the fish's lane, drop the rod slowly and move it downstream to allow a natural drift of the fly.

Whether a dry fly should be fished completely drag-free or with a bit of movement depends on what the real bugs are doing. Fishing to rising trout is classic hatch matching, which means mimicking both the appearance and the *behavior* of the real insect with your imitation. Careful observation pays dividends. If the real bugs move and flutter a bit as they drift, you should make your imitation do likewise. The downstream dry-fly method is best for adding the subtle upstream twitches that so often drive trout crazy.

The downstream dry-fly method is also good when you want to drift a dry underneath bankside vegetation. From a position upstream, you can drop the fly above the brush and allow it to drift in underneath the branches. You can't do that from downstream. It's also a great way to get a natural drift over a fish rising in the narrow band of slow water right against a bank.

How close your fly must come to the fish depends on how actively the fish is feeding and how abundant the natural bugs are. A fish that's rising every few seconds won't move far out of its way, so your fly must come within a foot or less of its position. A fish that has fewer naturals to choose from will expand its range and move a couple feet to get one. This is especially true if the natural bugs are big.

When using the downstream dry-fly method, take special care to avoid striking too soon or too hard when a fish takes your fly. If you strike too soon, you'll probably take the fly away from the fish. If you strike too hard, you'll surely break it off. In either case, you won't be happy. Wait until the fish comes up and turns down before tightening gently. It's easier said than done.

The Straight-Upstream, Short-Drift Method

George Anderson of Livingston, Montana, is regarded as one of the world's most skilled fly fishers. He spends a lot of time on the delicate spring creeks of Montana's Paradise Valley, where the downstream dry-fly method is used extensively. But if you ask George about this method, he'll say something like, "Yeah, you can fish downstream if you want, but you really don't have to." You must understand that what this really means is that *we* might want to fish downstream, but *George* doesn't have to. On the flat, slow water of Armstrong Spring Creek, for instance, while most anglers work carefully down and across to rising fish, catching the occasional one, George sneaks in quietly directly below the trout and begins catching them one after another. It's quite a distraction and somewhat of an annoyance to the other anglers, who can't help but notice this. Even the local guides, watching yet another one of these performances, will say, "Well, that's just George."

But I know his secret. It's in the casting. He can consistently drop his fly delicately six to twelve inches upstream of the fish's nose. The last bit of tippet does go right over the fish, but it's there so briefly that its presence doesn't seem to sink into the fish's brain. The fish is rising to naturals, a new bug appears right in front of its face, and before the fish realizes it, the fly is in its mouth. The fish doesn't have enough time to process the data that might cause it to refuse the fly. It seems to play on the fish's greed instinct.

This sounds pretty easy, and as with most things that sound so, it is not. There is plenty that can go wrong. The fly can land too far above the fish, thereby giving it too much time to notice the leader, inspect the fly, process the data, and refuse; or the fly can land too hard and spook the fish right off the bat. As well, false casts can scare the fish if they're made right over its head or if they spray water onto it. It's important to resist the temptation to make a bunch of false casts over the trout in order to gradually and carefully measure the casting distance. George makes one or at most two false casts, which are a few feet short and a few degrees off to the side of the fish. He shoots line on the delivery, and the fly comes in low and quick and appears suddenly on the surface just upstream of the fish's position.

This method is characterized by precision, and it requires very good casting skills—not for distance, but for accuracy, delicacy, and consistency. Most anglers who try this conclude that it's easier to fish down and across to difficult fish in flat water, but persistence will eventually pay off with the development of confidence in yet another way to skin a cat—or catch a trout.

I gave this method a good test on the Missouri River below Holter Dam one September morning when Trico spinners were thick on the water. I could have fished downstream to most of the trout, but I wanted to see what would happen if I worked at this upstream, short-drift business. There were fish rising everywhere, so I knew I would have plenty of volunteers to try it on. For a while not much happened. Fish were rising in singles, pairs, and pods, and I fished diligently and carefully from thirty feet or so downstream. I was trying to drop the fly a couple feet in front of the fish so they could get a nice look at it, but they didn't appreciate my efforts. I tried a couple different flies, but still nothing happened until I made a cast a little shorter than planned. The fly nearly landed on the trout's head, and just as I was starting to curse my incompetence, the fish took the fly.

As the morning went on, it became clear that the only way to fool these fish from downstream was to drop the fly less than twelve inches ahead of them. If they got more than about one second to look it over, they wouldn't take. If the fly landed four inches ahead of them, they took nearly every time. My fly was a #16 Adams and my tippet was 5X. What's interesting is that this was a situation for which the "correct" fly would have been a #20 or #22 spinner, the "correct" tippet would have been 6X or 7X, and the "correct" position to fish from would have been up and across from the fish. As the morning went on, I found that I could predict which casts would produce a take—they were the ones that very nearly hit a fish on the nose. It took many attempts to get it right, but when I did, the fish ate.

This method is best used on fish that are feeding very actively during a heavy hatch and are either in very shallow water or holding just under the surface and really pigging out. The more actively they are feeding, the shorter the drifts can be and the better this method is likely to work. When the circumstances are right for its use, this method also seems to reduce the need for a detailed imitation of the natural insect.

Fishing to Pods

On rich spring creeks and tailwaters, it's common during heavy hatches to find fish rising in tight groups. These can vary from three or four fish to a dozen or more, gulping greedily in an area the size of a hot tub. It's a behavior often exhibited by large fish, and it can make quite an impression on an angler who hasn't seen it before. I recall another Missouri River experience, when I was fishing the same stretch of water two consecutive days. The second day, I was working my way along the bank, casting to individual rising fish, when I noticed a riffle a hundred yards or so up the river. This puzzled me because there hadn't been a riffle there the previous day. As I got closer, I saw that it was a pod of about twenty big trout rising so greedily they created a disturbance that looked like a riffle from a distance.

Pods of trout can be addressed from any direction, so long as you stay out of the fish's sight. It is my preference, however, to cast up or up and across. This is another example of how greed influences our approach—except that this time the greed belongs to the angler. By fishing from downstream and working on the fish nearest you and on the outside of the group, it's often possible to pick them off from the bottom up, catching several before the rest realize something's up. When a fish takes your fly, pressure it quickly and firmly toward the wide side of the river to try to keep it away from the rest of the group. With this firm suggestion from you, the hooked trout will usually peel off to the outside and go downstream, running and jumping and carrying on. If you fish from above or across, you'll have a very good chance of hooking a fish, but if it's one from near the front or inside of the pod, it will disturb the whole gang when it feels the sting of the hook. Because the biggest fish often takes the position at the head of the pod, fishing downstream is often a good way to catch that fish, if you don't mind sacrificing the rest of the pod to do it.

Trout feed in pods only when the bugs are very abundant. They try to get as much food as they can as quickly as possible, perhaps inspired by competition from the other fish. They are generally quite difficult to frighten and will allow an angler to approach fairly close and cast to them without becoming alarmed. They seem to compensate for this by cranking up the selectivity dial, and fish feeding in pods are often quite difficult to fool.

Prospecting with Dry Flies

Fishing dry flies to trout that aren't rising is often called prospecting, fishing blind, or fishing the water. It can be a random method of simply throwing a dry fly here and there and hoping it crosses paths with a willing trout. This works, but it doesn't work as well as fishing with a plan.

Prospecting with dry flies works well in summer after the fish have been gradually conditioned to feed on the surface by long-lasting, sporadic hatches of big flies. Large stoneflies in early summer and grasshoppers later on can prompt this behavior. Over time the fish see and eat enough of these bugs to recognize the next one that comes down the pike. This probably explains why trout are sometimes willing to come to the top for an artificial, even when there are few or no rises to natural bugs. Water temperature seems to be an important factor in this type of fishing, and the window of acceptable temperature is narrower for prospecting than it is for other types. It seems to work best when the water is between 50 and 60 degrees F. On high-elevation cutthroat streams, the water often doesn't enter this range until afternoon. A standard strategy on these streams is to fish with streamers or nymphs until lunch, and then begin prospecting with drys during the warmest part of the day. Conversely, on lower-elevation streams where the water is warmer, the best time for prospecting may be early and late in the day when the water is cool enough for the fish to come to the surface.

In order to persuade a fish to come to the surface for your dry fly, you must put the fly in a place where a fish can see it. With this method, you are trying to catch fish that are not actively feeding, or at least are not actively feeding on the surface, so it makes sense to concentrate on holding water and prime lies—the places where the fish have shelter from current and safety from predators. It's most effective in water less than three feet deep. In most western streams, there is plenty of holding water deeper than that, but fish rarely come to a dry fly from that depth.

In general, prospecting with dry flies works best in quick water with a somewhat broken surface. This isn't because the fish don't occupy other types of water, but because it's easier to predict the fish's location in this kind of water, and because fish in these places are used to making quick decisions as food items drift over. They don't get a clear look at the imitation and are more likely to fall for your sales pitch. In big rivers, the best prospecting areas are along bankside deflections, along undercut banks, or in midstream depressions, or buckets. In smaller streams, drys can be cast along undercut banks, around midstream rocks, and wherever the water is moving and deep enough to hide a fish. Some of the best places for prospecting in any size stream are areas of pocket water, where fast water is interrupted by numerous rocks. Any of the holding water described in chapter 5 can be fished effectively at times with dry flies, as long as it isn't too deep.

There are places where prospecting with a dry fly is a good choice simply because it's the only type of fly you can fish without fear of getting hung up on something. Examples are along brushy banks or in weedy water where it's nearly impossible to fish a sunken fly. Another example is in water with an abundance of deadfall. You can fish a dry fly around and over top of all this trash, but fishing a nymph or streamer there is little more than a depletion of your fly inventory. Of course, a whole new set of problems crops up when you hook a big fish from beneath a brush pile or on the far side of a sunken log. About all you can do is pull hard and hope for the best.

Perhaps the best place to prospect with a dry fly in any size stream is the riffle at the head of a major pool, because fish move up there in anticipation of food coming through. It's always a good idea to fish farther up the riffle than you think you need to. The biggest fish are often farthest up. They apparently want to get the first shot at the food when it arrives. And like belligerent people in a lineup at the grocery store, the big trout elbow their way to the head of the line, and none of the smaller, meeker citizens do anything about it.

In spite of all these theories, prospecting with dry flies sometimes doesn't work when it seems it should and other times works better than you would expect. The strangest case of the latter was in early summer many years ago on Alberta's Crowsnest River. I was fishing with John Glenn, a superb Pennsylvania nymph fisherman. I picked a good stretch of choppy stonefly water, with plenty of big rocks on the bottom. John went up the river first with a golden stone nymph, and I followed him with a golden stone dry. The short version of the story is that I caught fish and John didn't. I mention this partly because it was a surprise, and partly because I want everyone to know that I'm not always on the short end of these kinds of operations. What puzzled us both was why the trout would ignore a nymph drifting by at eye level yet come to the surface through three feet of turbulent water to take a fly on the surface. It's one of the many questions about fly fishing that we'll likely never answer. It's also one of the reasons we keep doing it.

The standard upstream or up-and-across-stream method is the easiest way to obtain a drag-free drift, and it is probably the method most frequently used when prospecting with dry flies. In all likelihood you won't see the fish before you cast, so you must rely on your ability to read the water to identify a target. The fly is cast three to five feet upstream of this spot and allowed to drift over it. This is generally a rapid-fire approach, and a couple of good drifts through each spot are all that is required before moving on. Fish in these situations usually take the fly on the first few casts or not at all.

This is not to say that other dry-fly methods won't work when prospecting. Any technique that results in a good drift through a fishy spot is worth trying, and competence in "fishing the clock" is an asset.

A drag-free drift forms the foundation of dry-fly prospecting, but trout sometimes respond better to flies that are fished with a bit of movement. This is especially true when the fly is imitating a bug that twitches and wiggles when it's on the water. Good examples are caddisflies, stoneflies, and grasshoppers. Caddis and stoneflies hop and skitter, especially when laying eggs. Grasshoppers are very unhappy when they find themselves in the water and show it with much wiggling and kicking. As a general policy, I try for a drag-free drift on the first cast, and on the next cast make the fly twitch slightly just as it approaches the spot where I think the fish is lying. It's best to make the fly twitch very slightly in an upstream direction. This seems to be the way real bugs do their twitching, and it's easiest to do when you're fishing across or across and down with an upstream reach cast.

An interesting question arises when prospecting regarding how the fly should hit the water. If the surface is slow and flat, the fly should land gently so it doesn't frighten the fish. If the water has a broken surface, it probably doesn't hurt—and may help—if the fly makes a bit of a splat when it lands. The disturbance can draw the fish's attention to the fly.

You can employ a variation on this when fishing with terrestrial patterns. If you're casting to a place where the natural bugs are likely to fall into the water, it makes sense to have your fly land with a nice plop the way the real ones do. But if you're casting to a place where natural bugs are more likely to drift into the fish's view, you should drop your fly gently some distance above the expected lie of the fish so that your fly arrives the same way the naturals do.

I don't know whether this fits under the heading of prospecting with a dry fly, but it certainly works often enough that it needs to be mentioned somewhere. Some down-winged dry flies, like Stimulators and grasshopper patterns, make pretty respectable streamers when they are pulled under the surface and retrieved with a jerky swimming motion. This is a great way to fish in areas of heavy cover, such as along fallen trees. The fly can be drifted into a tight spot along an undercut bank or against a fallen tree as a dry fly, and then retrieved back out as a streamer. I like this because it's easier to get a floating fly to drift into a tight spot than it is to make a pinpoint cast to the same place with a streamer. In addition, the fly doesn't land hard and spook fish the way a streamer might. My friend Bob Scammell has been working on a dry-fly-streamer hybrid for years, and his J & H is the result (see chapter 10).

Flies for prospecting
Prospecting has been defined as fishing dry flies to trout that aren't actively rising. But this doesn't mean that our flies aren't chosen to imitate something. While we aren't matching a hatch in the usual sense, we are still trying to ring the Pavlovian bell of recognition in the trout's slimy little brain. So though a fly can be chosen for any reason the angler likes, it's best to know a bit about what's gone on in the stream before you arrived. To find out, you can shake streamside bushes to see what kind of bugs fall out; watch the surface of the stream and the shoreline for hints of bug activity; and keep an eye on the birds that live around the water to see if they're feeding on something the trout also like to eat.

Prospecting is often good when stoneflies are around. Many of the larger species, including golden stones and salmon flies, as well as the smaller skwalas and yellow sallies, are available to the trout for several weeks, which helps condition the trout to taking flies off the surface. If you see a lot of stonefly nymph shucks on the rocks along the stream, you know there are a lot of adult stoneflies somewhere nearby. It doesn't matter how many adults you see, or how often you see trout eating adult stoneflies, if you see shucks on the rocks, you're being given a hint that it could be a good time to fish with a dry stonefly.

Imitations of terrestrial insects are also good flies to use for prospecting, especially in late summer, when these critters are large and active. If you see or hear grasshoppers or notice a lot of beetles or ants in the vegetation along the stream, it might be worth trying an imitation. One year on my home stream, there was a near infestation of ladybugs. I noticed it and thought it was a little odd but didn't see any significance to it in my fishing. A more astute angler than I did, though, and presumed that the fish must be eating some of them. He had great fishing that year with a ladybug pattern he devised for the occasion. He hasn't needed it since, but his observation and ingenuity paid off when the ladybugs were abundant.

Quite frequently your streamside sleuthing will turn up several possible food items. In this case, it's usually best to choose an imitation of the largest fly you think the fish have been seeing lately. If you see two sizes of stonefly shucks on the rocks, fish with a fly that imitates the adult of the bigger one.

One of my best days of prospecting with dry flies occurred last season on a foothills brown trout stream. This creek is notorious for its wide range of angling temperatures—that is, the fishing is either hot or cold, and more often the latter. It does, however, have the tantalizing habit of being hot just often enough to keep me coming back. It was June and there were a few bugs of various persuasions in evidence—some pale morning duns, a few small caddis, the odd small stonefly. I was fishing with a friend who has a cabin on the creek, and as usual he was pointing out the places where he knew big fish lived. We saw no surface action from the fish until we stopped in a place inhabited by big rocks and deep water. I was fishing a Trude or something like it among the rocks, when Bob directed my attention to the far side of the run. "A fish rose along the edge of the current," he said. I cast a few times without incident, and then noticed a big bug dive down onto the surface of the water. It was a large, pale caddis—about size 10—and though it was the only one we had seen, I changed to a Yellow Stimulator of the same size. I caught the fish, took photographs of it, and then Bob and I continued up the creek. I stayed with the Stimulator and proceeded to have a memorable afternoon with brown trout somewhat bigger than I usually catch, and a good deal bigger than I ever deserve. I continued to look for bugs, and about every ten minutes I saw one of the big caddisflies fluttering over the water. I hooked a dozen or so fish in the next couple hours, most of them coming from holding water to sip the dry unannounced. It was clearly prospecting, but about every third fish helped me out by rising once first, which I suppose made it informed prospecting. Though the fish didn't actually say so, I was convinced that they had seen enough of the caddisflies in previous days to know what they were. It's a circumstance that often makes for very good prospecting.

Another principle of fly selection is matching the type of fly to the type of water. My belief here is simple: The bigger and brasher the water, the bigger and brasher the fly should be. On tumbly, choppy streams like the Madison River below Quake Lake or the Deschutes in Oregon, I like the fly to be chunky and visible. Stimulators, Tarantulas, large Humpies, and Trudes are good choices. Even a vile-looking bug like the Rubber-Legged Double Humpy draws fish from this kind of water. Here you need a fly that floats well, is noticed by the fish, and is visible to you. The likelihood of frightening a fish with your fly is very small.

Conversely, if the water is moving slowly and is flat on top, it is very possible to frighten a fish by dropping a big fly on the water near it or even by simply drifting a big fly over it. Generally, the slower, flatter water produces smaller natural insects, and the sight of a giant Stimulator or Turck's Tarantula drifting into view on a glassy pool of a small stream may send the fish fleeing simply because they have never seen anything like this before. Instead of wanting to eat it, they are afraid it might be planning to eat them.

On smooth, slow-moving water, prospecting is best done with smaller, subtler flies. A #16 or #18 Parachute Adams can be a great choice in small meadow streams. Another good one is a #16 or #18 ant imitation in black, brown, or red, or a #16 black beetle.

There's a whole category of western flies whose role is primarily fulfilled when prospecting. These are commonly called attractors, which is a handy catchall name for flies that work well without any apparent reason. The best example is the Royal Wulff, which has been around for a very long time. It works as well today as it ever has. The debate will continue as to whether this fly represents an item of natural food to the trout or is simply a fishy version of strawberry shortcake, as Lee Wulff himself has said. Other attractors of that vintage include some variations on the Royal Wulff, like the down-winged Trude series. Still other buoyant, visible drys are the H & L Variant and the Humpy in all its disguises (Royal, Double, Rubber-Legged, Foam). More recently, the Stimulator series of flies, created by Oregon fly fisher Randall Kaufmann, has become extremely popular. And more recently yet, the prospecting world seems to have been conquered by flies made of foam and rubber. Some of these patterns, like the Turck's Tarantula, use a combination of synthetic and natural materials, while others, like the Chernobyl Ant and Chernobyl Hopper, are entirely foam and rubber hackle.

A fun way to prospect is with two dry flies, as long as it's legal where you're fishing. I like to use a large fly and a small fly, such as a grasshopper and an ant. The big fly is tied onto the leader, and the smaller fly is joined to it by a piece of tippet a couple feet long. The connecting tippet is tied to the eye or the bend of the big fly. If trout show a clear preference for one fly, you can remove the unproductive fly and carry on with the one they like. Or, to demonstrate the aforementioned greed, you can fish with two of the ones they like. With any two-fly rigs, extra care must be used when unhooking fish. It's easy to find yourself in the painful situation of having one fly in the trout's mouth and the other one in your thumb.

NYMPH FISHING

For decades, nymphing has been described in the outdoor press as difficult and even mysterious, requiring Zenlike skills and a lifetime of dedication and practice on the part of the angler. But recent refinements in tackle and technique have helped burst that bubble, and nymphing is now a method used successfully by both veterans and newcomers to fly fishing.

To really understand nymph fishing, one should understand nymphs. Studying the life cycles, habitat, and behavior of the immature stages of mayflies, caddisflies, stoneflies, midges, and other bugs will help you catch trout. Two of the best sources of this information are the books *Nymph Fishing for Larger Trout,* by Charles E. Brooks, and *Nymphs,* by Ernest Schwiebert. If you want to go deep into this part of fly fishing, you'll do well to track down these books. Most of us today, however, are interested in achieving quick results without putting in as much effort as Messrs. Brooks and Schwiebert did.

The preferred rod for nymphing is an 8½- or 9-foot rod for a 5- or 6-weight line. This is one type of fishing where a long rod is an advantage, because it allows more control of the line after the cast is made. People who fish mostly nymphs on larger rivers sometimes choose 9½- or even 10-foot rods.

At its simplest level, nymph fishing can be viewed as dry-fly fishing under water. This is because most nymph fishing has the same physical objective as most dry-fly fishing—that is, obtaining a drag-free drift of the fly. In each case, we are trying to make the fly behave as if it is being carried by the current alone, with "no strings attached," even though there is one very important string—the leader.

The difference between dry-fly fishing and nymph fishing, of course, is that one takes place at the surface of the water, in full view of the angler, and the other takes place beneath the surface, completely out of view of the person at the controls.

A good dry-fly angler watches his fly carefully. He does this to know when a fish has taken it, but also to know when the fly is behaving properly and when it's not. The nymph fisher watches also, but because he can't see the fly, he must watch other things to obtain the same information. Before casting, he looks into the water to determine depth, speed, and the presence of structure that attracts trout. After the cast, he watches the leader, the fly line, the strike indicator if he's using one, and the water currents.

The big problem that must be overcome in nymph fishing is determining when a fish has taken your fly. There must be a certain amount of slack between rod tip and fly in order for the fly to drift without drag, but this slack prevents you from feeling a fish take the fly. And because the fly is some distance under the water, you won't see the takes either. This is where the mysterious Zen stuff starts. Between the time the fish picks up the fly because it looks good and spits it out because it isn't what the fish thought it was, the fisherman must tighten the line to set the hook in the fish's mouth. Experienced nymph fishers do two things better than beginners in this area. First, rather than being surprised by strikes, they *expect* strikes. This allows them to stay ready to react at any moment. Second, they react to small, subtle indications of takes from fish. An inexperienced nymph fisherman strikes when his indicator twitches. A veteran nymph fisher strikes when he thinks the indicator might be getting ready to twitch.

There's really not much mystery to nymph fishing, but there is an inherent Catch-22: To be successful, you must have confidence in the method; yet to have confidence, you must first be successful. It can be frustrating to try to break into this cycle, but stubborn persistence with the methods that follow should help.

Most nymph fishing is done at one of two levels in a trout stream: just below the surface or just above the bottom. When fishing near the surface, the fly is usually small and light, and the game is much like dry-fly fishing. When fishing near the bottom, there are a number of additional factors to take into account.

Deep Nymphing

Nymphs can be fished successfully down to about ten feet in moving water. Water deeper than that is, in my opinion, beyond the practical range of fly tackle. And even water half that deep is not very pleasant to fish. So for our purposes here, let's say we're deep-nymphing when we're trying to fish near the bottom in water three or more feet deep. Fish feed in this water opportunistically unless there is some significant insect activity going on, so this is a method most useful in holding water. It is most effective in water of medium speed with a broken surface. It works well in the hearts of big pools, in deeper pocket water, and along deep current seams. Though the opportunities for deep nymphing occur most often in bigger rivers, the method also works well in the suitable parts of smaller streams.

Fishing nymphs in this kind of water is a consistent and effective way to take trout. There is no time when it is not a logical method to try. There are, however, certain times when it is the most effective method, such as when large stonefly nymphs begin their migration from the deeper water toward the banks in preparation for emergence. Knowledge of the insect life in the stream is always valuable.

Though sinking lines can be used for deep nymphing, floating lines are most commonly used today. The flies should be weighted and tied to an 8- to 10-foot leader, with the tippet diameter matched to the size of the fly. A strike indicator is optional, depending on which deep-nymphing method is used. The indicator can be a small piece of yarn, a stick-on type, or a "corkie" float. Where it is legal, many anglers like to use two flies in order to check the effectiveness of a couple different patterns simultaneously. There are a number of ways to set these up, shown in the illustration. My favorite is the eye-to-eye method, as it seems to cause fewer tangles. I especially like the fact that I can remove both nymphs by undoing one knot, should I come across a rising fish in the middle of a nymphing session. When casting two nymphs, it's especially important to remember the principles outlined in chapter 4 for casting weight, especially opening up the casting loop in order to minimize the possibility of tangles.

A popular way of rigging two flies is sometimes called the crappie rig. Two nymphs are attached to droppers, and the weight is put on the bottom. The tippet to which the weight is attached should be thinner than the rest of the leader. It is most often the weight that hangs up on the stream bottom, and when it becomes necessary to break off, the thinner tippet will break and you'll lose the weight but not the flies. It works thusly part of the time. Another way to achieve this is to put a simple overhand knot in the tippet above the split shot, which creates a weak spot in the monofilament and allows it to break just above the weight.

Aside from not knowing when they've had a strike, the most common mistake people make when fishing nymphs is not getting the fly deep enough. Some anglers think that if the fly is weighted, it will sink to the bottom of the stream. In truth, sometimes it will and sometimes it won't. A good rule of thumb is this: If you're catching neither fish nor the bottom of the stream, add weight to the leader or change to a heavier fly until you start

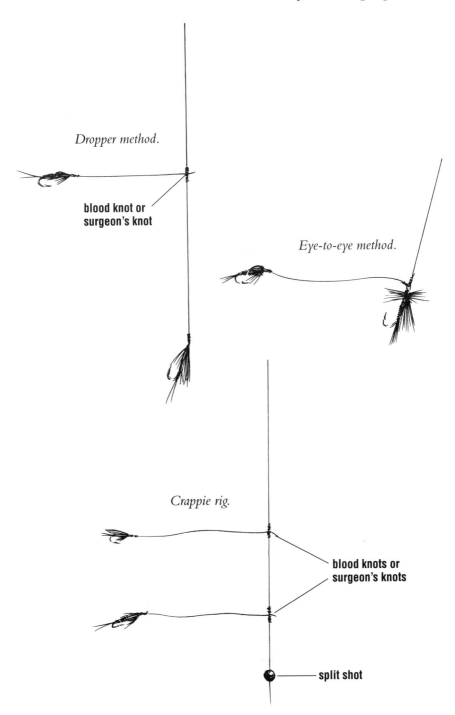

Dropper method.

**blood knot or
surgeon's knot**

Eye-to-eye method.

Crappie rig.

**blood knots or
surgeon's knots**

split shot

Two-fly rigs.

to catch one or the other. Once you're occasionally catching the bottom of the stream, you'll know you're in the proper zone to also catch trout.

Additional weight can be added in the form of shot (lead, tin, or tungsten), soft putty, twist-on lead strips, or tungsten beads threaded on the tippet. The additional weight is normally placed about twelve inches above the fly, or if two flies are used, it can be put above the top fly or between the flies.

There are two basic ways to fish nymphs deeply: the short-line method and the long-line method. Some details apply to deep nymphing with either method. First is a basic principle of stream hydrology: The water near the bottom of the stream moves slower than the water at the surface, due to the friction between the streambed and the water. This means that in order to move at the correct speed—that is, the same speed as a natural nymph drifting near the bottom—your fly must move more slowly than the current at the surface. Your strike indicator or leader can tell you about this. If it's moving at the same speed as the surface, it's trying to tell you that your fly isn't deep enough. The fly is not yet in the slower-velocity zone near the bottom. When you've got things operating properly, you'll notice that the indicator or leader moves slightly slower than the water it's resting on. It's when this is happening that you'll get the most strikes.

Second, frequent adjustments must be made to the terminal tackle. It's not enough to simply put a fly, indicator, and split shot on and leave it like that for a whole day's fishing. If you do this, you'll catch fish only when your setup happens to match the water you're fishing. Adjustments must be made—every few minutes, in come cases—to the amount of weight on the leader and the distance between the fly and indicator to ensure that you are getting a natural drift near the bottom.

The short-line method

Short-line nymphing was developed by Ralph Smith in the Cheeseman Canyon section of the Colorado's South Platte River in the 1960s and was popularized by Chuck Fothergill and others through the seventies and eighties. In the right situations, short-line nymphing is a great method. First, you must be able to identify very specifically the spot where the fish will be lying. Second, you must be able to wade to within about fifteen feet of the fish without frightening them. For both these reasons, short-line nymphing is most effective in fast, somewhat turbulent water. It is perhaps the best method of all for fishing rocky pocket water.

The cast is made so the fly lands five to fifteen feet directly upstream of the place where you think the fish are. As soon as the fly lands, raise the rod to keep as much fly line as possible off of the water. This prevents the

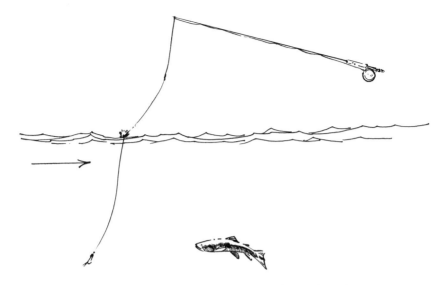

Proper setup for short-line nymphing with a strike indicator.

currents at the surface from pulling the fly line and dragging the fly. As the fly drifts downstream, follow it with the rod tip, gradually dropping the tip to allow the fly to continue drifting naturally. With this method, you fish with the line almost tight. There must be no more slack between rod tip and fly than that required to achieve a natural drift of the fly. A strike indicator is optional, and if used, it is positioned far enough up the leader to allow the fly to reach the bottom of the stream (typically with a distance of one and a half to two times the water depth between fly and indicator). Most of the time there should be no fly line at all on the water with this method. The line–leader connection should be between the rod tip and the surface of the water, and the leader should go straight to the indicator without lying on the water. If no indicator is used, you watch the spot where the leader enters the water.

Takes from trout can be detected in a couple different ways. The indicator or leader may hesitate, slow down, stop, or move sideways. Sometimes there will be a flash beneath the surface, indicating a take from a fish. Sometimes you'll feel a short, light tap. If any of these occur, you must set the hook with a short, quick upward flick of the rod tip.

As the fly approaches the end of its drift, I like to do one of two things. Sometimes I pick it up with a sharp lift of the rod tip, which I call the just-in-case pickup. This is a combination of a new cast and a hook-setting motion, used just in case a fish has taken the fly without my knowing it. Once in a while I do this and find a fish that I had no idea was there. When it happens, I pretend I planned it that way all along. Other times I let the fly swing below me on a tight line until the fly has moved to the surface. This mimics the movement many natural nymphs make as they begin to ascend to the surface for emergence.

You can fish the short-line method very effectively without a strike indicator, especially if you use a leader with a fluorescent-colored butt section. This is very visible at the point it enters the water and down a few inches into the water. You control the depth of the fly by raising or lowering the rod tip, rather than depending on perfect placement of the indicator on the leader. Deep nymphing without an indicator is a bit more difficult at first, but with practice it is a more versatile method, because you don't have to stop fishing to adjust the position of the indicator every time the depth of the water changes.

Short-line nymphing is a method where the drifts are short and the casts are many. The fly spends the first part of its drift sinking to its destination near the bottom. Then it drifts near the bottom of the stream until the line comes tight and lifts it off the bottom. Because of the short drifts, more weight is often needed with the short-line method than with the long-line method. A tuck cast can provide additional help in getting the fly to the bottom quickly.

The Brooks method, developed by the late Charles E. Brooks for fishing stonefly nymphs in the fast, broken water of the Madison River, is a variation of the short-line method. It uses a sinking fly line, short leader, and no strike indicator. Slack is controlled by raising the rod as the fly drifts toward you and lowering the rod as it moves downstream past you. Strikes are detected as light taps.

The long-line method
This method has helped more new fly fishers catch trout than any other. It is a way of covering a lot of water thoroughly. The long-line method is best in large areas of good holding water that are fairly uniform in depth. When you find yourself thinking, "This is all good water; the fish could be anywhere," you've probably found a good place for this method. The best places are long, bouncy runs; long current seams on big rivers; and in the hearts of pools on small streams.

The terminal tackle is the same for the long-line method as it is for the short-line method, with one important exception: A strike indicator is essential with the long-line method, because longer casts are used and the fly is usually some distance away from the angler. As well as being an indicator of strikes, the indicator also takes on the job of depth regulator. For this reason, the best indicators are large and buoyant enough to stay afloat no matter how much weight dangles below them. Many experts prefer large corkies—some nearly the size of Ping-Pong balls—or large, fuzzy yarn indicators that are attached with small rubber O-rings. The indicator is placed on the leader at a spot about twice as far from the fly as the water is deep. This is a generalization, and each piece of water will demand much adjusting of weight and indicator placement.

Though I've called it the long-line method, it doesn't really mean that the casts are long; they're just long compared with those used with the short-line method. Thirty- to fifty-foot casts are usually most practical. The cast is made up and across-stream so the fly drifts downstream through the good holding water. A tuck cast can be used to help the fly sink to the bottom quickly. As the fly and indicator drift downstream toward you, strip away the accumulating slack line exactly as you do when fishing a dry fly up and across. About the time the fly gets halfway back to you, a downstream belly often begins to form in the line between the rod tip and indicator, which, if left unattended, will accelerate the drift of the fly and ruin everything. When this happens, or better yet, *before* it happens, you must make an upstream mend that repositions the fly line upstream of the indicator, thereby allowing the fly to continue drifting at the proper speed. A perfect mend is one that adjusts the fly line and leader all the way down to, but not past, the indicator. Big corky-type indicators are best for this because their weight keeps them stuck to the water, making them effective "mend killers." This prevents the mend from going beyond the indicator and jerking the fly unnaturally. Often several upstream mends must be made as the fly moves downstream in order to maintain the drag-free drift.

If the cast was made at a fairly steep angle out into the stream, line can be fed out as it moves downstream past you. Mends are made as required to keep the indicator moving downstream ahead of the line. Think of the indicator as a dry fly, and do what you must to have it drift without drag. Near the end of the drift, it's advisable to let the fly swing toward the surface a bit before recasting, in case there's a fish ready to be duped by the nymph's rise toward the surface.

Throughout the drift, watch for the indicator to do something that the surface currents alone wouldn't make it do. This can be anything from a slight shudder to a subtle slowing down, a twitch, a change of direction, or a sudden submersion. Set the hook to find out what's making it do that. Don't wait until you're sure it's a fish, strike to find out if it's a fish. When I'm teaching this method, I find it helpful to tell students, "Find a reason to set the hook sometime on this drift." This intensifies their concentration on the indicator and develops the habit of expecting a strike rather than being surprised by one.

Flies for deep nymphing

Though there are times and places when small midge larva patterns like the Brassie and Serendipity are effective as deep nymphs, the best flies for deep nymphing are more often in the medium to large range (#14 to #4).

Most often the fly is chosen to represent something currently available to the fish. Turn over rocks in the riffles at the heads of pools to see what the fish's choices are. If the water is broken and has big rocks on the bottom, it is probably stonefly water, and brown or black stonefly nymphs in #4 or #6 should be good choices. As well, caddis larvae, Gold-Ribbed Hare's Ears, Pheasant Tails, Prince Nymphs, and San Juan Worms are good choices for deep nymphing just about anywhere.

Shallow Nymphing

Let's define shallow nymphing as fishing nymphs two feet or less beneath the surface. This can be in water less than two feet deep, or it can be in the top two feet of deeper water. If fish are in either of these places, it's because they're feeding. They don't feed all the time, of course, so shallow nymphing has less frequent application than deep nymphing. It is one of the most entertaining ways of catching trout, however, because of the delicate nature of the tackle, approach, and casting. Also, because it is a method most useful when fish are actively feeding, when it works, it often works very well.

Shallow nymphing is technically very simple to do. The biggest challenge is knowing when to use this method. There are several occasions when it works well. The first is when the fish are feeding actively on nymphs in shallow water. So how do you know when that is happening? Take it as a hint if you spook fish out of the shallows when you're wading. You can also sometimes see fish feeding in shallow water if the water is clear and the sun is behind you. Other times you'll just see an occasional flash from a shallow riffle. You might climb a high bank or a tree to get a good look down into the water. Knowing something about the insect hatches on the stream is particularly helpful for this type of nymphing. If you know, for instance, that pale morning dun mayflies have been hatching daily around noon, and if you know that the nymphs emerge from gravelly riffles, you could postulate that the fish will feed on the nymphs as they get active in the riffles in late morning. In short, know the bugs that are currently hatching, know what kind of water they emerge from, and fish there with nymphs prior to and in the early stages of the hatch.

The best shallow feeding areas are the riffles at the heads of pools and slight depressions in otherwise shallow water. Try small nymphs here prior to a hatch, or during a hatch if you see adult bugs but few rises. It may be that the fish prefer the emerging nymphs over the adults. Maybe they taste better. I find this method best on cloudy, dark days and especially good on autumn afternoons. The fall blue-winged olive mayflies are punctual and reliable on most streams, and this hatch is the key to late-summer shallow nymphing.

The second occasion when shallow nymphing is effective is when fish are feeding on nymphs just below the surface. You will sometimes see fish bulging or occasionally showing their backs, dorsal fins, or tails as they turn near the surface. If the fish disturb the surface but never show their heads, they are feeding on nymphs just beneath the surface and are perfect candidates for this method.

Shallow nymphing is also a good way to fish to trout that are taking adult bugs off the surface but only sporadically. My theory—unproven— is that such fish may be feeding occasionally right at the surface but are probably feeding quite regularly a foot or so beneath the surface. Shallow nymphing is also a good way to fish alongside or in narrow channels between weed beds.

It takes a simple rig to fish with this method. Although some anglers do it without indicators, by simply watching the leader (which might be greased with fly floatant), most people use strike indicators. Because the fly is generally small, the indicator should be as small and unobtrusive as possible. The best ones for shallow nymphing are small pieces of buoyant yarn attached to the leader a couple feet from the fly. A small, visible dry fly, like a #14 Parachute Adams, can also be used as an indicator. The dry is tied to the end of the leader, and the nymph is added with a second piece of tippet tied to the dry fly, either at the eye or the bend of the hook. With this method the distance between the indicator and the nymph is usually 1½ to 3 feet.

Shallow nymphing is almost always done in an upstream direction and is nearly identical to upstream dry-fly fishing. The fly is cast above the spot where the fish is known or suspected to be and is allowed to drift back toward you without drag. The indicator usually does its job very well in this situation, because it is quite close to the fly. When a fish takes the nymph, the indicator simply stops suddenly in the midst of the drift. The tricky part is setting the hook. It must be done quickly but not violently. It takes practice to develop a sharp but *short* flick of the rod tip. If you do it properly, the fly won't come out of the water when you set the hook. If the fly or the fish ends up in the river or a tree behind you, it might mean that you struck a bit too hard.

Flies for shallow nymphing

In this type of fishing, it's important that the fly is a decent representative of a bug the fish are seeing frequently, that it lands on the water without spooking the fish, and that it sinks quickly to the fish's depth. I'm probably oversimplifying here, but I find few flies better than the various members of the Pheasant Tail Nymph family. It can be any of the versions, from Frank Sawyer's original, which is tied with nothing more than pheasant tail fibers and copper wire, to the one that's become standard in North America today, which has a peacock herl thorax and pheasant tail legs.

Perhaps an even more popular and more common choice today is a beadhead version of the Pheasant Tail. I carry some tied with brass beads and some with tungsten beads. Tungsten is much heavier and sinks the fly much more quickly, without requiring additional weight on the leader. The only problem is identifying which flies have tungsten beads and which have standard brass beads. If you tie your own, you can use a different color thread for each, or you can simply keep them in different fly boxes.

I also like Pheasant Tail Nymphs tied with pheasant tail fibers dyed olive or red. Other patterns work well too, especially versions of the Gold-Ribbed Hare's Ear, A. P. Nymph, and caddis pupa patterns, either with or without beads at the head.

Sight Fishing

One of the most entertaining methods in still or moving water is casting to visible fish. When a feeding fish is spotted, a small nymph is cast ahead of it. The angler usually watches the fish rather than an indicator for a sign of a take. Sometimes the fish moves toward the fly and stops, and other times it opens its mouth at just the right moment. Either of these is the cue to set the hook. With this method, it's critical to get the fly to the fish's depth, and sink rate is an important consideration in fly choice. The Beadhead Pheasant Tail, Beadhead Prince Nymph, and Brassie are favorites for this.

Of course, before you cast to a visible fish, you must find one, and that is a skill all its own. Good polarized sunglasses will help you see into the water, and persistent practice will help you interpret what you see down there so you can tell what's a trout and what's a rock or a stick lying on the bottom.

Fishing for Stillwater Cruisers

Many western spring creeks and some freestone streams have sections of stillwater. Some of these are natural ponds and others are man-made. Some are nothing more than places where the stream's gradient flattens out and the water stops flowing. Many of these places hold trout that feed all day long. The fish cruise back and forth, rising occasionally and feeding subsurface frequently. Sometimes they can be seen cruising just beneath the surface. A favorite technique on the stillwater sections of Montana spring creeks is to use a midge larva pattern, like the Brassie, and a small yarn indicator attached to the tippet about three feet above the fly. The fly is cast into the path of a cruising fish and is simply left hanging. The angler watches the indicator closely and occasionally twitches the fly slightly to draw the attention of a passing trout.

STREAMER FISHING

Fly fishing is a sport well cluttered with lore, which a cynic might define as "statements made without the benefit of corroborating facts." You know the ones: "Day in and day out, trout do 80 percent of their feeding under the surface." "Day in and day out, nymphing is the most effective way to catch trout." You've got to be careful with statements that begin like that. However, one of these pearls is true most of the time: "Big fish eat little fish (feel free to add 'day in and day out')." The practical corollary of this is the fact that the biggest trout are usually caught on flies that imitate little fish. In the past, there were two types of flies tied to imitate baitfish. Those tied with feathers were called streamers, and those tied with animal hair were called bucktails. Today, however, the term *streamer* is used for both.

Leeches can also be imitated with streamers. Leeches live in many waters, both moving and still, and are food for the trout that also live there. Generally leech imitations are tied with soft materials like rabbit fur or marabou, which naturally mimic the undulating swimming motion of a leech.

It may take a few hundred small insects to provide a trout with the protein it can get in one gulp from a single leech or juicy sculpin minnow. I suppose it's simply more practical for a large trout to take a few big bites rather than a bunch of tiny ones. So in most streams, the best way to catch the biggest trout is with streamers.

Streamer fishing was probably an American invention and attained high stature first in the Northeast, in places like Maine, where famous fly-dresser Carrie Stevens developed a series of elegant streamer patterns, including the venerable Gray Ghost.

In the West, streamer fishing was, if not pioneered, at least practiced and publicized in the mid-twentieth century by anglers like Dan Bailey and Joe Brooks. Brooks's books and magazine articles related his experiences streamer fishing in Montana rivers like the Yellowstone, with flies like the Muddler Minnow and later a variation called the Spuddler.

As with other methods, the tackle you choose for streamer fishing depends on your overall angling philosophy. If you plan on using a variety of flies, including streamers, you'll choose a versatile outfit—probably a 5 or 6—and will carry both a floating and sinking-tip fly line. If you plan to fish exclusively with streamers you'll choose an outfit that is a bit more specialized.

Big river streamer specialists usually use 6-, 7-, or 8-weight outfits and prefer rods that are light yet powerful. The lightness helps minimize fatigue during a long day of long casts, and the power helps launch big flies with a minimum of false casting. The rod should be 9- or 9½-feet long, though some anglers like them even longer. It should be relatively stiff, which helps develop the line speed required to make big casts into big winds with big flies.

There are times when trout will take streamers fished near the surface, but it's usually more effective if you take the fly down to the fish, rather than ask the fish to come up to the fly. This can be done with a floating line, long leader, and weighted fly, but in the deeper water of big rivers sinking-tip lines are preferred. As well as keeping the fly deep, a sinking-tip mends easily after the cast and allows you to control the speed and depth of the fly's swim, which are critical to success. The sinking-tip should have 10 to 20 feet of fast or very fast sinking line on the front end.

Your standard reel will work for streamer fishing, but make sure it has at least 50 yards of backing on it. Backing isn't needed often in trout fishing, but if you're going to do much streamer fishing, you'll need it sooner or later. And when you need it, you need it badly. The reel should have an adjustable drag so you can control the amount of resistance the fish has to pull against.

Though there are several theories on leaders for streamer fishing, it's generally agreed that they shouldn't be too long, especially when a sinking or sinking-tip line is used. Some anglers, notably Lefty Kreh, are advocates of extremely short leaders for this kind of fishing. The first time Lefty fished the Bow River he used a sinking-tip line and a 6-inch leader. This was a bit extreme, but it did prove his point—fish don't swim up the leader to measure it. While you don't have to go that short, it's usually a mistake to use a leader that's too long. Even a weighted fly is pushed toward the surface when it's held against a tight line, so if the leader is too long the fly is much closer to the surface than the tip of the line is. This defeats the purpose of using a sinking-tip line. A short leader keeps the fly near the end of the line and, consequently, deeper in the water where you want it to be. Most streamer aficionados use leaders between 3 and 6 feet long when using sinking-tip fly lines.

It's also a mistake to fish with a leader that's too thin. Most of the takes occur when the line is tight and the rod tip is low, and if you strike too hard, like most of us do, you'll either launch the little fish into the trees behind you or break the big ones off. Leader visibility isn't often a deterrent to streamer fishing because the water is often turbulent, and the flies are fished with motion. You can usually use a stout tippet of 1X or 2X, and rarely should streamers be fished on tippets lighter than 3X. In very slow,

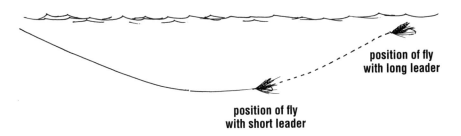

When fishing streamers with a sinking or sinking-tip fly line, a short leader keeps the fly deeper in the water.

clear water it may be wise to use a fluorocarbon tippet because it is less visible underwater than standard nylon monofilament.

There are no bad times to fish with streamers. It makes more sense at some times than at others, but it truly is a method for all seasons. An especially good time is when the water is cloudy but not completely muddy. When the stream is clearing after being dirtied by a storm or spring runoff, the trout seem particularly vulnerable to streamers. The cloudy water seems to make them bolder and more willing to chase things. Periods of low light are also good. Early mornings, late evenings, and cloudy days are made for streamer fishing. Those few anglers who specialize in fishing at night often do so with streamers. They catch the biggest fish in the stream, along with a few bats.

Fall is a favorite time for streamer fishermen who pursue the big brown trout that move out of large reservoirs in preparation to spawn. Streamers are also a good choice through the winter months and during other periods of little insect activity. Fish have to feed whether the insects are cooperating or not, and a properly presented streamer will usually get at least a look from a fish.

Streamer fishing is a good way to search for fish. These flies cover a lot of water and attract trout from some distance. It is generally a method for fishing holding water rather than feeding water, and some of the best places are in the heads of big pools and in current seams along the insides of big corners. Streamers can also be used in pocket water, in sections of still water, and in reverse-flowing eddies. They can be used anywhere you suspect fish to be holding.

Three basic principles are important in streamer fishing. The first is to always have a target in mind. This is the place where you expect the fish to be. It's sometimes difficult to identify a target in a long, uniform run, but look closely at the water and try to find the small areas where the velocity is slightly less, the depth is slightly more, or the nature of the surface is slightly different. Be sure your streamer swims through these places. The second principle is to have your streamer arrive at the hot spot by water, not by air. If there's a great-looking spot behind a boulder, don't cast so the streamer lands there, but cast so you can make the fly swim into the area. Remember that you're trying to imitate a small fish, and they don't arrive in a trout's living room by parachute. The third principle is to try to visualize where your streamer is and what it's doing. If you can make it appear to be in trouble, it will help your cause. Make it swim erratically as if it's injured or frightened. In short, if you make it behave like Little Red Riding Hood in the presence of the Big Bad Wolf (or the big bad brown trout), you'll probably witness an act of gratuitous violence.

Streamer fishing is associated with big rivers but is effective on all types of western streams—freestoners, tailwaters, and spring creeks. With the exception of the down-and-across method, the techniques described below are good on streams of all sizes.

The Down-and-Across Method

This is the traditional and preferred method for fishing streamers, and trout anglers inherited it from Atlantic salmon fishermen. It works well in all but the smallest of streams. To do it, choose a long run or a long current seam, and begin at the upstream end of it. Position yourself above and to the inside (the bankside) of the water you think the fish are in. Make a medium-length cast across stream followed by a couple of upstream mends, and let the fly swing down below you on a tight line. Follow the swing of the fly with the rod tip, which is held low to the water. When the fly has finished its swing and is hanging straight downstream, retrieve it until you can see it in the water, and then make another cast slightly longer than the first one. When you've reached the limit of your casting range take a few steps downstream and repeat the process. Most of the strikes occur in the second half of the drift, when the fly is moving across the river. The first half of the drift is essentially a preparation period, during which the fly sinks into the fish's range. You proceed downstream, covering the water in a thorough, fan-like pattern. Most of the fish in the run will eventually see the fly, which is one of the reasons the method is effective.

It's best to fish streamers deep in the water column, and you can do a number of things to get them down where they belong. The first is to add weight to the leader. I like to attach split shot or lead putty on the leader right against the eye of the streamer. This imparts an up-and-down, jig-like movement to the fly when it's retrieved.

Another way to get the fly deeper is to make the cast slightly upstream. This gives the streamer more time to sink before it comes tight against the line and starts to move across the stream. Additional depth can also be gained by making more upstream mends after the fly has entered the water. These mends release tension on the fly and allow it to sink longer and deeper.

You can also steal a trick from nymph fishermen and use a tuck cast. This puts the fly into the water ahead of the line and leader and gives it a head start in sinking (see chapter 4). But perhaps the best way to get a fly deep quickly is to use Doug Swisher's stack mends. These put slack line right on top of the fly and allow the streamer to dive quickly to the bottom. They are described in chapter 4 and demonstrated in Swisher's video, *Advanced Strategies for Selective Trout.*

Once the cast and mends are made and the fly is beginning its trip down the river, you are in control of the fly and the way it swims. You can begin the retrieve as soon as the fly hits the water or you can wait until it has swung completely downstream before retrieving. If the fly is dressed with soft materials like marabou or rabbit fur, or if it is a leech imitation, you might do nothing other than let the fly swing on a tight line, trusting the current to make the fly wave and undulate seductively. Or, you can pump the rod slowly up and down to vary the fly's speed. You might use the rod tip to impart twitches to the fly as it drifts to suggest the darting movements of an active baitfish. Or, you might do both of these together.

When the fly reaches a point directly downstream from you, you can retrieve it immediately, or you can let it hang there awhile first. You can also diddle with it by retrieving a couple feet of line and then letting it drop back a bit, then retrieving a bit more, and so on. It's a good idea to try a number of these variations because the recipe that works on one stream one day might be ignored on a different stream or a different day. For me the problem comes after I've hooked the first fish. I have to ask myself, "What exactly was I doing to the fly when he struck?" Usually I can't remember what I was doing, so I guess it helps to pay attention.

Most of the strikes will be apparent because they occur when the line is tight. Some of them will be downright vicious, and the first time an over-enthusiastic trout jerks the rod completely out of your hand you'll look over your shoulder to see if anybody is watching. But not all the strikes will be violent. If the fish is moving toward the rod tip when it takes the fly, slack will be pushed into the system between the fly and rod, and you won't feel anything beyond a slight hesitation. Stay alert for slight bumps or taps while the fly is swinging, and set the hook when you think something's going on out there at the fly.

The Straight Upstream Method

This barely qualifies as a method, but it's worth trying when more conventional approaches are ignored. Throw the fly straight upstream or up and across, and retrieve it immediately and quickly, so that it swims toward you a bit faster than the current. To get the best motion from the fly, use a lead-eyed streamer like the Clouser Minnow or Gartside Leech, or attach a split shot to the leader right against the eye of the fly. This causes the fly to hop-scotch its way back toward you with a pronounced up-and-down motion that fish seem to like. I have no suggestions on when to use this method, and I don't know why it works when it does. I simply know that it sometimes catches fish when the regular methods don't. The fish will let you know.

Swisher Method

The late Joe Brooks advocated something called the *broadside float* for streamer fishing. He believed a streamer was most effective if it traveled down the river perpendicular to the current, thereby showing its profile to the trout. He speculated that the fish were better able to identify the fly as an item of food when it approached them this way rather than head-on.

A good way of achieving the broadside float is the method developed by Doug Swisher. For this method, use a floating or sinking-tip line and a weighted fly. Cast across or up-and-across stream, and as soon as the fly lands, make several stack mends, which allow the fly to sink quickly to the bottom. As the fly begins to drift downstream, make a series of downstream mends, and with each mend feed slack line through the rod so that the line doesn't begin to pull on the fly. The downstream mends turn the fly perpendicular to the current, and the addition of slack line allows the fly to drift downstream without rising in the water column. When the fly is downstream from the angler, the line begins to take a curved path from the fly to the rod tip. This curve allows the fly to stay broadside in the current and is maintained by additional mending and feeding as the fly drifts. It's a good way to fish a fly deeply through a run. Strikes are often less violent than with the conventional down-and-across method because of the slack line between the rod and fly. The method is demonstrated and described clearly on Swisher's video, *Advanced Strategies for Selective Trout*.

Dead-Drift Method

At times streamers work best if they're fished with little or no motion. Simply treat the streamer as if it were a nymph, and dead drift it near the bottom. You can use a sinking-tip line and do it by feel, or you can use a floating line, conventional leader, and strike indicator. Good patterns for this are sculpin imitations and realistic flies that look like little fish even

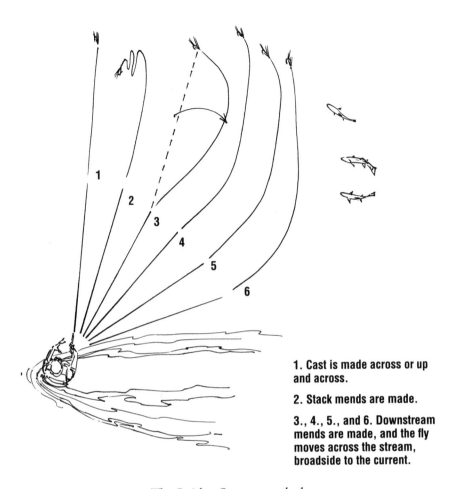

1. Cast is made across or up and across.

2. Stack mends are made.

3., 4., 5., and 6. Downstream mends are made, and the fly moves across the stream, broadside to the current.

The Swisher Streamer method.

when they're not moving. Wooly Buggers and Clouser Minnows also work when fished this way. A nice benefit of this method is that a little drag on the fly doesn't hurt, and might even help by attracting a fish's attention. Be sure to fish the casts out completely, and let the fly swim and swing at the end of the drift so that you can present two different types of movement in the same cast.

Fishing Streamers in Small Streams

Small streams seem to have become the domain of the dry-fly and nymph angler. Streamer fishing in small creeks is something of a forgotten art, and that fact alone makes it worth trying. Streamers work well in small streams, and as in most trout waters, they often attract a bigger class of fish. It's often a good idea to try streamers on your first visit to a small stream to take inventory on unfamiliar water. You'll probably catch some fish this way, but it's quite likely you'll see even more—chasing, boiling, and flashing at the fly. This helps you determine where the most productive parts of the new stream are.

In small creeks, the casts will generally be shorter and the flies smaller than what you would use on a big river, so your tackle doesn't need to be quite as specialized. It will probably be very similar to what you'd use to fish drys or nymphs in the same water. You might choose a slightly more powerful rod if you plan to do this a lot, but you can comfortably fish streamers on small creeks with any versatile small-stream fly rod. I prefer an 8½-foot rod for 3-, 4-, or 5-weight line.

A floating line will do usually do the job unless the creek has a lot of water more than four feet deep, in which case a sinking-tip is helpful. For occasional use, the Instant Sink Tip, marketed by Orvis and possibly other companies, is a good tool. It is a piece of sinking fly line that connects with loops to the end of the floating line. It provides the benefit of a sinking-tip line without the cost of a line, spool, and backing.

When fishing a streamer on a floating line in a small creek the leader should be 7½ or 9 feet long with a tippet of around 3X. Use a heavier tippet when you fish a fly larger than size 10 or if you expect especially large fish. There are no special reel requirements for this type of fishing.

Just as on larger rivers, streamer fishing on small streams is best when the sky or the water is less than perfectly clear. Many of us like to spend evenings searching for rising trout. I'm included in that group. But if there aren't many fish rising, the hour after the sun leaves the water can be especially good with streamers. The biggest difficulty is sometimes simply talking yourself into trying it.

You can fish streamers in any part of a small stream where you think fish are holding. All parts of pools are good, especially the heads. Bankside cover, both in the water and hanging over it, are good places to find fish. Areas of rocky pocket water hold trout if the depth is adequate. In the smallest of streams, finding a fish is simply a matter of finding water deep enough to hide a fish.

Though the principles are the same, the techniques and flies used for streamer fishing in small water are somewhat different than those used in larger streams. The first challenge in this type of fishing is figuring out how to let the fish see your fly without letting them see you. This is much more difficult in small creeks than in big rivers because everything happens in closer quarters. This largely rules out use of the standard down-and-across method in small creeks, first because you'd be very close to the fish and directly in their field of vision, and second because the debris you stir up with your wading would drift down and alert the fish. About the only time you can fish streamers down and across in small creeks is when you can stay out of the water and hide behind bushes or tall grass.

For this reason, I usually find it best to fish upstream or up and across in small streams. The straight upstream method is a great way to fish deeply along an undercut bank or along any sort of bankside cover. If the good bank is on your side of the stream, cast directly upstream and jig the fly back towards you so that it moves slightly faster than the current. If the good bank is on the opposite side of the stream, cast diagonally up and across so that the fly lands as close to the bank as possible and ten or fifteen feet above the best part of the lie. Use a downstream reach cast or make a downstream mend after the fly has landed to place the line near to and parallel with the far bank. When you retrieve, the fly stays close to the bank as it swims downstream, rather than immediately moving out into the middle of the creek. This is an especially good way to fish along and underneath sweepers that stick out from the far side of a narrow stream.

To fish pools, it's best to cast diagonally up and across and then retrieve so that the fly moves primarily across the current. You can retrieve the fly as soon as it lands, or you can let it sink first to gain more depth. Stack mends can be used to get the fly deeper still, and upstream mends can keep the fly perpendicular to the current during the retrieve. Be sure to fish streamers well up into the heads of the pools. Feeding fish will congregate there and will often mug a streamer that swims nonchalantly through the danger zone.

Streamer fishing in small water comes with an inherent problem. Because these flies imitate small fish, they are usually fished with motion. That motion is provided by retrieving the fly, and retrieving the fly brings it closer and closer to you. A fish that's following your fly will sooner or later notice you standing there, big and bold, and will suddenly lose its appetite. This is a bigger problem in small water than large. In a big river the whole episode takes place in a larger arena, and the fish will be some distance from you when it decides it's interested in your fly. But in a small creek you may have only cast twenty or twenty-five feet, and by the time a fish sees, follows, and decides to take the fly, it may only be ten or fifteen feet from you and getting closer by the second. There's not much you can do about this, except reduce your visibility as much as possible by wearing clothing that blends in with the background vegetation and by staying low to avoid silhouetting yourself against the sky. If you can, stay out of the water and hide in the streamside bushes. Do as little arm-waving and gyrating as possible when retrieving the fly.

In small-creek streamer fishing, the method is largely determined by the nature of the water. The overall approach is to find a way to swim the fly through the holding water without spooking the fish first. To do this, you'll find yourself using different methods at different times, including the Swisher method, the straight upstream method, and the dead-drift method.

Choosing Streamers

In any type of fly fishing, it's beneficial to know what you're trying to imitate with your fly. Information about the baitfish in a particular river is harder to obtain than the same data regarding insects. Most ardent fly fishers can tell you what bugs hatch when in their favorite rivers and can probably do so in a foreign language, but far fewer anglers can tell you much about the baitfish that live in the same streams. In light of this information gap, there are two approaches to streamer selection. The first is to learn something about the baitfish in the stream. You can be casual about it and simply pay attention to the size and color of the little fish that you scare out of the shallows with your wading, or you can go a little further and contact the nearest university or college to see if any research has been conducted on the ecology of the stream. This may sound a bit odd, but you'd be surprised what you can turn up if you dig a bit. Of course you should also lean on the experience of fly shops and other anglers, and though their information may or may not be based on science, it will likely be practical and proven over time. The other approach to fly selection is to simply choose flies that have worked for you in other similar streams.

Fly popularity seems to go in cycles, not unlike fashions in music or clothing. In the 1960s it was the Beatles, bell-bottoms, and Muddler Minnows. The Muddler was the most popular streamer in the West for a long time, but few anglers carry it today. Did it stop working? Did the fish vote about this? The truth is that new patterns come along, get publicity in magazines and on websites, and before long the new flies are popular and the old ones forgotten.

In big rivers, the basic rule of fly selection is anything goes. Large flies are often associated with large rivers, however, and streamers in sizes 2 and 4 are usually not too large. Most big rivers have big trout that are accustomed to eating baitfish this size.

If I were limited to four streamers for big rivers, they would be the Wooly Bugger in some form, perhaps the Bow River Bugger version, which has a clipped deer hair head; the Clouser Minnow; a leech pattern like the Gartside Leech; and a sculpin pattern like Dave Whitlock's Near Nuff Sculpin. I'd like to have each of these in black, brown, olive, and white, and in sizes 2, 4, and 6. I'd want them all to be weighted. With these in my fly box,

I'd be pretty confident that I could catch fish on most big rivers in the West, or at least if I couldn't catch them, it wouldn't be the flies' fault.

I've always wondered why it's common to see people fishing two nymphs or two wet flies together but rare to see anybody fishing two streamers together. The two-fly approach has the same advantages for streamer fishing as it does for wet-fly or nymph fishing—it's a time-saving way of trying two different patterns to see which one the fish like best. To do it with streamers, the first fly is tied to the end of the leader, and the second trails it by two to three feet at the end of a second piece of tippet that's tied to the bend of the first hook. Choose two different types of streamers, like a light-colored one and a dark one, a big one and a small one, or a sparse one and a bushy one. The drawback to this is that it's harder to cast two flies, and you might need to use a more powerful rod to handle the extra weight and air resistance.

In small streams you need to choose a streamer that casts easily with a light outfit, lands without making a big splat, sinks quickly, and moves well in the water. My favorite is a pattern I call the Spring Creek Bugger, which was developed with these objectives in mind. I like this fly in olive, brown, or black, and carry it in sizes 8, 10, and 12. I also like size 8 or 10 standard Wooly Buggers in olive or brown. I prefer the flies to be weighted, but I also add a single split shot to the leader at the head of the fly when it's necessary to get it down deeper still.

WET-FLY FISHING

A fly that sinks but is not a nymph or a streamer must be a wet fly. This is a pretty lame definition, but it will probably work. *Wet fly* is both a general term for any fly that is fished under the surface and the formal name for the particular category of sinking flies that we'll examine here. Wet flies are the oldest type of trout flies, having come to us from England, where they were originated and cataloged as early as the fifteenth and sixteenth centuries. They are simple patterns, consisting of either just body and hackle, in which case they are called soft-hackles, or body, hackle, wing, and tail, in which case we'll call them winged wets. They are usually tied with natural furs and feathers, which are soft and absorbent, allowing the flies to sink easily. Wet flies are generally tied on regular-length, heavy wire hooks and lack the specific imitative features we've come to think important today, like wing cases, segmented bodies, eyes, and antennae.

There was a time when it wouldn't have been necessary to explain what wet flies are. In the first half of the twentieth century, every angler on the stream would have carried patterns like the Partridge and Orange and Cowdung in their sheepskin and leather fly wallets. That time has passed, though, and wet flies are the least-used type of flies on western streams today. Modern fly pattern books show hundreds of drys, nymphs, emergers, and streamers, but very few wet flies. Except for a few soft-hackles that occasionally draw the assignment of imitating caddis pupae, you'll find few traditional wet flies in most anglers' boxes today. Wet flies' lack of popularity is likely a result of our demand for things complex and laden with technology. We no longer appreciate simplicity.

What's funny about this is the fact that nobody told the fish that wet flies went out of fashion. Wet flies still work, and they still work well. The fact that they are out of fashion is the main reason I'd choose to use them. Our fish are becoming harder to fool because of the increased pressure from fly fishers, and it's a good strategy to show them something they haven't seen. It's a pretty safe bet that most of our western trout aren't seeing many traditional wet flies these days. It's hard to know if wet-fly fishing is a method whose time has come and gone forever, or if it is simply in the low part of a larger cycle and will become popular again sometime in the future.

Wet flies probably work well because they can imitate so many of the trout's natural food items. Depending on the depth and the method with which they are fished, they can imitate emerging, spent, or drowned mayflies and caddisflies, as well as any number of terrestrial bugs that find their way into the water. It's interesting that our understanding of wet flies contradicts the usual sequence of modern fly development. Today we identify a problem and devise a pattern to solve it. In the case of wet flies, the solution was in use long before we knew what the problem was. For example, it has only recently been added to the body of general fly-fishing knowledge that adult females of a couple of the most common types of caddisflies— *Rhyacophila* and *Hydropsyche*—swim to the bottom of the stream to lay their eggs. And we've just also recently realized that some emerging mayflies escape the nymphal shuck well before reaching the surface of the water. Wet flies are very good imitations of both these creatures engaged in these behaviors. So instead of providing us with information to create new patterns, science has given us the reason why old patterns work. It reminds me of the medical profession's practice of determining what illness you had by noting which drug made you better.

In addition to imitating specific stages of aquatic insects' lives, wet flies can also simply imitate drowned bugs. Most fly fishers don't realize that adult insects eventually sink beneath the surface of the water. Mayfly duns and spinners, spent caddisflies, stoneflies, ants, beetles, and grasshoppers are all susceptible to being swamped by a wave, after which they drift along beneath the surface. It's valuable to remember that all of the insects we usually associate with being on the surface of the water are at least occasionally available to the fish a short distance beneath the surface. In all, there are plenty of critters drifting and swimming beneath the surface of a trout stream that can be imitated by traditional wet flies.

Wet flies are generally fished within a couple feet of the surface of the stream. It is a method well suited to the same circumstances as shallow nymphing. Wet flies are most appealing to fish that are already feeding, so their application makes the most sense in feeding water. Areas where riffles slow and deepen into pools, where pools begin to shallow into tailouts, and where depressions interrupt long shallows are good places for wet flies. It's a good time to try a wet fly when you see fish rising occasionally or bumping the surface while taking emerging nymphs, or anytime you see a lot of bug activity around the stream, especially caddisflies. When there are a lot of caddis flying, it probably means that there is either an emergence or an egg-laying flight, or both, taking place, which are great times to use wet flies. Even steadily rising fish can frequently be duped with wet flies, and sometimes more easily so than with a dry or an emerger.

The tackle for fishing wet flies is essentially the same as for dry flies. The rare wet-fly specialists prefer rods with fairly soft tips. These protect fine tippets when trout take flies aggressively on a tight line. But since this is a method employed more occasionally than exclusively, most anglers use whatever rod they have chosen for that day's fishing. It is another reason to select your rod with versatility in mind.

For wet-fly fishing, floating lines are used nearly exclusively, even though there's no law against using a sinking-tip or full-sinking line. Floating lines are preferred because they allow mending after the cast is made. Wet flies are generally tied without extra weight in the fly or on the leader, but there are no rules against that either. If the situation requires the fly to be fished deeper, extra weight will help.

The practice of using more than one fly at a time probably started with wet flies. The traditional setup consisted of what old-timers called a "cast" of two or three wets, with a point fly at the end of the leader and one or two other flies added on droppers, short pieces of leader tied to extend perpendicularly from the main body of the leader. The most common way to attach a dropper is to tie a blood knot and leave one of the tag ends about six inches long.

There are a number of methods of fishing wet flies, generally distinguished by the direction in which the flies are cast.

Traditional Wet-Fly Swing

The oldest and most common method of fishing wet flies is to swing them downstream. A floating line and conventional 9- or 10-foot leader are used, and the cast is made across and slightly downstream. No line is released after the cast, and the fly is allowed to swing around on a tight line. The angler plans the casts so that the swinging fly moves through the most productive parts of the stream. This method is effective with both winged wet flies and soft-hackles. As with many simple methods, it's the subtle variations that make it successful. It's important to visualize what the fly is doing during its time in the water, and a good objective, as related by Dave Hughes in his book *Wet Flies,* is Polly Rosborough's suggestion to try to keep the fly pointed upstream while it moves down and across-stream. This mimics the position and movement of natural insects in the water. The fly should not be held stationary in the current, because real bugs can't do that. You strive for something halfway between the swim of a streamer and the dead drift of a nymph. Mends are a means of achieving this, as they help control the speed of the fly's drift. Upstream mends, made periodically throughout the fly's drift, slow the fly down, and downstream mends accelerate it. Fished with this method, wet flies can imitate adult caddisflies swimming to lay eggs, as well as emerging caddisflies or mayflies.

The wet-fly swing is a good way to search for fish and is effective in feeding water in streams of all sizes. It works particularly well during late-spring emergences of the western march brown mayfly, one of the species that escapes its nymphal shuck well before it reaches the surface of the water.

Strikes are detected by feel and usually occur in the second half of the drift, when the line comes tight and the fly moves upward in the water column. A problem can arise when a robust strike occurs. With tippets of 4X or 5X, it's easy to break the fish off immediately upon the strike. Try to avoid hauling back on the rod when a fish takes. It also helps to hold the line loosely between a finger of your rod hand and the rod grip, such that line will slide out when a big fish surprises you with a vicious strike.

A variation of the traditional wet-fly swing can be used in situations where fish are rising steadily. Position yourself upstream and to the near side of the fish, far enough away to avoid being seen and to avoid sending dirty water down into its face. Cast the fly so it lands a few feet beyond and upstream of the fish's position. As soon as the fly lands, it must sink; if it doesn't, give the line a short tug to encourage the fly to break through the surface film. Then allow the fly to swing right in front of the fish's face on a tight line. This works very well and is best done with simple soft-hackled flies that match the size and color of the nymphal stage of the insect the fish is eating. The takes are usually strong, and one of the difficulties is avoiding breakoffs at the moment of the take.

The Upstream Method

The upstream wet-fly method is used almost exclusively on fish that are rising and eating flies at or just beneath the surface. Though they are largely overlooked by anglers when rising fish are encountered, old-fashioned wet flies often fool trout that turn up their noses, literally, at modern drys and fancy emergers. This is where the tortoise of tradition sometimes beats the hare of technology. This method is exactly the same as the upstream dry-fly method, except that the fly sinks slightly. The fly is cast a short distance above the rising fish and is allowed to drift down over it without drag. When the fly hits the water, the angler looks for the dent on the surface where the fly lands and watches this spot as the fly drifts down over the fish. If a fish rolls or porpoises at that spot, the fisherman raises the rod to set the hook. Sometimes the leader is greased with floatant to keep the fly from drifting too deep. An indicator—either a tiny piece of visible yarn or a small visible dry fly—can also be used with this method, thereby making it exactly the same as the shallow nymphing method. The best flies for this method are soft-hackles, in sizes and colors that match the natural bugs that are hatching.

Western Wet Flies
An angler need not have an elaborate collection of wets in order to cover the most important bases. A few winged wets and a few soft-hackles should do it. They are generally best in #12 through #16 and are usually tied unweighted. You should carry a few soft-hackles, like the Partridge and Orange and the Gray Hackle Peacock, and a few winged wets, like the Leadwing Coachman, March Brown, and Light Cahill.

HEAVILY FISHED WATERS
It's hard to believe that the trout that tips up slowly to inspect and finally refuse a size 24 Trico Spinner in Silver Creek is the same creature that races through three feet of water to slam a Stimulator in the chop of a high-country freestone stream. Yet they are the same, and their different attitudes toward feeding could be ammunition in the debate over acquired versus inherited behavior.

The wilderness hick trout has probably never seen an angler before and has no reason to be suspicious of a fly because it's never eaten a bug that's bitten back. It may rise to the cigarette butt a careless angler flicks into the stream. It is, however, very alert to danger from outside the stream. Wilderness trout are easy to fool but also easy to frighten and occupy one end of the trout behavior spectrum. At the other end are the heavily pressured fish that live in popular streams and develop a different defense mechanism.

It's possible that the word *selectivity* was first applied to the feeding behavior of trout by a befuddled spring creek fisherman. If it didn't happen that way, it could have. It is when trout feed on one food item to the exclusion of everything else that they are at their frustrating and exasperating worst. Or maybe their best. Selectivity is in some measure a natural behavior, but it is also a by-product of heavy angling pressure and catch-and-release fishing. Trout learn, after encountering pointy impostors a few times, to be more careful about what they eat. "If it doesn't look and behave *exactly* like all those other bugs, I won't eat it," seems to be their motto.

While angling pressure makes trout more selective, it also makes them more tolerant of human presence. Hard-fished trout become accustomed to feeding in the presence of anglers, simply because they'd go hungry if they had to wait until all the fishermen went home. It is possible to spook these trout, but when it happens it doesn't take long for them to recover and resume feeding. It is their extreme selectivity, rather than the flight reflex, that makes them difficult to catch.

Selectivity and tolerance of anglers are traits that develop most acutely in fish that see a lot of anglers. Streams like the Green, Bighorn, South Platte, Missouri, Silver Creek, Henry's Fork of the Snake, Depuy's Spring Creek, Fall River, San Juan, Hat Creek, Frying Pan, and others are all on the radar screen of modern fly fishers and are busy most of the year. Their fish are more like Las Vegas showgirls than small-town cuties. You can use your best lines, but these girls probably won't be impressed. Special techniques are required to fool the sophisticated trout in heavily-fished western streams.

It's both important and easy to learn about the hatches on a popular stream. Before visiting the area look at books, magazines, and websites, and when you get to your destination visit the local fly shops. It's also a good idea to carry a variety of imitations of the important bugs. Because the fish are so selective, the details of fly pattern are more critical on hard-fished waters than on other waters. Different fish lock in to different stages of the same insect, and different fish seem to require different triggering characteristics in the imitation. Many anglers believe good presentation will generally compensate for poor imitation, and in many cases they are correct. On heavily fished streams, though, both presentation *and* imitation are critical.

Flies for Heavily Fished Waters

Many hard-fished waters, especially spring creeks and tailwaters, are popular because of their abundant and reliable insect hatches and large numbers of rising trout. Consequently the normal procedure is to play the match-the-hatch game. This is the one where you make six casts, and then change to a smaller fly; make six casts, and then change to a lighter tippet; make six casts, and then change your position; make six casts, and then change to an even smaller fly. This is great fun and is the classic confrontation in fly fishing. But sometimes you just need to catch a trout.

When selective trout are feeding heavily on small flies, they can be nearly impossible to fool, no matter how good the imitation is. Sometimes though, these same fish completely lose their composure when a small, wiggly streamer swims enticingly through the feeding water. If the fly hits the water without spooking the fish and then works the audience like a shameless comedian, it often gets eaten. Flies like a size 10 or 12 Spring Creek Bugger are ideal. When you try this you'll probably find that the fish will either attack your streamer viciously the first time they see it, or they'll stop feeding altogether for a while. Fishing streamers to rising fish is not exactly a staple method on popular streams and might border on heresy, but I guarantee you'll crack a smug smile when one of these super-sophisticated trout bombs your little streamer.

You can also prospect with streamers. This often works well on dry-fly streams, simply because nobody else does it. Who'd want to go to a place like the Missouri below Holter Dam, which is famous for its rising fish, and throw streamers? Not very many fishermen, but those who do often catch fish. This provides welcome relief for a fisherman who's spent too much time crouching and squinting to see tiny flies. A word of warning: This method works very well until too many people do it too often. Once the fish become tuned in, it becomes just one more technique that works part of the time.

The San Juan Worm is a reliable fly on big, fertile rivers like the Missouri, Bighorn, and San Juan, of course, but it works other places too—especially in spring creeks. Some people neglect it for the same reason they neglect streamers in spring creeks—they think the fish are too sophisticated for that sort of stuff. But a size 14 Worm works well when fished in weedy sections of spring creeks, and a smaller one is deadly in stillwater when it's dangled beneath a tiny indicator.

If you're more of a purist and prefer to stick with matching the hatch, it can sometimes be a good strategy to find out what flies local shops are recommending and what most of the anglers are using—and then use something different. Fish get harder to fool when they see the same pattern too many times, and if everybody who goes into the fly shop leaves with exactly the same size 18 quill-bodied para-emergers, the pattern's effectiveness will diminish. Some anglers travel with a tying kit and create their own variations of the patterns that the fly shops recommend, changing a color or proportion slightly, so they can show the fish something a little different.

As trout streams receive more angling pressure, the fish seem to respond by feeding on smaller food items. Some places where the trout were pretty easy to catch before the stream became famous have developed into more technical streams under increased angling pressure. The Crowsnest River in southwestern Alberta is a perfect example. In the early to mid-1980s it was a Bitch Creek and Stimulator stream—a place where big nymphs and big drys were the order of the day. But as the river became more popular, it became necessary to fish with smaller flies, especially nymphs. The fish seemed to develop a greater degree of sophistication through the years, and smaller flies, finer leaders, and more precise tactics are now required to fool them.

It's sometimes hard to see the small dry flies that are required on many spring creeks and western tailwaters. One solution is to use a tiny orange, yellow, or even black yarn strike indicator with the dry fly. Use the smallest indicator that's visible and put it on the leader about twelve inches from the fly. You can also use a small, visible dry fly as an indicator (so long as two flies are legal where you're fishing).

Rising Fish

On our most productive dry-fly streams there are usually plenty of rising fish. Most anglers concentrate on the first ones they see, which are usually in obvious feeding lies like tailouts, flats, heads of pools, and channels in the weeds. Though these fish are the easiest to find, they are usually also the most difficult to fool, simply because they get the most attention from anglers. They are the masters of selectivity. It's always fun to test your skill with these fish, but once you're tired of being snubbed, an alternative is to look for the rising fish other anglers don't see. They are hard to find and will often be underneath or beside some sort of cover—a pile of weeds or debris, a fallen log, an undercut bank, or an overhanging willow bush. These fish are sneaky. They usually rise so gently that they're nearly impossible to see. But if you watch the debris edges carefully you'll notice the occasional white "wink" at the surface, which is a brief opening of the feeding fish's mouth. Your first reaction will probably be to wonder whether you actually saw something or just imagined it. Watch a little longer, and if you happen to be carrying a small pair of binoculars, point them at the spot and watch some more. You'll find some fish this way, and the ones you find will be the ones most anglers miss. This is true on small spring creeks as well as on large rivers like the Henry's Fork and Missouri.

It's difficult to get a fly into these tight spots and even more difficult to get a good drift once you do. But if they are rising, these fish are almost always easier to fool than the trout that feed out in the open. It's more important to get a perfect drift than to show them a perfect imitation, and they often take the first reasonable imitation that you put over them properly. These fish see very few artificial flies in the first place, and most of those they see are behaving badly. If you break that pattern, you've got it made.

It's easy to be stubborn and continue casting to a rising fish until you either hook it or spook it. But selective fish seem to get their guard up once they realize they're being fished over, and though they probably won't quit feeding, they will become even more careful about what they eat. Your best opportunity to fool one is in the first three or four casts. So the longer you work on an individual fish, the less chance you have of getting a take. A better idea is to make a few good casts to a fish, and if it doesn't take, leave it alone and find another one. Give the first fish a ten- or fifteen-minute rest, and then try it with a different fly. While you're gone the fish will forget all about you, and you can get a fresh start when you come back later.

Tippets

The flat-water portions of hard-fished streams are some of the most difficult places to fool trout. Not only do the fish see plenty of anglers, but they also very clearly see the flies and leaders that the anglers throw at them. The slow flat right in front of the fishermen's hut on the O'Hair property of Armstrong's Spring Creek is a good example. Fish feed there on midges all day long, in plain view of every angler that puts on waders. Everybody has a go at these fish, but few anglers catch them. In this situation it's a good idea to adopt a lake-fishing trick, and use fluorocarbon tippet material. Fluorocarbon is much less visible in the water than nylon, and flat-water experts believe they get more takes with fluorocarbon than with conventional monofilament. There is an environmental concern with fluorocarbon, however, because it never breaks down. If you use it, don't leave any on the ground or in the water.

WADE-FISHING ETIQUETTE

There are more fly fishers than there have ever been in North America, just as there are more automobiles than there have ever been. In both cases, an increase in use causes an increase in problems—problems relating to space. The traffic issues are addressed with the construction of more and bigger roads. But they don't build more trout streams, so the problem of trout stream congestion must be handled differently.

In some ways, fly fishers in eastern North America have it easier than those in the West, at least in the fact that they have come to expect encounters with other anglers when they go fishing. This has prompted the development of a general code of behavior and accepted rules about how much space an angler is entitled to. In the West, there are some heavily fished waters where the eastern customs are suitable and accepted, but there are also areas well off the beaten path, where encounters with other anglers are less common and different rules need be applied. Solitude has largely disappeared from the eastern trout stream experience, but there are places in the West where it is still available, and the anglers who go to these places are often drawn to them specifically because of the solitude. This makes it disappointing when they find another fisherman somewhere out back of beyond, because one of their reasons for being there has just disappeared. But this is happening more often now, and some thought about how to deal with it is warranted.

The governing philosophy for all encounters with other anglers is the golden rule: Treat them the way you'd want them to treat you. Along with this must be an understanding that the "rules of engagement" are different in different places. The protocol on a particular stream can usually be determined by asking anglers who have frequently fished that water or by inquiring at local fly shops.

Failing outside help, my suggestion is that you simply realize the difference between a famous trout stream and a relatively unknown one. If there are books, videos, and frequent magazine stories about the stream, or if there are fly-fishing products, fly shops, or websites named after it, it's probably safe to consider it famous. This will be quickly confirmed when you see large numbers of other anglers. Here it's usually acceptable to conduct your fishing much closer to one another than on a less heavily used stream. But you still must not interfere with someone else's angling. Stay far enough away that you don't cross casts with others, and don't disturb the fish they're trying to catch. This often means moving back from the streambank as you walk along it. And it is never OK to cast to a rising fish that another angler is working on. It's better to give anglers more room than they need rather than less than they expect. Put yourself in the other person's position. Would you want another angler breathing down your neck?

Observe the behavior of the other anglers on a popular piece of water. Though you can't presume that everybody's following the rules, if you adopt the behavior of the majority of those fishing, you'll probably be all right. It's always a good idea to talk to other anglers if there is any chance they won't approve of what you want to do. This is a way to head off possible misunderstandings before they start. If someone is fishing in a particular spot and you want to walk past him to another spot, tell the angler that you're going past, rather than letting the person think you are butting in on his water.

If the stream you're fishing is not famous and heavily used, you'll know that right away also, because you won't see many other anglers. But you might see the occasional one, and when you do, the rules are different. Because there are fewer people at the party, they each get a bigger piece of the pie. Give another angler at least a couple of pools on a small stream and at least a few hundred yards on a big river.

Some rivers, like the Henry's Fork of the Snake in Idaho, have both types of water. The Harriman Ranch section near Last Chance is a famous piece of water, and on a typical summer day, anglers are scattered throughout the river. It's common and acceptable (and mostly unavoidable) to have a dozen other anglers within your sight at all times. On this marvelous piece of water, this works because there are plenty of fish for everyone to cast to. In fact, this becomes part of the Henry's Fork experience, for there are few other trout streams on which you may hear frustrated fly fishers cursing in so many different languages. Other, less accessible portions of the Henry's Fork have far less angler traffic, and on these sections, the "not famous" rules apply.

Familiarize yourself with the trespass laws in the state or province where you plan to fish. In some places access is provided to the public by law, and in other places permission is required of landowners. In some places the stream bottom is public land, and in other places it is not. The fact that these laws differ from one jurisdiction to another does not make ignorance of them acceptable. Check with the angling regulations and local fly shops for clarification of the trespass laws.

CHAPTER 7

Western Methods for the Driftboat Angler

In all likelihood, the idea of fly-fishing a river from a moving boat was not conceived in western North America at all. It probably traces back to Atlantic salmon fishermen who poled canoes in rivers of eastern Canada and the northeastern United States. But within fly-fishing culture today, float trips are most strongly associated with large trout streams in and near the Rocky Mountains. The common image is of a McKenzie River driftboat, either stationary in the parking lot of a small-town bar or chasing a pickup truck that's going a little too fast down a gravel road toward the Madison, Deschutes, North Platte, Snake, or Elk River. The driftboat is now a cultural symbol, and images of its elegant profile are frequently used by the outdoor press as a means to evoke the western fly-fishing experience.

The modern McKenzie River driftboat was developed on the West Coast for use in whitewater rivers like the McKenzie, Rogue, and others, but the boat's heritage lies on the East Coast. The sharply elevated bow and stern, which made the East Coast fishing dory safe in the stormy Atlantic, provide the same capabilities to a fly fisher on the rough-and-tumble rivers of the Rockies. McKenzie driftboats float in very shallow water, are very maneuverable, and are stable platforms from which to cast. They are also resistant to rocks (taken in moderation) and have keelless hulls that flex when the riverbed makes an unexpected arrival from below. Today's luxury versions have plenty of dry storage and are available in different configurations as required by different fishing situations. There are steeply curved models with high sides for use in extremely rough water, and there are more elongated, lower-sided versions that are easier to get in and out of and handle more easily in strong winds. McKenzie boats are made of fiberglass, aluminum, or wood, and each type has its advantages and disadvantages relating to cost, durability, maintenance, and weight.

There is little doubt that a well-equipped McKenzie boat is the most convenient boat from which to fly-fish a trout river. But other factors may lead a prospective owner to different choices. Most McKenzies require that at least one or possibly both anglers stand while fishing. This is great if you want to stand, but if you can't or don't want to stand, it's not great. If the river doesn't have a boat ramp, or at least a place where a boat trailer can be backed to the water's edge, the McKenzie won't work. If the fisherman wants to put a motor on the boat or hunt ducks from it, he may also choose another type.

Inflatable rafts meet many of these additional requirements. Compared with driftboats, they generally don't have as many comfort features, such as knee braces or drink holders, or as much space for dry storage, but when deflated, they are easy to haul in the back of a pickup truck and to store in the basement over the winter. A big advantage is the fact that they bounce off rocks in the river much better than hard-sided boats. They can also be tossed down and dragged up steep riverbanks where there are no formal boat ramps.

A modern McKenzie-style driftboat is the most comfortable boat from which to fly-fish a trout river.

There was a time when flat-bottomed aluminum johnboats were quite popular on gentler western rivers, but those days seem to be disappearing. I spent many years fly-fishing from a drifting johnboat and only recently and somewhat reluctantly graduated to the ranks of the McKenzie boat crowd.

The most recent addition to the western river boat repertoire is the inflatable pontoon boat. These started as souped-up float tubes that were propelled and steered by the feet of the driver, but they have quickly developed into sophisticated, riverworthy craft that are equipped with small oars, which make them much easier to steer and move about.

Pontoon boats are a good choice for the angler who usually fishes alone, for unlike the other types of boats, they allow you to steer and fish at the same time. If you've ever tried to do this in a conventional boat, you know the problems: make a couple of oar strokes; pick up the rod and make a cast; put the rod in your mouth while you pull on the oars; make a couple strips on the fly line while holding the oars with your knees; make a cast into the first great spot as you drift by at eighty-five feet; then make a cast to the next great spot as you drift by at two and a half feet. I'm sure you get the picture, and I'm not even going to mention the complications that arise when a fish gets involved.

Other types of boats, such as simple car-toppers, are sometimes used in rivers, and they can work well so long as the boat is capable of handling the water. Don't presume that any kind of boat is safe in any kind of water. Always investigate before getting the boat wet. This advice also applies to the skill of the rower. Make an honest appraisal of your rowing ability, and inquire about the difficulty of the water before you put any boat into it.

There are two philosophies concerning the use of boats for fly-fishing rivers. Some people use them primarily as a means of getting from one good spot to another, preferring to get out of the boat to fish the good water thoroughly on foot. Others consider the boat a fishing platform and enjoy fishing on the drift. On a big river, the advantages of using a boat may seem obvious: You can get access to the whole river, including both banks, all islands, and most anyplace you can't reach by wading. But there is more to it than that. Some parts of some big rivers are much more effectively fished from a boat, especially with certain methods. The boat can also be anchored in water too deep to wade, which allows the anglers to fish where others can't.

Sometimes boats are used not because the rivers are large, but because foot access is minimal or wading is prohibited. In some western states and provinces the bottoms of navigable rivers are public land, even where the streams flow through private property. In these rivers, wading is generally legal. In other jurisdictions, however, the stream bottoms belong to the landowner whose property the stream flows through. In many of these places wading constitutes trespass, so all fishing must be done from boats.

ROWING A BOAT IN A RIVER

Whichever type of boat is used, the principles for controlling it in flowing water are the same. Only the basics of rowing will be covered in this book. The fine points are best learned through experience or through instructional videos such as the one produced by Hyde Driftboats, and through the personalized instruction offered by some fly shops and outfitters. There are also a number of books dealing with the topic in detail, including *Driftboat Strategies* and *Driftboat Fly Fishing,* both by Neale Streeks.

The first principle of piloting a drifting boat is that the driver must face downstream. It's more important to see where you're going than where you've been. In a McKenzie boat, this means that the boat goes down the river bowfirst. In some other types of boats, like the johnboat, it means that the boat goes down sternfirst. The basic rowing techniques are the same for all boats, including pontoon boats. For the remainder of this discussion, however, we'll presume that a driftboat is being used.

To control a boat that's drifting in a river, you must understand that the river's current provides mobility, while the oars are used for control. Think of the river as the engine and the oars as the brakes and steering wheel. For steering, maneuvering, and positioning, the rowing is always done against the current. To move the boat toward one bank, point the stern of the boat (the part behind the rower) diagonally toward that bank, and row against the current with both oars together. The boat will continue to move downstream, but it will move toward the bank as it does. In effect, you're trying to row the boat upstream toward the bank, but because of the current, the boat moves downstream toward the bank. To make the most direct move toward that bank, point the boat toward the bank at a forty-five-degree angle. To make slight adjustments in position, point the boat at a less severe angle toward the bank. To simply slow the boat, point the bow straight downstream and row straight upstream.

It's important to realize that the boat will continue to slide toward the bank after you stop rowing. You can't put the boat the correct distance from the bank and then stop rowing any more than you can get your car in the center of the lane and then take your hands off the steering wheel. The only vehicle that doesn't need to be steered is a train. Small adjustments must be made constantly to both cars and driftboats.

In places where the water is more demanding, such as in tight corners and rough water, precise placement of the boat in the river channel is

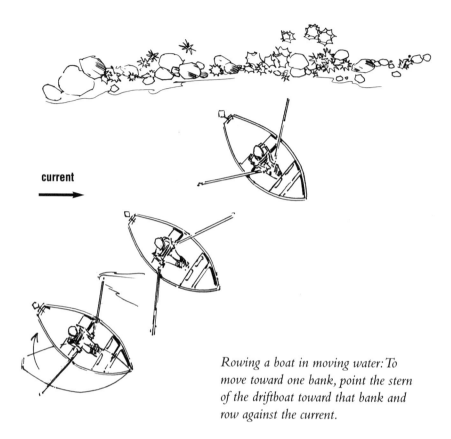

current

Rowing a boat in moving water: To move toward one bank, point the stern of the driftboat toward that bank and row against the current.

critical. Always enter tight corners in the correct part of the river with the boat already set up to row out of the corner. Go through rough water and standing waves with the bow pointing straight downstream, while slowing the boat with direct upstream rowing. In areas of large rocks, plan your route through before you start, even if it means beaching the boat and thinking about it for a minute. Go through these boulder gardens slowly, with a lot of direct upstream rowing. Don't let the boat get perpendicular to the current in areas of big waves or big rocks. If the water is particularly difficult, have the fisherman in the bow stop fishing and start watching for rocks that you might not see.

There are refinements to rowing, such as knowing when to drag an oar and when to use the oars in opposite directions, which will become apparent with experience. Most of these are subtle ways to control the boat's position to the benefit of the angler. If you're new to rowing, watch carefully when you're in the driftboat with a more experienced oarsman, and ask him to explain any maneuvers that you don't recognize.

The rower has two jobs if he's got fishermen in the boat: steering the boat and helping the anglers with their fishing. The first one is the most important, and the oarsman must make worrying about what the river is doing a higher priority than worrying about what the fishermen are doing.

It's sometimes a good idea to hurry through the less productive parts of rivers. In a johnboat or inflatable raft, it's usually simplest to turn the boat around and row downstream. Because of its shape, it's best to leave a McKenzie boat in its usual position and use the oars to push it downstream with the current.

All types of flies can be used effectively from a driftboat, with the possible exception of wet flies. They are rarely used, because the precise down-and-across swing is difficult to reproduce from a moving boat.

DRY-FLY FISHING FROM A DRIFTBOAT

In a general sense, dry-fly fishing from a drifting boat is simple. The rower steers the boat while the fishermen cast toward the good water and let the flies drift with the current. But this is a little like saying golf is a sport where you knock a ball into a hole with a stick. The art is in the details.

The tackle for driftboat dry-fly fishing is much the same as that used for wade-fishing in a big river. A 9- or 9½-foot rod is better than a shorter rod, because it allows fewer false casts and keeps the line away from the oars. The line should be a floater with a 9- or 10-foot leader at the end.

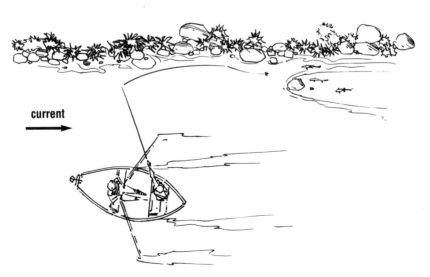

When dry-fly fishing from a drifting boat, the cast is made in a downstream direction using an upstream reach cast.

Driftboat fishing requires teamwork between the two casters and the rower. The oarsman must keep the boat a comfortable and relatively constant distance from the target water, which is often near the bank of the river. It's imperative that the two anglers cast more or less parallel to one another to avoid crossing lines and tangling. This is easy to remember when you're at home thinking about it, but not quite so easy when you're in the boat with a rod in your hand. When a great spot comes along, it's tempting to make one or two or three casts at it, reaching back upstream a little farther each time as the boat passes the spot. Unless the other angler is succumbing to the same temptation, this is a recipe for a big tangle.

Fishing from a driftboat allows you to get exceptionally long drag-free drifts with dry flies—if you do things correctly. Fish often lie in the quiet water along the banks of the river, but if you make a standard delivery straight across to the bank, the fly will drag soon after it lands, because it is in slower water than the boat is. Even if the oarsman slows the boat, a downstream belly will form in the line and the fly will drag. But if the fisherman casts the dry fly toward the bank at a downstream angle with an upstream reach cast, the fly not only will arrive at the target ahead of the leader and line, but will drift much longer without drag.

If the cast is made a bit too far, the fly can be drawn back toward the boat with an gentle upward motion of the rod, in order to place the fly in the perfect drift line. This is very much like the downstream dry-fly method used by wading anglers in flat-water situations. Upstream mends are made to reestablish a good drift and avoid drag whenever a belly begins to form in the fly line. The fly is left on the water as long as it stays in a good lane and doesn't sink or drag. With this method, it's possible to get drifts of a hundred feet or more. It's often a good idea to impart occasional slight twitches to the drift of the fly with the rod tip. Give the bug a little extra life just as it approaches a fishy spot, and get ready for a strike.

It's easy to tell if someone is inexperienced at fishing from a driftboat. Generally, the more false casts you see, the newer the angler is to this game. In my guiding career, I was convinced that some of my clients were training for the World False Cast Championships. It's always important to minimize the number of false casts, but even more so when fishing from a moving boat. Because you're passing water constantly, every false cast you make is a fishing cast you don't make. The experts usually make just one or two false casts between drifts, which maximizes the amount of time their flies spend on the water. This, in turn, maximizes their chances of catching fish. Keep your fly on the water.

For most dry-fly fishing, the rower allows the boat to move at the same speed as the current or slows it just slightly. The angler's job is to keep one

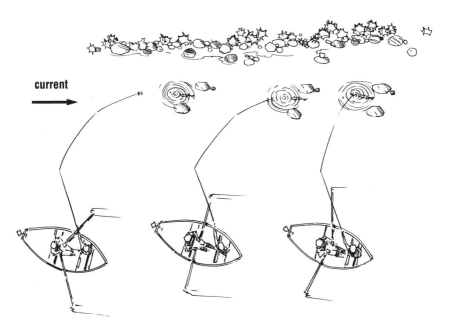

When casting to a rising fish from a moving boat, remember that the fish is not moving downstream with the riseform, but is still in the spot where the riseform was created.

eye on the drifting fly and another on the water downstream so he's ready when the boat approaches a particularly good spot. As the boat nears one of these hot spots, the rower may slow the boat further or even stop it altogether so the fishermen can make several casts to it. When the boat is held stationary in the current, the casters direct their casts upstream and allow the flies to drift back toward them, much as they do when standing in the river or on the bank.

Dry-fly fishing from a drifting boat is a type of prospecting, because the target is usually identified by reading the water, rather than by seeing a fish. It is most effective in holding water along the banks of the river. Though this method is generally used when there aren't many fish rising, it's not uncommon to see the odd rise as you drift along. When this happens, you should cast above the rise so that your fly drifts into the fish's view. Keep in mind that your frame of reference is skewed. The boat is moving, the water is moving, the fly is moving, and the riseform of the fish is moving. The fish, though, is stationary. Don't keep casting at the riseform as it drifts downriver with the boat. The fish is back upstream where the riseform was created.

If somebody in the boat sees a big fish rise as you're going along, the fishermen should stop casting and the oarsman should slide the boat quietly a safe distance past the fish before stopping and anchoring the boat. The fishermen can then get out and stalk the fish on foot. This is a more efficient way to work on risers and allows you to change flies when you need to and spend the additional time it usually takes to fool the big guys.

Driftboat Dry Flies

I suppose you could fish a #22 Trico Compara-dun or some kind of technical surface-film emerger from a drifting boat, but it usually makes more sense to fish larger and more visible flies. The light and water conditions vary from spot to spot along a river, and it's an advantage to use a fly that can be seen in bright sun, deep shade, broken water, and all combinations thereof. Buoyant flies in colors that contrast with the water are preferred. Most driftboat drys are more attractors than imitators, because they are used for searching good water rather than fooling rising fish. They are often larger versions of the attractors you use when fishing on foot. Many western driftboat guides like Stimulators and Turck's Tarantulas, as well as foam flies such as the Chernobyl Ant and Hopper. Members of the growing family of white-winged flies are also good choices. This group includes the Royal Wulff, H & L Variant, Coachman Trude, and Royal Humpy.

Another type of fly that's particularly good from a driftboat is a grasshopper pattern. High banks on outside bends of big rivers are great places for hoppers in late summer but are difficult to fish on foot because of high vegetation or difficult wading. Fishing a hopper from a boat in these places is almost like cheating. It's amazing how much easier it is to fish to the bank, rather than from the bank. While some anglers fish two hoppers, others like to use a hopper and a smaller dry, and still others use the increasingly popular "hopper-dropper" method, where a small nymph is dangled a couple feet beneath a buoyant hopper.

Fishing on the drift is also great with imitations of adult stoneflies during their hatching period. Entomology-wise this is different from hopper fishing, but execution-wise it is the same.

NYMPH FISHING FROM A DRIFTBOAT

In the days when all the driftboats were made of wood, most of the fishing from them was done with dry flies and streamers. But in recent years, good methods of fishing nymphs from drifting boats have been developed.

The usual tackle for this job is a 9-foot rod for a #5 or #6 floating fly line, a 9- or 10-foot leader, a buoyant strike indicator, a weighted nymph, and possibly extra weight to attach to the leader. It is the same outfit you'd use for nymphing a big river from your feet.

The Rocky Mountains have profound influence on western freestone streams, making them more productive but less predictable.

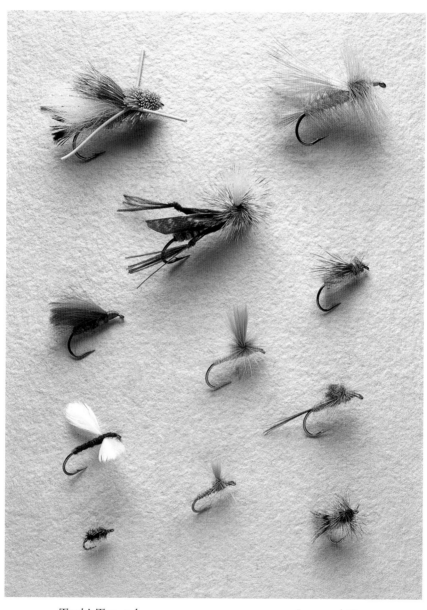

Turck's Tarantula

Parachute Hopper

Glenn's CDC Caddis

Hen Spinner

Griffith's Gnat

Parachute

R. S. Quad

Improved Stone

LaFontaine Emergent
Sparkle Pupa

Floating Nymph

Spent Partridge Caddis

J & H Streamer   Gartside Leech

Bow River Bugger

San Juan Worm

Spring Creek Bugger   A. P. Nymph

Leadwing Coachman

Brassie   Beadhead

Flashback Pheasant Tail

Driftboats are used for fishing on the drift and moving from one good spot to another for wade fishing.

The placement of the indicator on the leader is always a tricky issue, for the depth of the water changes as the boat moves down the river. Usually it's better to have too much distance between fly and indicator, rather than too little. The indicator is placed close to the end of the fly line when the water is three to five feet deep, and a little closer to the fly if the water is shallower.

The oarsman has an important part to play in this type of fishing. First, he must keep the casters within a comfortable distance of the good water. Often the good water is along the banks of the river, but a good rower should also position the boat where the casters can cover depressions, slots, drop-offs, current seams, buckets, and converging currents in midriver. Second, the oarsman should be aware of the anglers' terminal tackle so he can direct the boat through areas of suitable water. For instance, if the fisherman is rigged with the indicator three feet from the fly, the oarsman should try to find holding water where that setup will be effective.

As in dry-fly fishing, the boat is allowed to drift about the same speed as the current or is slowed slightly. If the boat is moving the same speed as the water you want to fish, the cast is made perpendicular to the current. If the rower is slowing the boat and the boat is moving slower than the water you want to fish, the cast should be slightly upstream of perpendicular. If the boat is moving faster than the water you want to fish, the cast should be slightly downstream of perpendicular.

The objective doesn't change when you do your nymphing from a boat. You're still trying to make the nymph drift naturally near the bottom of the river. The first step to achieving this is to make a big upstream mend immediately after the fly hits the water. If done correctly, the mend will extend right down to the indicator, and the line will lie on the water upstream of the indicator. Additional mends are made to maintain this relationship. An indicator that is buoyant, visible, and a good mend killer is very helpful.

The oarsman has an additional contribution to make for his nymph-fishing companions. He can help achieve a natural drift by watching the strike indicators and slowing or turning the boat to allow the flies to work their way into the best holding spots. As he does when rowing for dry-fly anglers, the oarsman may choose to slow the boat or stop it altogether to allow multiple casts into the best holding water. He can also anchor the boat in places where it would be difficult or impossible for the anglers to wade, and they can work nymphs into good water that doesn't otherwise get fished.

Driftboat Nymphs

Just about any nymph that works for wade-fishing also works from a boat. Ideally, the pattern should represent something that the fish have been eating recently, and that information can be researched before you launch your boat. Fishing two nymphs from a driftboat is very popular, and in these situations two contrasting patterns are often chosen. A San Juan Worm is often paired with a Prince Nymph on many rivers. In other places, smaller and more technical flies are preferred, such as a Serendipity, caddis pupa, or Brassie.

STREAMER FISHING FROM A DRIFTBOAT

Streamer fishing a big western river from a driftboat is the most macho form of trout fishing I know. A powerful, 9-foot rod for a 6-, 7-, or 8-weight line is used, usually with a fast-sinking-tip line. Big flies, stout leaders, and thousands of casts are the ingredients for this type of fishing. There are a couple themes and a dozen variations.

The first method is the rapid-fire, "bombing the banks" method. The rower keeps the boat a comfortable cast from the bank and slows it so that it moves downstream about half the speed of the current. The fishermen fire casts at a slight downstream angle toward the bank, choosing deflections and current seams as their targets. The flies are thrown beyond the current seams into the quiet water right next to the bank and are retrieved immediately with short, fast strips. Because the objective is to make the streamer swim across the current seams at a right angle, it's important for the fishermen to continue to cast slightly downstream of the boat, resisting the temptation to reach back upstream. If the boat is in fast water, the line is stripped only three or four times before the next cast is made. This is because the fish won't chase the fly very far out into heavy current. In slower water, the fly can be retrieved until the angler can see that there isn't a fish following. In either case, it's imperative that the rod tip be held low, pointing at the water, so the stripping motion of the line hand is transmitted into a darting motion of the fly. If the rod tip is held high, the stripping of the line will make the rod tip bounce up and down, but it won't provide much action to the fly.

When this method is working well it is very exciting. Fish turn up everywhere, boiling, slashing, and chasing the fly every few casts. It's easy to be oblivious to everything else when you're fishing this way, and you might forget to stop for lunch. I've never calculated how many casts you make in a full day of this kind of fishing, but I do know that the combination of big rod, sinking-tip line, heavy flies, and nonstop casting takes a toll on the body. You can wake up the next morning with a big headache and a sore arm. It's full-contact fly fishing. It's also a method that sometimes gets a lot of action but few hookups. Some days dozens of fish boil and chase your streamer, but few of them actually take it. I've been given much advice on what to do about this and am happy to pass all of it on here. Some people favor speeding up the retrieve to simulate a greater degree of fright and panic in their streamer. Other guys suggest stopping the retrieve altogether, on the theory that big trout try to stun their prey with the first strike, and then come back and eat it a moment later. This is probably a pretty good idea, but after so many years of telling myself to strike quickly when a fish takes, I find it hard to refrain from striking when a fish shows up at my fly. It's also been suggested that a smaller fly or a fly of a contrasting color might increase the rate of hookups. All these ideas work—sometimes.

When bombing the banks doesn't work, I like to try a method that was shown to me by Alberta guides George McBride and Eric Grinnell. The oarsman slows the boat, and the angler casts back upstream to the very top of a current seam. The fisherman makes a couple upstream mends and then begins a slow stripping retrieve with a low rod. The fly slowly passes the boat and eventually comes tight against the line. The objective is to make the fly move downstream right in the current seam and quite deep in the water column. The fisherman retrieves slowly, trying to just stay in touch with the fly. It is nearly a dead-drift method, but not quite. With this method, the streamer is fished deep and slow and moves along the full length of the current seam, rather than swimming across the current seam. When bombing the banks works, many anglers prefer it because it is a high-energy, high-excitement method. But when the fish won't chase, this slower, deeper method of fishing streamers right in the current seams is often more effective.

Streamers can work well anytime, especially in low-light periods, but the best time is just as the river is clearing from runoff. As the water reaches marginal fishing condition after being "too thick to drink and too thin to plow," streamer fishing usually becomes very good. The best streamer fishing I've had has been when there was one to two feet of visibility in the water.

Driftboat Streamers
Any good western streamer can be used from a drifting boat, but flies that show a strong silhouette, sink quickly, and cast easily are best. The bugger family predominates in most western rivers. Also good are the Clouser Minnow and leech patterns like the Gartside Leech, which has a great silhouette and swimming motion. I carry both dark and light streamers and try both before I give up on the method. Some anglers fish a tandem streamer rig from a boat, usually pairing a small one with a big one or a dark one with a light one. While they are effective, I don't care for woolhead sculpin patterns or rabbit strip streamers for use from a driftboat. They absorb and hold so much water that they cast like wet sponges.

Though they may not work as well overall as dark patterns, I enjoy fishing white streamers from a driftboat. Late in the season, you can often fish them near the surface with a floating line, which is very exciting. A white streamer remains visible for the whole retrieve, and you'll see most of the fish that come after it.

PLAYING AND LANDING FISH FROM A DRIFTBOAT

There are various opinions on the best way to handle and release fish when they're hooked from a drifting boat. In truth, the approach should be determined by the situation, and the objective is to do what's best for the fish. Small trout can be landed and released quickly without stopping the boat. The fish is skidded to the side of the boat, and the angler reaches down the leader to the fly, gives it a twist, and the fish is gone almost before it knows what's happened.

It's a more difficult decision when the fish is large. Some people insist that the boat should always go to the shore as soon as it becomes apparent that the fish is bigger than average. This may or may not be the best idea. If the water is slow and gentle, and if wading is allowed, it works well. In this case, after the boat is landed, the angler can move downstream with the fish on foot, and if need be, one of his companions can net the fish for him.

If the fish is hooked in fast water, though, landing the boat often puts the fisherman in a poor position. He is stuck on the bank while the fish continues to roar off downstream. The shore-bound angler has to deal with both current and the strong fish, and he must sometimes chase the fish down the bank. It often takes a long time to land a fish this way. When big fish are hooked in fast water, my suggestion is to stay in the boat and drift with the fish until late in the fight, and then pull in to land, revive, and release the fish on foot. If the angler is incapable of getting out of the boat to complete the fight on foot, one of his companions should get out of the anchored boat to land the fish for him. Often you'll want to fish the water on foot after the fish is released, so you'll want to pull in to land the fish even if it isn't big enough to require it.

Whenever possible, a fish that has fought long and needs reviving should be released in slow current by an angler who is on foot. Reviving a fish for any length of time from a boat is difficult. The simple act of bending out over the gunwale is uncomfortable, and you may be tempted to release the fish before it's ready simply because your back is sore from leaning out over the water.

Of course, other factors enter into the decision of how to handle a big fish. If wading is not allowed, all fish must be landed and released from the boat. If a fish is hooked along a steep or rugged bank it may be difficult or dangerous to beach the boat and try to wade. In this case, keep drifting with the fish until you can land the boat safely, or else use the long-handled boat net that you brought with you. (You did bring it, didn't you?) It is very difficult to land big fish from a boat without a net.

DRIFTBOAT ETIQUETTE

When you're drifting a river, you'll encounter other people doing a number of different things. There may be other anglers in boats, other anglers on foot, and nonanglers in boats or other water craft.

Other anglers in boats should be given plenty of room. Never drift close enough that you can cast to the same water. It's generally OK to follow people through the good water, but stay far enough behind them that they don't think they've picked up new companions for the day. Don't row past another boat and then cut in front of it to get first shot at the good water. This is a huge no-no and a possible prelude to river rage.

The potential for problems with other boats is greatest early in the day, when there's a lot of congestion near the put-in spot. In this situation, I like to get my boat in the water and then stop early and fish on foot for an hour or two while most of the other boats go by. Then I can continue on with less traffic around me. This works surprisingly well. Even though it's sometimes beneficial to be the first boat down the river, other times it's better to go through a little later.

When a driftboat encounters wading anglers, the waders have the right-of-way. The boat should be steered past the waders in the way least likely to disturb their fishing. If they're wading some distance out into the river, it may be best to take the boat behind them. When in doubt, ask them what they prefer. Leave wading anglers plenty of water to fish before you move the boat back into casting range of their bank.

Some rivers have small side channels where the fishing is especially good. Avoid taking a boat down these channels. Not only will it disturb the water for later anglers, but you may round a corner and suddenly find yourself in a wading fisherman's lap. The only gracious way out of this is to stop the boat and ask the wading angler what he would prefer you do.

When a driftboat encounters other boats inhabited by nonfishermen, the rule is simply to be polite and not crowd them. They may not understand what you're doing and as a result might crowd you occasionally, but realize that this occurs through ignorance, not malice.

Etiquette becomes important at both ends of the float trip, where the rule is simple: Don't clog up the boat ramp. At the beginning of the day, get your tackle ready and your waders on well away from the ramp so that you spend as little time as possible on the ramp itself. At the end of the day, land the boat quickly and then move your vehicle out of the way so somebody else doesn't have to wait for you.

If you're floating a river for the first time, ask at local fly shops about any local boating practices you should know about. The overriding rule of driftboat etiquette is the same as wading etiquette: Treat the other guy the way you'd like him to treat you.

CHAPTER 8

Western Trout Stream Seasons

The cycle of seasons is the same for all western trout streams, but the magnitude of difference between seasons is influenced by altitude, latitude, and type of stream. Those in the north and at high elevations face longer, colder winters and have more pronounced seasons than low-elevation or more southerly streams. Freestone streams have more pronounced seasons than tailwaters and spring creeks. There are also great differences in the timing of the seasons because of latitude and elevation. When it's early summer in Colorado and New Mexico, for instance, it's barely spring in British Columbia and northern Montana. Likewise, when it's early summer at two thousand feet, it might still be late winter at seven thousand feet.

FREESTONE SEASONS

For fly-fishing purposes, let's define spring on freestone rivers as the period between the departure of ice on the stream and the arrival of spring runoff. Most streams get dirty for a short time when the ice leaves the stream and the snow along the banks melts. But between this "little runoff" and the big runoff that follows later is a window of low, clear water up to several weeks long. This is a time of change in the life of a trout stream. Canada geese return from wintering grounds, and lifelong pairs look for nesting sites close to the water. Meadowlarks on barbed wire sing of renewal, and the ruffed grouse you couldn't find last October materializes from the swamp to drum on his fallen log. The weather is unpredictable, and the sky carries the blustery, squally look of an unhappy child. Daytime temperatures are often pleasant, though the dusting of fresh snow on the mountains reminds you that the nights are still cool above timberline. On spring days like these the sun is intense, but so are the clouds. Fishermen, golfers, and farmers spend an inordinate amount of time putting on and taking off jackets. The snowfall that comes after we think it's too late for such nonsense briefly covers the blooming prairie crocuses.

Freestone trout streams emerge from a long, cold winter the same way I awaken from a long, deep sleep—slowly and reluctantly. The water is low, clear, and cold. Midges have been hatching sporadically all winter, but their activity increases in early spring. The first mayflies of the season begin to emerge from the gravel on warm afternoons. The western bookend hatch of *Baetis,* or blue-winged olive, is the first mayfly of the season on most western streams. On some streams, like the Yellowstone, the fish rise nicely to this spring hatch, but on others the bugs hatch profusely but are largely ignored in what seems to be some kind of piscatorial protest. The good fishing is restricted to a few hours during the warmest part of the afternoon and is often best with small nymphs like the Brassie or Pheasant Tail Nymph.

Spring is a time for an angler to be aware of water temperature. Early in this period, when it's very cold—below 45 degrees F—the fish are reluctant to move far to pick up food. They need to eat, but they eat less, and less often, because their slowed metabolism makes the food last longer. They also take holding positions in slower current than they do in summer. I often find the best fish at the heads of the pools or in pockets amid the faster water through the summer. In the cold water of spring, they're positioned a little farther downstream, near the middle or deepest parts of the pools. Successful fly fishing at this time of year is largely a matter of stubborn persistence. Because the fish won't move very far for food, you must take the food—or the imitation thereof—to the fish. The universal fly-fishing rule is to make it easy for the fish to take your fly, but it's even more important in times of cold water. Nymphs and streamers must be fished near the bottom, and this requires plenty of tinkering with your terminal tackle. Adding and removing weight, adjusting the position of the strike indicator, changing from a floating to a sinking line are all part of the ritual of prerunoff fly fishing. Some people can't be bothered with all this tinkering; they're the ones who don't catch many fish.

In the last weeks prior to runoff on freestone streams, the water warms, more insects hatch, and the fish begin to spread out through the stream, creating more possibilities for dry-fly fishing. The first caddisflies of the year, called the Mother's Day caddis on the Yellowstone and other rivers, arrive in swarms, accompanied on many waters by western march brown mayflies. Some streams, like the Bitterroot in western Montana, have good hatches of Skwala stoneflies.

In the time leading up to runoff, rainbows and cutthroats spawn in the gravelly tailouts of the pools. It's important to recognize the nests, or redds, that fish build for spawning, and avoid wading in or around them. A redd can be identified quite easily if you know what to look for. It appears as an oval- or teardrop-shaped area of gravel where the fish have dug a shallow depression. The gravel in the redd is cleaner and paler in color than the surrounding gravel. Redds can be anywhere from a couple feet to more than ten feet long.

To fly fishers, spring seems to have been designed as a way to break us in, to ease slowly into the main event, much as preseason games do for baseball players and fans. We probably aren't ready for the serious stuff yet, but we're keen to get to the water, and if the fishing regulations say it's OK to fish, we usually do, even if at the end of the day we ask ourselves why we insisted on starting so early in the year.

The spring fishing on western freestone trout streams generally comes to a rather sudden halt with the arrival of runoff. Spring runoff is the most traumatic event of the year for a freestone trout stream. The basic principle of spring runoff is simple: When the weather warms up in spring, the snow in the mountains melts and drains into the rivers. The rivers rise and become discolored until the majority of the snowmelt in the mountains is complete. The details of the mechanics of spring runoff, however, are complex. How long runoff lasts, when it begins, and how severe it is are dependent on many factors and are influenced by differing conditions in different parts of the watershed. Heavy rain in the headwaters of one small tributary, for instance, can bring runoff sooner from that area of the drainage. If the weather is cool and dry, there might be a long, gentle runoff that anglers can fish right through. Or if spring brings both hot weather and precipitation, runoff might be brief but heavy. Predicting the timing and severity of spring runoff is a touchy business, for Mother Nature is notoriously contrary, especially near the Rocky Mountains. So even when things look like they should be straightforward, they might not turn out that way.

There is frequent wintertime debate in fly shops over the length and severity of the upcoming runoff, and the prognostications vary widely. When I was a young fly fisher with a summer job in such a shop, my boss had a pragmatic view of these things. When I said one day that I didn't think runoff would amount to much, he pointed toward the white western mountains and said, "See all that snow out there? Every bit of it has to come under the Center Street Bridge."

A full-scale runoff in a big western river is an impressive event. It is a confirmation of the Jekyll and Hyde personality of western rivers. Such a stream in late summer is exuberant but charming; enthusiastic yet gracious—the Mary Tyler Moore of flowing water. The same river in spring spate is chocolate brown, carrying grass, branches, and logs, and producing the roar of churning current and the low groan of grinding gravel. This river is dangerous and snarly—the Hulk Hogan of trout streams.

From our viewpoint beside and above the water, it's easy to presume that spring runoff is a stressful time for the fish in a river. Visibility is next to nothing, and the velocity and strength of the current increase greatly, requiring more effort for the fish to swim against it. Yet in many streams, fish seem to come out of spring runoff in great physical condition. Unless they've spawned, the fish are often fat and feisty after a week or two of high, dirty water.

So perhaps runoff might not be so bad for a trout. It would be bad if they had to stay in the heavy current all the time, but the fish are not required to stay put, and in heavy runoff, they move to the edges of the stream, even if those edges are not where they normally would be. The stream may now flow through the willows and grass that grow along the top of the normal streambanks. But it matters not where the edges are, the current is slower there, and trout can find the relief they need. Trout are also equipped to locate food with senses other than sight. They can track it down by smell, which is an adaptation that's particularly useful at this time of year. During runoff, there is plenty of "junk" drifting with the current. Some of this junk is edible—worms, beetles, ants, mice, and more that are washed in off the banks and are carried by the current.

Perhaps Mother Nature had runoff trout in mind when she created one of the most spectacular entomological events of the trout stream season— the salmon fly hatch. Giant stonefly nymphs, nicknamed salmon flies, migrate to the banks of fast, rocky freestone streams each spring to emerge as adult flies. While this is an impressive display, with thousands of nymphs arriving at the shore at the same time, it is often the most frustrating event of the season for anglers. Why? Because the salmon fly hatch often coincides with spring runoff and dirty water, making fishing nearly impossible. But the trout make out fine. Maybe it's not coincidence that the biggest nymphs in the stream become most readily available at a time when the trout need some help finding food. And even though they can't find them by sight, they do find them.

So while runoff can be a traumatic time in the life of a trout stream, in the big picture it has an important role to play. It cleans out the streambed, exposing gravel bars, removing silt, and allowing sunlight to penetrate farther into the streambed. It carves new channels, digs new holes, and promotes the process of renewal that is critical to the life of a freestone stream.

The next significant change on freestone streams is the recession of runoff. On many western freestone streams, this signals the end of training camp and the beginning of the games that count. The dominant color along the stream is now green rather than brown, and the scuddy gray clouds of the spring sky have been replaced by tall cumulus columns that mature into thunderboomers in the warm evenings. The tall cottonwoods in the river bottoms begin to drop their fluff, and the wild roses bloom in the ditches along gravel roads.

After runoff, good fishing returns sooner than many anglers think. Once the water has cleared to the point of having two feet of visibility, it is ready to be fished again. On some of the larger western rivers, the biggest fish of the year are taken on streamers and big stonefly nymphs when the water is still a little high and a little colored from the dregs of runoff. The fish seem bold and are attracted to bold flies and bold methods. One of my favorite early-summer flies is a flamboyant pattern called the Bitch Creek Nymph. It's a big yellow-and-black contraption, the kind of fly nonanglers think is supposed to imitate a bumblebee, and has attention-getting white rubber legs wiggling about at both ends. In the fast, cloudy water of receding runoff, trout—even the supposedly shy brown trout—can't get enough of a #4 Bitch Creek that's bouncing and flouncing along the bottom. Later in the summer, when the water is lower, clearer, and warmer, trout flee in terror from a fly this gaudy. I like to get my licks in early, though, because I know these same fish will get the best of me before the year is over.

Through this postrunoff period, the water in the freestone rivers continues to recede, warm, and clear. Weed growth appears in the richer streams, bug life gets busy, and fishing is good with a variety of methods. On many streams, the best hatches of the season are crammed into a six- or eight-week period in early summer. Pale morning dun mayflies, western green drakes, brown drakes, salmon flies, golden stoneflies, and caddisflies all take their turn in the spotlight of early summer. The hatch-matching scholars are in their glory, and even the pragmatic types who scoff at such trifling create fishing stories of their own with streamers and nymphs. The days are longer, and the productive fishing time is longer as well. In spring the fishing often shuts down in late afternoon, but by early summer the water is warm enough that good activity continues well into the evening and beyond. Water conditions on freestone streams can be affected by rain or severe showers, but early summer is generally a time when the differences between freestoners, tailwaters, and spring creeks are less apparent. On all waters, all systems are go.

In the West, there have long been farming towns, railroad towns, and tourist towns. And now you can add to the list the new category of trout towns. Anywhere else, these would be typical small towns with one grocery store, one gas station, two churches, and six bars. But when there's a high-profile trout river or two nearby, you can add a few fly shops to the list of businesses, and you can begin to see fly-fishing culture affect the town's personality. A wader-clad housewife pushing a shopping cart through the aisles of a grocery store doesn't even draw a second glance in places like Dillon, Montana, or Basalt, Colorado. Fly shops are important parts of the economy in trout towns, and the shopkeepers work long hours and stay busy updating their Internet fishing reports and hatch hotlines; selling waders, fly floatant, and fly lines; guiding anglers; renting driftboats; shuttling SUVs; and tying more of this year's hot fly patterns. In short, they're making their hay while the sun is shining.

Western summer evenings are long, and bleary-eyed anglers gather in small cafés the mornings after to commiserate over strong coffee. They don't gather early, though, for the best fishing, especially during caddis and brown drake mayfly hatches, lasts until and beyond sunset. In the higher latitudes of Alberta and Montana, there is enough light for old eyes to change small flies at 10:00 P.M. Squinting into the pale western sky to find an Elk Hair Caddis riding the last bit of silver reflection is a long-standing tradition on trout streams on the east slopes of the Rockies.

By August, water levels are usually low and clear, the rush and anxiety of early season is over, and western fly fishing takes on a sense of stability. The early hatches, like brown drakes and salmon flies, have come and gone, and while they provide some of the best fishing of the year, they are difficult to predict and meet successfully. By late summer, the remaining hatches and the fishing to them, if not entirely predictable, are at least less changeable.

The arrival of summer's core is announced by the first buzzing chatter of grasshoppers on a south-facing riverbank. In dry years, hoppers are the most important bug of late summer and are the reason many fly fishers plan their western trips between late July and early September. *Tricorythodes* mayflies and caddis play supporting roles throughout most of the West until the nights begin to freeze hard again in September. These bugs conveniently provide the trout with three square meals each day. The Tricos are important mainly for their early-morning spinner fall. Grasshoppers become active during the warmest part of midday, and the caddis usually arrive after the sun drops behind the hills each evening.

Late summer is the most anticipated time of year for anglers whose passion is high-country cutthroat fishing. On streams like the Snake in Wyoming and the Elk in British Columbia, it seems to take forever to arrive, but when it does, it's time to begin tossing Trudes, Turck's Tarantulas, and Stimulators to the banks from driftboats. Studious hatch matching is only occasionally required on these waters, but late-summer hatches of stoneflies and green drake mayflies help keep the fish focused on the surface.

In September, the days begin to shorten, and almost imperceptibly the sights and smells of western rivers begin to change. The green of summer is joined by tinges of brown on the pastureland and gold on the grain-growing benches above the river breaks. The scent of the wolf willow is long gone, replaced by the dry, acrid aroma of August. Evening fishing is now over by the civilized time of 8:00 P.M. Somewhere in a snarly draw that climbs out of the river valley, a willow has turned the color of blood, underscoring the inevitability of what is to come.

I respectfully submit that Mother Nature made an error when she gave the West so much winter and so little autumn. I'd happily trade all of January or even April for just a couple additional weeks of October. Some people see autumn as a sad and bittersweet season because it is a time of ever-approaching endings. But I see it as the focal point of the cycle that defines western life. Autumn is the centerpiece of nature's big production, and for art as well as fishing, the climax occurs just a little closer to the end than we'd prefer.

I like the way trout streams look in autumn. The sun stays low to the horizon, and the rich amber light, prized by photographers and painters, stretches through the whole day. The cloudless October sky becomes an indigo backdrop for fields of sagebrush and limber pines and the first white on the Bighorns and Absarokas.

I like the way trout streams smell in autumn. Some perceive it as the scent of death and decay, as the grass shrivels and the leaves fall, but it's also the scent of harvest, when the air carries the bite of frost and the gentle hint of cut grain.

Autumn on a freestone trout stream is the time when fishing conditions are their most reliable. Poor conditions are not impossible—this is the West, after all—but they are unlikely. Water levels are low, and the stream bottom has accumulated a full season's growth of algae and weeds. The water is very clear, and the frosty nights are beginning to take the water temperature down. Fall on a trout stream is a time of transition, when the summer hatches of hoppers, Tricos, and caddisflies fade and are replaced by the second coming of the small blue-winged olives. Dry-fly fishing becomes less complex but no less difficult. The fish have seen it all by the end of September, and their selectometers are cranked to the max. Lower, clearer water means longer, finer leaders, precise casting, and plenty of brief—often too brief—encounters with rising fish.

On some streams, autumn is brown trout season, when dark and mysterious fish move quietly out of lakes and reservoirs into the rivers in preparation for spawning. Fish that would have been the highlight of the summer are considered annoyances now, for there are fish from five to fifteen pounds available to the dedicated. On these streams, small cadres of loyal brown trout hunters dress in fleece and neoprene and start at dawn, working big rods and sculpin imitations in an attempt to find the fish of a lifetime.

One of the best things about fall in the West is the fact that no matter what the weather is like, some type of fishing is generally good. If the usual cold autumn nights bleed into the usual warm, sunny days, expect good fishing with nymphs and grasshoppers. If the day breaks overcast and dreary and stays cold, resist the temptation to stay home instead of going fishing. Cool, overcast weather in September brings the blue-winged olives out in droves and also inspires the fish to feed on them the most heavily. Such a day might be the best dry-fly day of the season. And even if you're not a dry-fly junkie, cold fall days are also the best times to catch those big browns on streamers. So don't be a sissy. Take some gloves.

It's pretty easy to describe a pure freestone stream in a cold winter. Frozen. End of story. But some parts of some streams remain open and fishable through the year. These are portions of rivers where introductions of warmer water keep the water temperature above freezing. The sources of the warmth are usually springs, which contribute water directly to the river or through a tributary, or some type of human activity. The best example of the latter is the Bow River in Alberta, which receives the warm outfall from the city of Calgary's water treatment plant. This keeps five to fifteen miles of the river open and fishable through the winter.

Trout are cold-blooded creatures, and because of it, their lives are ruled by water temperature. The portions of freestone streams that stay open and fishable through winter are still very cold. This water is liquid, but just barely. Temperatures between 33 and 40 degrees F are common. This greatly influences the trout's behavior and, by association, the angler's fishing methods.

Trout are like senior citizens. In summer they're spread all over the countryside, but in winter they congregate in places with the best habitat. To a senior, this means an October migration from Wisconsin or Ohio to Florida or Arizona; to a trout, it means a move from the pockets and riffles into the slow, deep pools sometime in early winter. On big rivers, these winter pools might be four to six feet deep or deeper. On smaller streams, they might be two to three feet deep.

The bad news about fishing freestone streams in winter is that the trout are sluggish and don't feed aggressively, and consequently, you must fish slowly and thoroughly. The good news is that when you find one trout, you'll probably find a bunch of them.

In water this cold, it makes sense to fish with sunken flies. There may be midges hatching on the warmer days, but rising fish in such conditions will be a pleasant surprise rather than something to plan on. Streamers should be fished on sinking or sinking-tip lines with the down-and-across method and a slow retrieve. Nymphs can be fished with any method that gets the fly to the bottom of the stream. A trout in cold water will not chase its food. It will take a fly if it's easy to do so. Successful winter anglers pay particular attention to the job of getting the fly to the bottom and keeping it there. There is no penalty for fishing deep, but there is a severe one for not fishing deep enough.

Good winter fly patterns on freestone streams are the Beadhead Flashback Pheasant Tail Nymph, San Juan Worm, Brassie, Bow River Bugger, and Gartside Leech.

It's important to dress suitably in winter. Neoprene waders have long been the preferred choice of winter anglers, but many are finding that breathable waders worn over good heavy fleece or pile pants are equally comfortable in cold conditions. It's wise to wear multiple layers of good-quality outerwear so you can adjust your insulation as the weather changes through the day.

I don't fish in winter unless the air temperature is above 40 degrees F. This is partly because I'm becoming an old fud and partly because I find it annoying to have to chip the ice out of my rod guides every few minutes. But even on pleasant winter days when old fuds make it to the river, gloves are still usually necessary. The three best choices are fingerless fleece, fingerless wool, and full neoprene. Neoprene offers the most insulation but provides the least dexterity for changing flies.

Wading safety becomes a critical issue in winter. It's never fun to fall down in the water and get wet, but what might be a minor annoyance in July can be big trouble if it happens in February. The best advice I can offer is to suggest that you fish with a friend so you can keep an eye on each other, and that you be very conservative in your wading. When you're out a bit too deep and your grip on the stream bottom gets a bit too tenuous, listen to that little voice in the back of your head. You know, the one that says, "I don't like this . . ."

Carry a thermos of coffee and a waterproof container of matches in your vest if you're fishing in the winter. If you get wet, it usually makes more sense to build a fire and warm up than to walk back to the car, unless the car is close at hand.

For me the greatest attraction of winter fly fishing is not simply the fact that I can occasionally catch a couple fish. Instead, it is the opportunity to see the "other side" of a trout stream. It's like getting a backstage pass at a concert or going for the first time to the home of someone you work with. There's an interesting mix of surprise and revelation. A winter visit helps me gain a better understanding of these things we call trout streams.

SPRING CREEK SEASONS

It's hard to say just when spring begins on a spring creek. We can't define it as the time when the ice goes out, because on most spring creeks there won't be any ice to go out. We can't quite say it starts with the first insect hatches, because some insects will hatch every day of the year. You can't tie it to water reaching a certain temperature, because the water comes out of the ground at the same temperature in January as it does in August.

OK, so maybe it's best to trace spring creek seasons by the arrival and departure of certain mayflies. In this case, you could say spring starts with the first of these, which are usually a species of *Baetis* that shows up as early as February or March.

Confirming the arrival of spring is the arrival of anglers suffering from cabin fever. I've spent many pleasant March and April mornings wandering around Montana fly shops, drinking coffee with companions, waiting for the air to warm up to the point where fishing seemed possible. We knew that the trout were ready, but we had to get ourselves psyched for it first.

The fishing at this time of year can be very good on spring creeks, especially if you're used to the long, slow spring seasons that are the norm on freestone water. On spring creeks, there are often good midge hatches throughout the day and short periods of *Baetis* activity in midday. Some streams, like DePuys Spring Creek, have an occasional early hatch of caddisflies. These hatches can all bring fish to the surface to feed. And when the fish aren't rising, imitations of *Baetis* nymphs, midge larvae, and scuds are good choices. Popular spring creek nymphs are the Pheasant Tail and its variations and the Brassie. Other good flies are small egg imitations and small streamers like the Spring Creek Bugger. Spring creeks are some of the most challenging of trout streams, and though they are still technical and demanding in springtime, the fish are usually a bit more cooperative before they've faced the onslaught of anglers later in the year.

It's probably reasonable to say that spring creek summer begins with the pale morning dun hatch. This is an important insect on most western streams of all types, and many anglers plan their fishing trips to correspond with this hatch. Angling pressure is heavy on the popular spring creeks through the summer, and the fish become a little tougher to fool each day.

And if the fishing isn't tricky enough with size 16 Pale Morning Duns, in late summer many spring creeks get blizzard hatches of the tiny, white-winged, black-bodied *Tricorythodes* mayflies. These are even smaller bugs, requiring imitations from #20 to #26. Trico duns emerge through the night and molt into spinners that mate and lay eggs early the next morning. These insects are very abundant, and a common sight on good Trico streams is an early-morning swarm of spinners that drifts over the water like smoke. The spent flies fall to the water, and the fish hold just beneath the surface and bob up and down like pistons, taking the spinners in greedy gulps.

Summer is also a good time for terrestrial fly patterns on spring creeks. Beetles, ants, and grasshoppers are important fish food in the warm part of the year.

Throughout the Rockies, a sure sign of fall's imminence is when the first cottonwood trees begin to turn yellow in the river bottoms. On spring creeks it's the return of the *Baetis* mayflies that marks the turning of a season. These flies are joined by hatches of back swimmers and water boatmen in the quiet parts of spring creeks in autumn. Later yet, the brown trout begin to darken toward spawning, the evenings get cool, and fresh snow appears overnight on the mountains. The fishing slows on freestone streams, but it doesn't on spring creeks. The midges and *Baetis* continue to hatch, and trout continue to rise. Spring creeks extend our fishing season at both ends of the summer.

Perhaps it's not far from true to say that on a spring creek the year passes this way: spring, summer, fall, spring. The great contrast in seasons that defines human life in the West is softened and blurred in a spring creek to the point where winter seems almost absent—at least, in the watery world of the trout. Because we're tracing the seasons via mayflies, perhaps winter on a spring creek should be defined as the time when no mayflies are hatching. This is often quite a short window, a period between December and February, but even then there is good fishing. Nymphing with midge larva and scud patterns is consistently productive, and many days have midge hatches and a chance of rising fish through the middle of the day. The stillwater portions of the streams can be especially good during midge hatches. The weather may be cold, but under the water, life proceeds quite happily in those remarkable streams called spring creeks.

TAILWATER SEASONS

Because tailwaters have stable flows and temperatures, their seasons are much like those of spring creeks. And as on spring creeks, the first mayflies of the year are usually a species of *Baetis* that anglers have long called blue-winged olives. These flies typically join hatches of midges that occur through the winter. The spring blue-winged olive hatch is an afternoon event that comes on best on days that are overcast, blustery, and sometimes damp—the kind of days that come along frequently in the Rocky Mountain West in March and April.

Most tailwater streams get little or no spring runoff, because the flow of water is controlled by the dam. The river above the dam will be subject to runoff, but the dirty water settles in the reservoir and clears before being released to the river downstream. Some tailwaters have freestone tributaries that join the river below the dam, and if large enough, these can dirty the main river. But typically tailwaters fish well when most freestone streams in the area are high and dirty from full-bore runoff.

Both freestone streams and tailwaters respond to summer weather with increases in water temperature. But the water close to the dam on a tailwater stays cold through the summer, and consequently, hatches like pale morning duns and caddisflies sometimes begin later on tailwaters than on other types of streams.

About the same time these insects begin to hatch comes a noticeable increase in weed growth on the bottom of the stream. Three factors are responsible for this: The water of tailwater streams is rich in nutrients, which stimulate plant growth; the longer days of summer provide more sunlight to the plants; and there is no spring runoff to interrupt the growth of weeds on tailwaters, as there is on freestone rivers. The weeds continue to grow through the summer and become a significant factor in the fishing as the season goes on. Some streams, like the Bighorn and Missouri, occasionally have plant growth heavy enough to become a nuisance for anglers. The problem is not so much with the plants that stay connected to the stream bottom, as it is with those that drift in the current and hang up on lines, leaders, and flies. The severity of the problem corresponds to releases of water from the dams. When the water level rises even a small amount, weeds are dislodged from the river bottom and begin to drift in the current. The drifting weeds cause more problems for sunken flies than for dry flies. Streamers are worst, because they are usually fished against the current, which allows weeds to drift into the line or leader and slide down to the fly. During heavy periods of drifting weeds, experienced tailwater anglers fish both streamers and nymphs with the current rather than against it, and sometimes use flies tied with monofilament or wire weed guards.

Autumn on a tailwater trout stream is no less attractive than on any other type of stream. The season is marked by the turning of the trees and bushes in the river bottom and the autumn encore performance of the *Baetis* mayflies. These bugs follow the same rules as on other types of streams, hatching heaviest on the cold, blustery fall days that make some anglers change their plans. The fishing is much like autumn fishing on spring creeks. The fish that were dunces in the spring are scholars now, and fishermen must do everything right to fool them.

Winter on a tailwater stream is much like winter on a spring creek. There is usually open water, at least for a few miles downstream of the dam. Nymph fishing with small flies is the bread-and-butter method, as the fish's winter food consists primarily of small insects. The benefit of the tailwater situation is perhaps most apparent in winter. While January water temperatures on freestone streams can hover just above the freezing mark, the temperature immediately below the dam on a tailwater will be the same as it was in the summer—probably somewhere between 40 and 50 degrees F. This is a difference that makes a difference. Midges hatch most days of the winter, and on the best tailwaters, dry-fly fishing is a possibility at any time. It's entirely possible for the water to be warmer than the air, and in a cold winter, a tailwater stream may be at its warmest right near the dam and may get cooler as it moves farther from its "source" into the grip of a Rocky Mountain winter.

CHAPTER 9

Western Hatches
and Other Trout Food

A nd now the author will attempt to do the impossible: to provide read-
ers with useable information about important insect hatches on trout
streams from British Columbia to New Mexico, in three simple charts. I'm
reminded of the disclaimers pharmaceutical companies must now include in
their TV and radio advertisements. Along with telling us how great the drug
is and how much it will improve our lives, it seems they must also tell us that
the product might not work for everybody, and that in fact there are a number of possible side effects, including bleeding, coughing, liver trouble,
blurred vision, diabetes, genital defects, heart failure, itchy teeth. These ads
hardly inspire confidence in the product being promoted, and the drug
companies must wonder whether it's worth advertising this way at all. I
know how they feel. I've got about a thousand words planned to introduce
the hatch charts that appear later in this chapter, and I'll probably use half
of them to tell you that those charts aren't going to help you as much as
you think they are. There are so many factors influencing the hatch dates
that we have nearly as many rule-breakers as rule-followers. Nevertheless, it
seems equally impossible not to address in some manner the topic of which
bugs hatch when and where, and what you can tie on your leader to imitate them.

I have chosen three geographic regions in order to reflect the general
differences in timing of the hatches. The hatches on streams in the coastal
region generally occur earlier than the same hatches on rivers farther inland
near the Rockies. This is because of the milder coastal weather and lower
elevation. The trout streams along both slopes of the Rocky Mountains have
many of the same hatches, but with different timing because of latitude and
altitude. Generally, the farther north or the farther up (the higher in elevation) the stream is, the later the hatches occur.

166

You'll notice that the hatching periods for most insects in the charts are quite long. This is done to reflect the usual range of these hatch periods within the geographic zone and is unlikely to reflect the actual hatching period of any one bug on any one stream. Please view these hatch charts as starting points only—as a way to get you into the ballpark. Remember that everything about western fly fishing is variable, and the term applies as much to insect hatches as anything else.

It's more difficult to predict hatches on freestone streams than on other types of streams because they are influenced by so many factors. Along with altitude and latitude, local conditions have a big impact on hatch dates. A long, cold winter means colder water temperatures and later hatches in the spring. An unusually heavy spring runoff can delay hatches, whereas a modest runoff can bring the bugs out early. The weather through the summer can also influence the hatches. Unusually cold weather can delay things, and hot weather can bring on activity early.

As an example of the variability of bug hatches in the West, let me tell you about western green drakes. These are very important insects wherever they occur, because they are large and hatch quite heavily. Through most of the northern Rocky Mountain region, the hatch generally begins sometime between early June and late July and generally lasts two or three weeks. I said "generally," and I said it twice. On the lower-elevation brown trout streams two hours northwest of my home, the green drakes follow those rules very nicely. But on some high-country cutthroat streams two hours southwest of my home, I've fished good green drake hatches as early as mid-June and as late as early September.

Hatch times are more consistent from year to year on spring creeks and tailwaters because of their stable flows and steady temperatures, but a hatch may occur earlier or later on a tailwater stream than it does on nearby freestone streams.

If you're new to the sport of "hatch chasing," or even if you're not, there is an interesting tool you can use to help predict the insect hatches. It's the phenological approach, and though it has been used by astute outdoor people for generations, one of the first fly fishers to write about it was Bob Scammell in *The Phenological Fly*. Phenology is "the study of the timing of events that happen every year in the lives of plants and animals." As it applies to trout streams, it means noticing which wildflowers and plants are in bloom while certain aquatic insects are hatching. For example, on many western streams, the wolf willow blooms around the same time that the golden stoneflies hatch. This association has become strong enough for me that the first time the pungent odor of the flowering wolf willow reaches my nostrils, it evokes images of late spring on a trout stream, with backlit stoneflies fluttering down from spruce trees. Though the correlations aren't the same on all streams, the matchups between flower and bug on any one stream will be consistent from year to year. By keeping track of this, you'll find you can use the plants to tell you what stage of the yearly cycle the trout stream is in. This phenological approach is of most benefit on streams you fish regularly and frequently over a period of years. It is a great way to become more intimate with the ecosystem on your home water.

The hatch charts in this chapter contain general information on hatches throughout the West. Specifics about hatches on individual streams are best taken from books dedicated to particular streams or areas, like *Deschutes,* by Dave Hughes, or *The Yellowstone Fly Fishing Guide,* by Craig Matthews, and from magazine articles or fly shops near the rivers.

Specific information on particular western insects can be gathered from a number of good books, including *Mayflies,* by Malcolm Knopp and Robert Cormier; *Caddisflies,* by Gary LaFontaine; and *Western Hatches,* by Dave Hughes and Rick Hafele.

Where possible, the insects in the hatch charts are identified by both common anglers' names and more formal Latin names, even though few anglers and even fewer trout are bilingual.

Not included in these charts are a number of nonbugs that are important fish food on certain streams. Minnows, leeches, and scuds are in this category, as is the aquatic worm. The imitation of the latter is usually referred to as the San Juan Worm, named after the New Mexico tailwater where it is a popular pattern. Another example is the crayfish, which is common and important on some western streams, such as the Missouri River, but completely absent from entire drainages in other parts of the West.

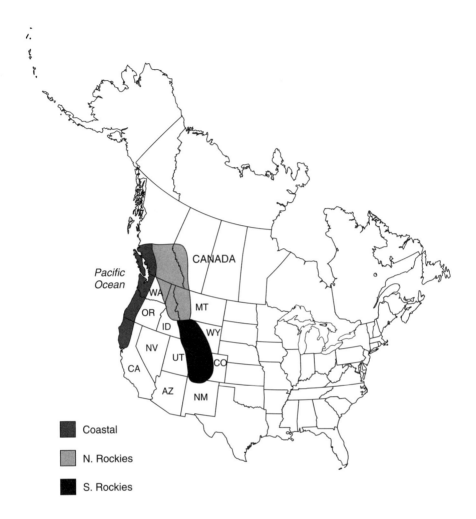

Coastal

N. Rockies

S. Rockies

COASTAL REGION HATCH CHART

Insect	Hatch Period	Nymph (Larva)
MAYFLIES		
BLUE-WINGED OLIVE *(Baetis)*	All Year	Pheasant Tail Nymph (natural or olive) **A. P. Nymph (black/brown)** Sizes 16–20
WESTERN MARCH BROWN *(Rhithrogena)*	March 1–May 30	Pheasant Tail Nymph **A. P. Nymph (black/brown)** Sizes 12, 14
GRAY DRAKE *(Siphlonurus)*	May 1–September 30	Gold-Ribbed Hare's Ear **A. P. Nymph (black/gray)** Sizes 8, 10
PALE MORNING DUN *(Ephemerella infrequens* and *inermis)*	May 1–October 15	Pheasant Tail Nymph **Beadhead Flashback Pheasant Tail** **A. P. Nymph (black/brown)** Sizes 16, 18
CALLIBAETIS	May 1–October 15	Pheasant Tail Nymph Gold-Ribbed Hare's Ear Sizes 14, 16
HEXAGENIA	June 1–July 15	**A. P. Nymph (black/cream)** Gold-Ribbed Hare's Ear Size 8
WESTERN GREEN DRAKE *(Drunella grandis)*	June 1–July 30	Pheasant Tail Nymph (olive) **A. P. Nymph (black/olive)** Sizes 8, 10

• Highlighted patterns are featured in chapter 10.
• First color is of wings or wing case; second color is of body.

Emerger (Pupa)	Dun (Adult)	Spinner (Spent Adult)
Floating Nymph (gray/brown) RS2 Sizes 16–20	Adams **R. S. Quad (gray/olive)** **Parachute (gray/olive)** Sizes 16–20	**Hen Spinner (white/brown)** Sizes 16–20
Floating Nymph (gray/brown) Partridge and Brown Sizes 12, 14	Adams **R. S. Quad (gray/brown)** Sizes 12, 14	**Hen Spinner (white/brown)** Sizes 12, 14
Floating Nymph (gray/gray) Sizes 8, 10	**Parachute (gray/gray)** **R. S. Quad (gray/gray)** Adams Sizes 8, 10	**Hen Spinner (white/gray)** Sizes 8, 10
Floating Nymph (gray/brown) Partridge and Yellow Sizes 16, 18	**R. S. Quad (gray/pale olive)** **Parachute (gray/pale olive)** Sizes 16, 18	**Hen Spinner (white/rust)** Sizes 16, 18
Floating Nymph (gray/gray) Sizes 14, 16	**Parachute (gray/gray)** Adams Sizes 14, 16	**Hen Spinner (white/gray)** Sizes 14, 16
Floating Nymph (gray/cream) Size 8	Cream Paradrake **R. S. Quad (gray/cream)** Size 8	**Hen Spinner (white/cream)** Size 8
Floating Nymph (gray/olive) Sizes 8, 10	**R. S. Quad (gray/olive)** Olive Paradrake Sizes 8, 10	**Hen Spinner (white/olive)** Sizes 8, 10

	Insect	Hatch Period	Nymph (Larva)
M A Y F L I E S	SMALL WESTERN GREEN DRAKE (*Drunella flavilinea*)	June 1–August 15	Pheasant Tail Nymph (olive) **A. P. Nymph (black/olive)** Sizes 12, 14
	BROWN DRAKE (*Ephemera simulans*)	June 1–July 30	**A. P. Nymph (black/brown)** Gold-Ribbed Hare's Ear Sizes 8, 10
	TRICO (*Tricorythodes*)	July 1–October 15	**A. P. Nymph (black/black)** Sizes 18–22
C A D D I S F L I E S	MOTHER'S DAY CADDIS (*Brachycentrus*)	May1–June 30	Gold-Ribbed Hare's Ear **Beadhead Flashback Pheasant Tail** Sizes 12, 14
	SUMMER CADDIS (*Rhyacophila, Hydropsyche,* and others)	May 1–August 30	Gold-Ribbed Hare's Ear Peeking Caddis Sizes 14–18
	FALL CADDIS (*Dicosmoecus*)	September 1– October 30	Gold-Ribbed Hare's Ear Sizes 6, 8
S T O N E F L I E S	SKWALA	March 1–April 15	**A. P. Nymph (black/brown)** Gold-Ribbed Hare's Ear Sizes 8, 10
	SALMON FLY (*Pteronarcys*)	May 1–July 30	**A. P. Nymph (black/black)** Kaufmann's Stone Sizes 4, 6
	GOLDEN STONE (*Acroneuria*)	May 1–June 15	**A. P. Nymph (black/brown)** Yellow Stone Sizes 4–8

Emerger (Pupa)	Dun (Adult)	Spinner (Spent Adult)
Floating Nymph (gray/olive) Sizes 12, 14	R. S. Quad (gray/olive) Parachute (gray/olive) Sizes 12, 14	Hen Spinner (white/olive) Sizes 12, 14
Floating Nymph (brown/brown) Partridge and Brown Sizes 8, 10	R. S. Quad (brown/yellow) Brown Paradrake Sizes 8, 10	Hen Spinner (white/tan) Sizes 8, 10
Floating Nymph (white/black) Sizes 18–22	Parachute (white/black) Trico Thorax Sizes 18–22	Hen Spinner (white/black) Poly-Winged Spinner Sizes 18–22
LaFontaine Emergent Sparkle Pupa (brown) Sizes 12, 14	Glenn's CDC Caddis (gray/brown) Elk Hair Caddis Sizes 12, 14	Spent Partridge Caddis (brown/brown) Partridge and Brown Sizes 12, 14
LaFontaine Emergent Sparkle Pupa Partridge and Orange Sizes 14–18	Glenn's CDC Caddis (gray/brown) Elk Hair Caddis Sizes 14–18	Spent Partridge Caddis (brown/brown) Partridge and Orange Partridge and Brown Sizes 14–18
	Orange Stimulator Sizes 6, 8 Sizes 6, 8	Spent Partridge Caddis (brown/orange)
	Improved Stone (brown/brown) Brown Stimulator Sizes 8, 10	
	Orange Stimulator Improved Stone (brown/orange) Sizes 4, 6	
	Yellow Stimulator Improved Stone (tan/yellow) Sizes 4–8	

Insect	Hatch Period	Nymph (Larva)
STONEFLIES YELLOW SALLY *(Isosperla)*	May 1–July 1	**A. P. Nymph (black/yellow)** Yellow Stone Sizes 12–16
OTHERS MIDGES	All Year	**Brassie** **San Juan Worm** Sizes 18–22
GRASSHOPPERS	June 15–October 15	

	Yellow Stimulator Sizes 12–16	
CDC Midge Emerger **Griffith's Gnat** Sizes 18–22	Griffith's Gnat Adams Sizes 18–22	
	Parachute Hopper **Turck's Tarantula** Dave's Hopper Sizes 6–14	

NORTHERN ROCKIES
HATCH CHART

Insect	Hatch Period	Nymph (Larva)

MAYFLIES

Insect	Hatch Period	Nymph (Larva)
BLUE-WINGED OLIVE *(Baetis)*	March–November	Pheasant Tail Nymph (natural or olive) **A. P. Nymph (black/brown)** Sizes 16–20
WESTERN MARCH BROWN *(Rhithrogena)*	April 15–May 30	Pheasant Tail Nymph **A. P. Nymph (black/brown)** Sizes 12, 14
PALE MORNING DUN *(Ephemerella infrequens* and *inermis)*	June 1–August 15	Pheasant Tail Nymph **Beadhead Flashback Pheasant Tail Nymph** **A. P. Nymph (black/brown)** Sizes 16, 18
WESTERN GREEN DRAKE *(Drunella grandis)*	June 1–July 30	Pheasant Tail Nymph (olive) **A. P. Nymph (black/olive)** Sizes 8, 10
SMALL WESTERN GREEN DRAKE *(Drunella flavilinea)*	July 1–September 15	Pheasant Tail Nymph (olive) **A. P. Nymph (black/olive)** Sizes 12, 14
BROWN DRAKE *(Ephemera simulans)*	June 1–July 30	**A. P. Nymph (black/brown)** Gold-Ribbed Hare's Ear Sizes 8, 10
TRICO *(Tricorythodes)*	July 15–October 15	**A. P. Nymph (black/black)** Sizes 18–22

• Highlighted patterns are featured in chapter 10.
• First color is of wings or wing case; second color is of body.

Emerger (Pupa)	Dun (Adult)	Spinner (Spent Adult)
Floating Nymph **(gray/brown)** RS2 Sizes 16–20	Adams **R. S. Quad (gray/olive)** **Parachute (gray/olive)** Sizes 16–20	**Hen Spinner** **(white/brown)** Sizes 16–20
Floating Nymph **(gray/brown)** Partridge and Brown Sizes 12, 14	Adams **R. S. Quad (gray/brown)** **Parachute (gray/brown)** Sizes 12, 14	**Hen Spinner** **(white/brown)** Sizes 12, 14
Floating Nymph **(gray/brown)** Partridge and Yellow Sizes 16, 18	**R. S. Quad** **(gray/pale olive)** **Parachute** **(gray/pale olive)** Sizes 16, 18	**Hen Spinner (white/rust)** Sizes 16, 18
Floating Nymph **(gray/olive)** Sizes 8, 10	**R. S. Quad (gray/olive)** Olive Paradrake Sizes 8, 10	**Hen Spinner (white/olive)** Sizes 8, 10
Floating Nymph **(gray/olive)** Sizes 12, 14	**Parachute (gray/olive)** **R. S. Quad (gray/olive)** Sizes 12, 14	**Hen Spinner (white/olive)** Sizes 12, 14
Floating Nymph **(brown/brown)** Partridge and Brown Sizes 8, 10	**R. S. Quad** **(brown/brown)** Brown Paradrake Sizes 8, 10	**Hen Spinner (white/tan)** Sizes 8, 10
Floating Nymph **(white/black)** Sizes 18–22	**Parachute (white/black)** Trico Thorax Sizes 18–22	**Hen Spinner** **(white/black)** Poly-Winged Spinner Sizes 18–22

Insect	Hatch Period	Nymph (Larva)
CADDISFLIES		
MOTHER'S DAY CADDIS *(Brachycentrus)*	May 1–30	Gold-Ribbed Hare's Ear **Beadhead Flashback Pheasant Tail** Sizes 12, 14
SUMMER CADDIS *(Rhyacophila, Hydropsyche,* and others)	June 1–September 30	Gold-Ribbed Hare's Ear Peeking Caddis Sizes 14–18
STONEFLIES		
SKWALA	March 15–May 30	**A.P. Nymph (black/brown)** Gold-Ribbed Hare's Ear Sizes 8, 10
SALMON FLY *(Pteronarcys)*	June 1–July 30	**A. P. Nymph (black/black)** Kaufmann's Stone Sizes 4, 6
GOLDEN STONE *(Acroneuria)*	June 15–August 15	**A. P. Nymph (black/brown)** Yellow Stone Sizes 4, 6, 8
YELLOW SALLY *(Isoperla)*	July 1–August 30	**A. P. Nymph (black/yellow)** Yellow Stone Sizes 12, 14
OTHERS		
MIDGES	All Year	**Brassie San Juan Worm** Sizes 18, 20, 22
GRASSHOPPERS	July 1–October 15	

Emerger (Pupa)	Dun (Adult)	Spinner (Spent Adult)
LaFontaine Emergent Sparkle Pupa (brown) Partridge and Orange Sizes 12, 14	**Glenn's CDC Caddis (gray/brown)** Elk Hair Caddis Sizes 12, 14	**Spent Partridge Caddis (brown/brown)** Partridge and Brown Sizes 12, 14
LaFontaine Emergent Sparkle Pupa (brown) Partridge and Orange Sizes 14–18	**Glenn's CDC Caddis (gray/brown)** Elk Hair Caddis Sizes 14–18	**Spent Partridge Caddis (brown/brown)** Partridge and Orange Partridge and Brown Sizes 14–18
	Improved Stone (brown/brown) Brown Stimulator Sizes 8, 10	
	Orange Stimulator **Improved Stone (brown/orange)** Sizes 4, 6	
	Yellow Stimulator **Improved Stone (tan/yellow)** Sizes 4, 6, 8	
	Yellow Stimulator Sizes 12, 14	
CDC Midge Emerger Griffith's Gnat Sizes 18, 20, 22	**Griffith's Gnat** Adams Sizes 18, 20, 22	
	Parachute Hopper Turck's Tarantula Dave's Hopper Sizes 6–14	

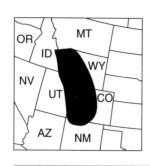

SOUTHERN ROCKIES
HATCH CHART

Insect	Hatch Period	Nymph (Larva)

MAYFLIES

Insect	Hatch Period	Nymph (Larva)
BLUE-WINGED OLIVE *(Baetis)*	January 15–March 31 May 1–June 15 September 15– November 30	Pheasant Tail Nymph (natural or olive) **A. P. Nymph (black/brown)** Sizes 16–20
BROWN DRAKE *(Ephemera simulans)*	May 1–July 15	**A. P. Nymph (black/brown)** Gold-Ribbed Hare's Ear Sizes 8, 10
PALE MORNING DUN *(Ephemerella infrequens* and *inermis)*	June 15–August 30	Pheasant Tail Nymph **Beadhead Flashback** **Pheasant Tail** **A. P. Nymph (black/brown)** Sizes 16, 18
WESTERN GREEN DRAKE *(Drunella grandis)*	June 15–July 30	Pheasant Tail Nymph (olive) **A. P. Nymph (black/olive)** Sizes 8, 10
SMALL WESTERN GREEN DRAKE *(Drunella flavilinea)*	July 1–October 1	Pheasant Tail Nymph (olive) **A. P. Nymph (black/olive)** Sizes 12, 14
WESTERN MARCH BROWN *(Rhithrogena)*	July 15–September 1	Pheasant Tail Nymph **A. P. Nymph (black/brown)** Sizes 12, 14
TRICO *(Tricorythodes)*	August 15–October 1	**A. P. Nymph (black/black)** Sizes 18–22

• Highlighted patterns are featured in chapter 10.
• First color is of wings or wing case; second color is of body.

Emerger (Pupa)	Dun (Adult)	Spinner (Spent Adult)
Floating Nymph **(gray/brown)** RS2 Sizes 16–20	Adams **R. S. Quad (gray/olive)** **Parachute (gray/olive)** Sizes 16–20	**Hen Spinner** **(white/brown)** Sizes 16–20
Floating Nymph **(brown/brown)** Partridge and Brown Sizes 8, 10	**R. S. Quad (brown/brown)** Brown Paradrake Sizes 8, 10	**Hen Spinner (white/tan)** Sizes 8, 10
Floating Nymph **(gray/brown)** Partridge and Yellow Sizes 16, 18	**R. S. Quad** **(gray/pale olive)** **Parachute** **(gray/pale olive)** Sizes 16, 18	**Hen Spinner (white/rust)** Sizes 16, 18
Floating Nymph **(gray/olive)** Sizes 8, 10	**R. S. Quad (gray/olive)** Olive Paradrake Sizes 8, 10	**Hen Spinner (white/olive)** Sizes 8, 10
Floating Nymph **(gray/olive)** Sizes 12, 14	**Parachute (gray/olive)** **R. S. Quad (gray/olive)** Sizes 12, 14	**Hen Spinner (white/olive)** Sizes 12, 14
Floating Nymph **(gray/brown)** Partridge and Brown Sizes 12, 14	Adams **R. S. Quad (gray/brown)** **Parachute (gray/brown)** Sizes 12, 14	**Hen Spinner** **(white/brown)** Sizes 12, 14
Floating Nymph **(white/black)** Sizes 18–22	**Parachute (white/black)** Trico Thorax Sizes 18–22	**Hen Spinner** **(white/black)** Poly-Winged Spinner Sizes 18–22

Insect	Hatch Period	Nymph (Larva)
MAYFLIES GRAY DRAKE *(Siphlonurus)*	August 15–October 30	Gold-Ribbed Hare's Ear **A. P. Nymph (black/gray)** Sizes 8, 10
CADDISFLIES MOTHER'S DAY CADDIS *(Brachycentrus)*	April 15–May 20	Gold-Ribbed Hare's Ear **Beadhead Flashback Pheasant Tail** Sizes 12, 14
SUMMER CADDIS *(Rhyacophila, Hydropsyche,* and others)	April 15–October 30	Gold-Ribbed Hare's Ear Peeking Caddis Sizes 14–18
STONEFLIES SALMON FLY *(Pteronarcys)*	May 15–July 30	**A. P. Nymph (black/black)** Kaufmann's Stone Sizes 4, 6
GOLDEN STONE *(Acroneuria)*	June 1–July 30	**A. P. Nymph (black/brown)** Yellow Stone Sizes 4–8
YELLOW SALLY *(Isoperla)*	July 1–August 30	**A. P. Nymph (black/yellow)** Yellow Stone Sizes 12, 14

Emerger (Pupa)	Dun (Adult)	Spinner (Spent Adult)
Floating Nymph (gray/gray) Sizes 8, 10	**Parachute (gray/gray)** **R. S. Quad (gray/gray)** Adams Sizes 8, 10	**Hen Spinner (white/gray)** Sizes 8, 10
LaFontaine Emergent Sparkle Pupa (brown) Partridge and Orange Sizes 12, 14	**Glenn's CDC Caddis (gray/brown)** Elk Hair Caddis Sizes 12, 14	**Spent Partridge Caddis (brown/brown)** Partridge and Brown Sizes 12, 14
LaFontaine Emergent Sparkle Pupa (brown) Partridge and Orange Sizes 14–18	**Glenn's CDC Caddis (gray/brown)** Elk Hair Caddis Sizes 14–18	**Spent Partridge Caddis (brown/brown)** Partridge and Orange Partridge and Brown Sizes 14–18
	Improved Stone (brown/orange) Orange Stimulator Sizes 4, 6	
	Improved Stone (tan/yellow) Yellow Stimulator Sizes 4–8	
	Improved Stone (tan/yellow) Yellow Stimulator Sizes 12, 14	

Insect	Hatch Period	Nymph (Larva)
MIDGES	All Year San Juan Worm Sizes 18–22	Brassie Griffith's Gnat Sizes 18–22
GRASSHOPPERS	July 1–October 15	

OTHERS

Emerger (Pupa)	Dun (Adult)	Spinner (Spent Adult)
CDC Midge Emerger Adams Sizes 18–22	Griffith's Gnat	
	Parachute Hopper **Turck's Tarantula** Dave's Hopper Sizes 6–14	

CHAPTER 10

Favorite Western
Fly Patterns

Deciding which patterns to include in a book like this is tricky business. I don't want to show the extreme oddball patterns that nobody will ever find in a fly shop, but neither do I want to show yet again the tried and true standbys like the Adams, Royal Wulff, and Woolly Bugger, the recipes for which are widely available elsewhere. By not including these old gems, I don't mean to imply that they don't work. I've included both old favorites and the patterns listed here in the hatch charts in chapter 9.

The flies whose photographs and recipes appear here have been chosen according to the following criteria: First, they work consistently throughout the West. Second, many are available in western fly shops. Third, they are adaptable, in that with color and size changes, they can imitate a number of species of insects or be used in a variety of situations. Fourth, fly tiers will be able to easily find the materials required to tie them.

You'll notice a lack of formal names for many of the flies. I've included as many "prototype" patterns as possible. For instance, the Parachute dry fly in the photograph is the PMD (Pale Morning Dun) Parachute, and it is identified as such in the photo caption. In the recipe, though, colors are omitted, as they can and should be changed to match the color of the particular mayfly being imitated. The details of size and colors needed to imitate specific insects can be found in the hatch charts in chapter 9.

In this chapter and in the hatch charts in chapter 9, I've adopted the method of color description used by Swisher and Richards in their book *Selective Trout,* wherein the first color is that of the wing or wing case and the second color is that of the body, as in Gray/Olive Hen Spinner.

PARACHUTE
The parachute-style dry fly is a universally successful imitation of a mayfly dun. It lands upright and shows the proper profile to the trout. It's a good pattern in quiet water where fish can look flies over carefully.

Hook:	Mustad 94840 (standard dry-fly hook) or equivalent, sizes 10–22
Tail:	Stiff hackle fibers or Micro Fibetts, color to match wing, tied split
Body:	Fine dry-fly dubbing
Wing:	Single upright post of turkey body feather (sometimes called "turkey flats")
Hackle:	Dun dry-fly hackle, tied parachute-style
Best colors:	Gray/olive; gray/pale olive; gray/brown; gray/tan; white/black

GLENN'S CDC CADDIS
The work of fly tier Glenn Smith (who tied the flies in the photographs), this is a very effective caddis pattern that is also easy to tie. It uses cul-de-canard (CDC) feathers, which float very well until the fly is taken by a trout. Then the fly must be refurbished by blotting it on a piece of tissue and treating it with desiccant floatant. It's a small price to pay for a great fly. This is a good caddis to use after the sun has set, which is when many western streams have their heaviest caddis activity. Surprisingly, black is often the most visible color late in the evening, because it contrasts with the silvery hue of the water.

Hook:	Mustad 94840 or equivalent (standard dry-fly hook), sizes 12–20
Trailing shuck:	A few strands of brown or gray Z-Lon
Body:	Fine dry-fly dubbing
Rib:	Extrafine gold wire
Wing:	Four to six CDC feather tips
Best colors:	Gray/brown; brown/brown; tan/tan; black/black

SPENT PARTRIDGE CADDIS
This pattern, from Idaho's Mike Lawson, is intended to imitate caddisflies that have laid eggs and died, and it does so nicely. In that situation, I fish it without floatant, which allows it to float awash in the film, just the way the natural spent caddis do. But this fly also works very well as an adult caddis when it's treated with floatant to make it sit high in the water.

Hook:	Mustad 94840 or equivalent (standard dry-fly hook), sizes 12–18
Tail:	None
Body:	Peacock herl or fine natural or synthetic dry-fly dubbing
Wing:	Two mottled brown partridge feathers
Thorax:	Peacock herl
Hackle:	Brown and grizzly dry-fly hackle, wrapped through thorax
Best colors:	Tan/brown; brown/brown; brown/orange

TURCK'S TARANTULA

This fly first achieved fame when it was the winning fly in the Jackson Hole One-Fly Contest in 1990. Since then, it has become a standard attractor dry on rivers throughout the West.

Hook:	Mustad 94831 or equivalent (3X long dry-fly hook), sizes 6–10
Tail:	Amherst pheasant tippets
Body:	Tan, brown, or gold hare's ear
Wing:	White calf tail, mixed with a few strands of pearl Krystal Flash
Overwing:	Natural deer hair
Legs:	White or brown rubber legs, tied X-fashion
Head:	Natural deer hair, spun and clipped

IMPROVED STONE

This is a good adult stonefly imitation that can be adapted to represent any species of stonefly by changing color and size.

Hook:	Mustad 94831, Tiemco 200R, or equivalent (curved, long-shank dry-fly hook), sizes 4–14
Tail:	Elk hair, natural or bleached
Body:	Gold, orange, brown, or black Antron or other synthetic dry-fly dubbing
Rear hackle:	Undersize dry-fly hackle, color to match body, palmered through body
Wing:	Elk hair, natural or bleached
Front hackle:	Dry-fly hackle, color to match body
Best colors:	Brown/orange; tan/yellow

PARACHUTE HOPPER

It shouldn't be difficult to see a fly as big as a grasshopper on the water, but in certain light conditions it is. Ed Schroeder's hopper helps solve the problem. Its excellent buoyancy and visibility also make this pattern a good candidate for the "hopper dropper" method, where a small nymph hangs beneath the dry on a short dropper.

Hook:	Mustad 94831 or equivalent (3X long dry-fly hook), sizes 6–12
Tail:	None
Abdomen:	Gold, tan, gray, or yellow Antron dry-fly dubbing
Rib:	Dark brown floss
Wing:	Brown mottled turkey feather, stiffened with Flexament and tied tent-wing-style
Parachute post:	White calf tail
Legs:	Cock ring-necked pheasant tail fibers, knotted
Hackle:	Grizzly, wrapped around parachute post
Thorax:	Antron dry-fly dubbing, color to match abdomen

R. S. QUAD

Roman Scharabun is the creative fly tier who developed the Quad series of flies to imitate emergent mayfly duns. It incorporates four of the most important triggering factors that seem to prompt a fish's acceptance of an imitation: a segmented body, an oversize wing, an enlarged thorax, and a trailing shuck. The fly will work as an attractor but is clearly at its best when trout are keyed in to adult mayflies. It successfully imitates mayflies of all sizes, including the large brown and green drakes.

Hook:	Mustad 94840 or equivalent (standard dry-fly hook) or Tiemco 2487 (curved dry-fly hook), sizes 10–20
Trailing shuck:	Brown, olive, or gray Z-Lon
Abdomen:	Turkey biot, wrapped
Thorax:	Antron dubbing, color to match body
Wing:	Single post of turkey body feather
Hackle:	Dun dry-fly hackle, wrapped parachute-style
Best colors:	Gray/olive; gray/pale olive; gray/brown; gray/tan; black/white

HEN SPINNER

There are a number of variations of this pattern in use today, including A. K. Best's, which uses a quill-bodied abdomen. With size and color changes, the Hen Spinner can be adapted easily to match any mayfly spinner.

Hook:	Mustad 94840 or equivalent (standard dry-fly hook), sizes 10–22
Tail:	Stiff dun hackle fibers or Micro Fibetts, tied split
Body:	Fine dry-fly dubbing
Thorax:	Same as body
Wing:	White, cream, or pale dun hen hackle tips, tied spent
Best colors:	White/rust; white/black; white/olive; white/cream; white/pale olive

FLOATING NYMPH

There are a great number of mayfly emergers available today. This one is effective and adaptable to any mayfly. It represents the nymph suspended at the surface in the first stages of emergence. The body color should match that of the nymph's body, and the wing case should match the color of the adult mayfly's wing.

Hook:	Mustad 94840 or equivalent (standard dry-fly hook), sizes 10–20
Tail:	Stiff dun hackle fibers or Micro Fibetts
Body:	Fine dry-fly dubbing
Wing case:	Ball of Fly Rite or other fine polypropylene dubbing
Hackle:	Dun dry-fly hackle, tied parachute-style around base of wing case
Best colors:	Gray/brown; gray/olive

LAFONTAINE EMERGENT SPARKLE PUPA

The late Gary LaFontaine was one of the true original thinkers in our sport. He wrote many important books, notably *Caddisflies* and *The Dry Fly: New Angles,* and created many succesful fly patterns, including this one. I always thought this fly looked like a little fuzzy blob on the surface of the water, but its effectiveness during caddis emergences has convinced me that real emerging caddis pupae must look like little fuzzy blobs too. Fish eat it.

Hook:	Mustad 94840 or equivalent (standard dry-fly hook), sizes 10–18
Underbody:	Dubbing made of brown, olive, or gray yarn mixed and blended with natural fur
Overbody:	Antron yarn a shade lighter than the body pulled forward in a loose envelope to surround the body; a small piece of yarn is left as a trailing shuck
Wing:	Light deer hair
Head:	Dubbed fur, same color as underbody
Best colors:	Tan/brown; tan/gray; tan/olive

GRIFFITH'S GNAT

This is a universally popular adult midge imitation. In larger sizes it can imitate a clump of midges, and in small sizes it can represent a single adult or emerging midge. The hackle can be trimmed at streamside to make the overall fly smaller and float lower in the surface film.

Hook:	Mustard 94840 (standard dry-fly) or equivalent, size 16–22
Body:	Peacock Herl
Hackle:	Grizzly hackle, palmered over body

BRASSIE

Sometimes called the Copper Nymph or South Platte Brassie, this is a very good imitation of a midge pupa. It is a great fly for sight fishing in both still and moving water.

Hook:	Mustad 94840 or equivalent (standard dry-fly hook) or Tiemco 2457 or equivalent (curved scud hook), sizes 14–20
Body:	Tightly wrapped copper wire
Head:	Peacock herl or black dubbing
Best colors:	Copper, red, green

SAN JUAN WORM

Named for the San Juan River in New Mexico, this fly imitates aquatic worms that live in the weeds and silt of rich tailwaters and spring creeks. In some places, it is a controversial pattern, partly because it almost works too well at times, and partly because it lacks the sophistication that some fly fishers think a fly must have. I have no problem with it, because it is made of artificial materials and imitates a natural food item that trout eat. There are many variations of this pattern in use throughout the West. It's not really a nymph but can be considered one because it is fished like one. It is sometimes tied on standard hooks in small sizes (16, 18) as an imitation of red midge larvae.

Hook:	Tiemco 200R or equivalent (long-shanked curved nymph hook), sizes 8–18
Tail:	Red floss
Body:	Flat red monofilament (Cobra) or V Rib

BEADHEAD FLASHBACK PHEASANT TAIL

It's hard to know which of the dozens of the variations of the Pheasant Tail Nymph to include here. I've chosen this one because it is relatively new and because it works well. It can be tied with natural or dyed pheasant tail fibers, and with beads of brass or tungsten.

Hook:	Mustad 9671 or equivalent (2XL nymph hook), sizes 10–18
Tail:	Cock ring-necked pheasant tail fibers
Body:	Cock ring-necked pheasant tail fibers, wrapped
Overbody:	Two or three strands of pearl Flashabou pulled over top of body
Rib:	Fine copper wire, counterwrapped over body
Thorax:	Peacock herl
Wing case:	Remainder of pearl Flashabou
Legs:	A few strands of cock ring-necked pheasant tail fibers pulled to each side of body
Bead:	Copper, brass, or tungsten bead behind eye of hook
Best colors:	Natural, green, red, gold

A. P. NYMPH

The A. P. stands for both André Puyans, the creator of this series of nymphs, and presumably All Purpose, which describes its versatility. By changing body color only, this single pattern can be used to imitate most mayfly and stonefly nymphs.

Hook:	Mustad 9671 or equivalent (1XL or 2XL standard nymph hook), sizes 6–16
Weight:	Lead or nontoxic wire wrapped on hook shank
Tail:	Dark moose body hair
Abdomen:	Dubbed beaver, muskrat, hare's ear, or other fur
Rib:	Fine copper wire
Thorax:	Same as abdomen
Wing case:	Dark moose body hair
Legs:	Three fibers from the wing case pulled to either side and secured with thread
Head:	Same as abdomen
Best colors:	Black/brown; black/olive; black/gold; black/black

BOW RIVER BUGGER

The Federation of Fly Fishers' *Fly Pattern Encyclopedia* shows fifty different variations on the Woolly Bugger. This is yet another. The signature streamer from my home river, Alberta's Bow, this fly is a composite of the best components from the Muddler Minnow and the original Woolly Bugger. First tied by guide Peter Chenier in the 1980s, it is now showing up in fly bins throughout the West.

Hook:	Mustad 79580 or equivalent (4XL streamer hook), sizes 2–8
Weight:	Lead or nontoxic wire wrapped on hook shank
Tail:	Marabou, mixed with a few strands of Flashabou in a contrasting color
Body:	Chenille
Hackle:	Soft black saddle hackle, palmered over body
Rib:	Fine copper wire, reverse-wrapped through the hackle
Collar:	Natural deer hair
Head:	White deer hair, spun and clipped
Best colors:	Brown, black, olive, white

SPRING CREEK BUGGER

This fly was designed to be a good small-water streamer. It is easy to cast, it enters the water with little disturbance, it sinks quickly, and it moves nicely when retrieved.

Hook:	Tiemco 2457 or equivalent (curved scud hook), sizes 8–12
Tail:	Marabou, mixed with Krystal Flash of a contrasting color
Body:	Remainder of tail material, wrapped forward
Overbody:	Remainder of Krystal Flash pulled over top of body
Eyes:	Brass eyes tied behind the eye of the hook
Hackle:	Soft hackle feather, color to match body
Best colors:	Brown, black, olive

GARTSIDE LEECH

A leech pattern is essential for western fly fishing, and this pattern is one of the best. It is extremely easy to tie and moves beautifully through the water.

Hook:	Mustad 79580 or equivalent (4XL streamer hook), sizes 2–6
Body:	None
Eyes:	Silver or plain lead eyes tied in behind eye of hook
Hackle:	One or two marabou plumes wrapped in front of eyes
Best colors:	Black, brown, maroon, olive, or a mixture

J & H STREAMER

The letters stand for Jekyl and Hyde, for this fly has a split personality. Alberta outdoor writer Bob Scammell devised it to be both dry fly and streamer. It is fished as a dry fly for the first part of its drift (probably imitating a stonefly or grasshopper); then it sinks and becomes a streamer when the fisherman begins to retrieve it. The great advantage to this fly is that it can be floated into tight spots where it would be very difficult to cast a conventional streamer. It also lands gently and is less likely to spook fish than a standard streamer.

Hook:	Mustad 94831 or equivalent (3XL dry-fly hook), sizes 6–10
Tail:	Red deer hair
Body:	Brown dubbing
Rear hackle:	Brown or furnace hackle, palmered over body
Rib:	Fine copper wire
Wing:	Gold elk hair beneath orange marabou beneath copper Krystal Flash
Thorax:	Red dubbing
Hackle:	Grizzly, palmered through thorax
Best colors:	The colors listed here are suggestions only. They can be changed to better imitate local insects or baitfish.

LEADWING COACHMAN

The leadwing coachman is one of the best traditional wet flies. These flies still take fish, even though they are somewhat out of fashion and lack the sophistication we've come to expect in more modern fly patterns.

Hook:	Mustad 3906B or equivalent (regular length wet-fly hook), sizes 10-18
Body:	Peacock herl
Rib:	Fine silver or gold oval tinsel
Wing:	Matched pair of mallard quill feathers
Hackle:	Brown or furnace

CHAPTER 11

Leftovers

HIRING A GUIDE

The occupation of guiding fly fishermen has a long tradition in the West, and a few of the veteran guides who helped build western fly fishing's reputation are still working their rivers. There is also a whole new generation of fly-fishing guides dragging driftboats up and down the interstates today. They are young, hip, passionate, capable, and extremely knowledgeable. They know where the trout are and what they are doing. Don't let an earring or tattoo put you off.

Hiring a guide is an obvious consideration for anglers who venture into a new and wild place to fish for the first time. One of the first questions to ponder is, "Who should hire a guide?" I'm tempted to say, "All the fishermen who think they don't need one," but that might come off as a bit cynical. I suppose a gentler answer would be to say that people who want to quickly learn how to catch fish in an unfamiliar area should hire a guide. Some people know they fit into this category but are unwilling to part with the money required. If that's you, think of it this way: In order to have good fishing in a new area, you have to spend something. It can be time or it can be money, but you won't get the fishing you want without parting with one or the other. If you're able to fish for a couple weeks or more in an area, you'll probably figure things out on your own, and for some people, this is far more appealing and satisfying than paying somebody to show them what's going on. Fair enough, but if you have only a few days to fish, consider hiring a guide. It might surprise you when I say that not just neophytes should do this. Many of the best anglers I know are consistently successful partly because they fish with good guides.

There are two ways guided fishing trips are arranged. The first is well in advance of the trip, and the second is on short notice, a day or two prior to the trip. Where possible, the former is preferred, if only because the best guides will probably still be available.

When considering a fly-fishing destination, you'll probably have a number of guides and outfitters to choose from. Don't simply pick the one who quotes the lowest price. There might be a reason he's $50 cheaper than everybody else. Instead, do some homework by asking the candidates for references and contacting these people for information. Ask them if the guide is personable, punctual, knowledgeable, and flexible. You can also solicit advice from angling friends who have hired guides in the same area.

Last-minute guided trips sometimes arise when you're in an area for other reasons—business, golf, sight-seeing—and you suddenly realize there's some fishing nearby. They also come about because of the bruised-ego syndrome. This happens when a group of fishermen go to a new area expecting the fabulous fishing they read about in a magazine, only to experience something less than that. Over a late dinner after another forgettable day on the water, somebody in the group says in a meek, apologetic voice, "Do you think we should hire some guides?" He says it as if he's telling the world he's a Viagra customer, but he's probably on the right track.

It's difficult on short notice to be sure you're getting a top-notch guide, and in fact, some people would say you can be fairly certain you aren't, simply because the good ones will have already been booked by the anglers who planned their trip the previous winter. But by speaking directly with the guide and assessing what he tells you, you can often do quite well. Listen carefully, and be suspicious if the candidate "guarantees" you good fishing: If it sounds too good to be true, it probably is. I'm most likely to hire the guy who asks me a lot of questions about where I've been fishing and what I expect, and who undersells rather than oversells. I'll go with the guy who says, "I think we can find a few fish," and stay away from the one who says, "Man, we kicked their butts yesterday!" I'm not concerned with the age of the guide one way or the other, if my intuition gives me the go-ahead.

Whether the trip is arranged well in advance or the night before, there are some things you should remember, most of which entail communication. First, tell the guide what your goals are. Tell him the specific methods you'd like help with, or the particular types of water you want to fish. If your main goal is for your less experienced companion to have a good time, say so. If you prefer the opportunity to catch a couple big fish rather than a bucketful of little ones (or vice versa), tell him. Inform him of your fishing preferences and any physical limitations you may have. For example, if you're arranging a float trip and you prefer to do a lot of fishing from your feet, tell him that so he'll choose a short stretch of river. If you find wading difficult, tell him. If you really prefer dry-fly fishing—or if you simply won't fish any other way—let him know that, and if he says the dry-fly fishing hasn't been very good, temper your expectations. If you insist on fishing dry flies anyway, don't be surprised or angry if the fishing turns out to be lousy.

Once you've booked a trip, most guides and outfitters will provide you with literature telling you what kind of tackle and gear to bring. Read this and presume that the guide has good reasons for his suggestions. If he says a 7-weight outfit is best, bring a 7-weight. If he says chest waders are essential, bring them. If he says you'll need a rain jacket, bring two.

You should never hire a guide simply to find the hot spots on the river so you can go back there the next day on your own. If the guide figures out what you're up to, you might find that for some strange reason the fishing isn't that great. And if he sees you and a few friends back there the next day, you might find yourself blacklisted for future trips with local guides.

Here's something you should always do: Be honest in your assessment of your own skills when arranging a guided trip. This is critical, and when in doubt, undersell your abilities rather than try to impress the guide with your complete mastery of the sport. On game day, it's better to surprise the guide with your skill rather than disappoint him with your lack of it.

When you're on the water, take the guide's advice and do what he says. You can do it your way anytime, and for free. You're buying access to the guide's expertise, so leave your ego at the door and take full advantage of what you're buying. I'm amazed how often people spend big money on guides just so they can try to prove that they don't need them.

Protocol requires some sort of gratuity at the end of the trip. It can be a gift or an item of tackle, but you can't go wrong with money. Your tip should not be the casual suggestion that the guide look you up next time he's in your neck of the woods.

WESTERN HAZARDS

There are probably more things that can go wrong on a fishing trip in the West than in most other places. Most of them can be blamed on the mountains and the creatures that live in them. All you have to do to familiarize yourself with these things is watch a good western—I think *Lonesome Dove* has them all. In no particular order, they are snakes, bears, cattle (especially bulls), heat, cold, dehydration, hypothermia, and quicksand.

The way to avoid difficulties with these things is to prepare ahead of time. When planning your trip, ask what to expect from the weather and other dangers, and carry the equipment that is required to counter them. Be sure to take enough proper clothing, including rainwear and warm stuff, and keep it where you can get at it. It won't do you much good in your basement or in your bag back at the motel.

Bears are probably the highest-profile creature with the potential to cause problems for fly fishers. It's important not to overreact to the idea of the presence of bears. They live in many of the areas we like to fish, yet the frequency of anglers' encounters with bears is very low. But it's also important not to be cavalier about their existence. They are capable of killing people. Inquire at fly shops or wardens' stations, asking if there have been any bears recently in the area you intend to fish. If there has been bear activity, consider carrying commercial bear spray with you. I carry it when I'm fishing in bear country, though I don't really know how well it works. I hope I never find out.

A way to reduce your chances of a close encounter of the bear kind is to avoid taking shortcuts through heavy brush, where it is easier to surprise a bear. Stay in or near the water, and make a lot of noise when you're moving along the river.

The presence of other creatures—mainly snakes and cattle—can usually be determined in advance by inquiring at fly shops. The only problem is that if a fly shop guy tells you not to fish someplace because of all the rattlesnakes, there is some chance he's just trying to keep you out of his favorite spot. Of course, he might be telling you not to go there because there really are a lot of rattlesnakes. Hmm . . .

The summers are hot in many parts of the West, and it's important to prevent heatstroke, sunburn, and dehydration. Wear a hat, carry sunblock, and either take extra water with you or carry a water purifier in your vest. You also need to be prepared for the possibility of cold weather any time of year. The weather is changeable, and cold fronts and storms can show up anywhere with little warning.

WESTERN TROUT STREAM CONSERVATION

Fly fishers should consider their sport a privilege rather than a right and should take an active role in protecting the wild places where we fish. For in protecting wild places, we protect much more than fish—we protect other species of animals and plants, of course, but we also protect rare and precious things like heritage, tradition, and integrity.

We have no shortage of things to protect our fishing from. There are physical threats like logging, mining, urban development, overgrazing, and pollution. The arrival in the West of Whirling Disease and the New Zealand Mud Snail has made it apparent that anglers are one possible way bad things can be transferred between watersheds. Conscientious fishermen rinse off wading gear and boats before moving from one river system to another. There are also social issues like overcrowding and the growing attention from the animal-rights movement. The specifics of how to address these issues are outside the scope of this book, yet to omit their mention altogether would be irresponsible. Thankfully, many organizations exist for precisely these reasons. My advice is simple: Support them, with both your body and your checkbook. There are large organizations in both the United States and Canada, such as Trout Unlimited, The Nature Conservancy, and Cal Trout, as well as small, grassroots organizations created to address specific issues that arise in specific watersheds. Get on their mailing lists, join them, and make your donations.

Many fly-fishing businesses are directly involved in the protection and restoration of fisheries habitat. It's good stewardship, and it's good business. The Orvis Company, in particular, has supported and initiated many such conservation projects throughout North America in recent years. The money that the Perkins family (who owns Orvis) and the Orvis Company has donated, raised, or caused to be raised for habitat conservation work in the last thirty years is staggering. Even if you don't use Orvis tackle, consider supporting its conservation projects. Other companies in the fly-fishing business likewise give back to the sport, including Patagonia and a great many individual fly shops.

I believe it's very important that we bring young people into the sport of fly fishing. I don't think we've done a very good job of this in the past. Please support clubs and organizations that promote youth participation, especially the Federation of Fly Fishers, which has great youth programs at its annual summer conclaves.

EPILOGUE

For me, two mental images, like bookends, give historical perspective to western fly fishing. The first is from the 1950s. A solitary man wades the Yellowstone River near the town of Livingston, Montana. The low sun highlights amber leaves falling from stately cottonwoods on the riverbank beneath the Absaroka Mountains. The fisherman's bamboo rod bends deeply, sending a Platinum Blonde streamer through the sharp October air into a powerful run in the river. Behind him on the bank lies a large, male brown trout, caught and killed an hour earlier. The angler is Joe Brooks, and he is hoping for another big fish before darkness chills the air and the line begins to freeze in his rod.

The other image is an early-twenty-first-century snapshot. Fifty or more anglers, wrapped in GoreTex and Supplex, held together with velcro, and armed with equipment made of barstock aluminum, titanium nitride, and nano-tech graphite, stand thigh-deep in the Henry's Fork of the Snake River, near Last Chance, Idaho. Feigning solitude, they pretend not to notice each other. They use downstream reach casts to deliver 4-weight lines, 14-foot fluorocarbon leaders, and size 22 CDC micro semi-emergers. The flies were designed and patented by a famous fly tier and marketed on the Internet. The big rainbows of the Henry's Fork are working a hatch of tiny mayflies and ignore the anglers' best efforts.

Perhaps our rivers haven't changed as much as we have. The Henry's Fork still has magnificent hatches, and the Yellowstone still flows undammed to the Missouri, but the numbers of anglers in the West, the tackle they use, and the ways they use it have changed a great deal. Whether you embrace or abhor the infringement of technology on our sport, fly fishing is still fly fishing. Swallows still tell us that bugs are on the water, and big rocks still hide stonefly nymphs and dent driftboats. And it's still important that we teach the sport with integrity, that we preserve and protect wild trout and the water they live in. Fly fishers are still having children.

INDEX

Page numbers in italics indicate illustrations.